The Crimean
War at Sea

The Crimean War at Sea

Naval Campaigns Against Russia, 1854–6

Peter Duckers

Pen & Sword
MARITIME

*This book is dedicated
to Anne*

First published in Great Britain in 2011 by
PEN & SWORD MARITIME
An imprint of
Pen & Sword Books Ltd
47 Church Street
Barnsley
South Yorkshire
S70 2AS

ISBN 978-1-84884-267-0

Typeset by Concept, Huddersfield, West Yorkshire
Printed and bound in England by CPI UK

Pen & Sword Books Ltd incorporates the Imprints of Pen & Sword Aviation,
Pen & Sword Maritime, Pen & Sword Military, Wharncliffe Local History,
Pen & Sword Select, Pen & Sword Military Classics, Leo Cooper, Remember When,
Seaforth Publishing and Frontline Publishing.

For a complete list of Pen & Sword titles please contact
PEN & SWORD BOOKS LIMITED
47 Church Street, Barnsley, South Yorkshire, S70 2AS, England
E-mail: enquiries@pen-and-sword.co.uk
Website: www.pen-and-sword.co.uk

Contents

List of Plates

List of Maps and Plans

Acknowledgements

The author would like to thank those publishers (or the descendants of the original publishers) who have allowed brief extracts to be taken from their works. In particular, he would like to thank the Navy Record Society for permission to use extracts from their published documentary collections on the naval campaigns of 1854–6. Where copyright has been unintentionally infringed, the author will be happy to acknowledge copyright in future editions of the book.

He also extends his sincere thanks to Mr Mark Cashmore for producing the main 'theatre' maps.

Note on Names and Illustrations

Many of the place names and personal names quoted in original sources in English are, of course, transliterations from other languages, like Russian, Finnish, Turkish etc. Many names occur in a variety of forms in contemporary accounts, a good example being Sveaborg, which occurs in a number of spellings. Many place names have changed considerably since 1856 (for example, Finnish place names replacing Swedish; Sveaborg, 'the fortress of the Swedes', is now Suomenlinna, 'the fortress of the Finns'). It has been decided to retain the most commonly used personal and proper names, since these will be more familiar to English readers; where there are significant differences in spelling or subsequent usage, this is referenced in the notes.

Unless otherwise stated, the illustrations are taken from the *Illustrated London News*, 1854–5. The *ILN* used sketches sent by officers and others 'on the spot', and also employed professional artists to produce what are often highly accurate drawings.

Introduction

War with Russia

In March 1854 Britain went to war with a major European power for the first time since 1815 when she joined France[1] in a campaign against Russia to support the integrity of the Ottoman Empire. The war's immediate origins lay in a long-standing dispute between France and Russia over the status of the Christian communities in the Ottoman Empire. In 1850, to gain conservative Catholic support, the French President Louis Napoleon had put pressure on the 'Sublime Porte', the government of Sultan Abdul Medjid II, to increase the influence of the Roman Catholic Church in the management of the Christian Holy Places in Palestine, then part of the Ottoman Empire. This was vehemently opposed by the Russian Tsar Nicholas I who supported the authority of the Ottoman Empire's 14,000,000 Orthodox Christians. But what superficially looked like a Franco-Russian dispute over the Ottoman Christians became a Russian demand for greater influence in the internal affairs of the Ottoman Empire and especially in the Balkans. Behind all the posturing were more important Russian territorial and strategic ambitions; Nicholas saw the opportunity to accelerate the fragmentation of the Ottoman Empire, to gain a Russian advantage in the Balkans, and was prepared to press the issue to the point of war to force Turkish concessions. In January 1853 Nicholas demanded the establishment of a Russian 'protectorate' over the Slavic Christians in the Balkans. When this and his request for 'substantial and permanent guarantees on behalf of the Orthodox Church' were rejected, diplomatic relations between the two countries were broken off. The drift into war – though not yet formally declared – began in July 1853 when Russian troops invaded the 'Danubian Principalities', the Ottoman provinces of Moldavia and Wallachia.[2] Intense and complex diplomatic efforts by all the European powers, led by Britain (and not least by the British Minister at Constantinople, Lord Stratford de Redcliffe), tried to broker a peace and force a Russian withdrawal. But with no such action likely, Turkey declared war on Russia on 4 October 1853 and on the 23rd Turkish troops under their Commander-in-Chief Omar Pasha crossed the Danube to engage the Russians. There followed a major Russo-Turkish land campaign in 'the Danubian Provinces' with a 'second front' to the east of the

Black Sea in the Caucasus – both campaigns now largely forgotten by popular historians of the Russian War – and the rapid destruction of Turkish naval power in the Black Sea.

For Britain and France, the preservation of the integrity of the Ottoman Empire was a matter of serious concern – and not for any inherent regard for 'the sick man of Europe'. The Ottoman Empire was regarded as a permanent barrier to Russia's southwestward expansion and to her ambitions in the Balkans and Mediterranean. The Tsar's demands indicated a desire for far greater influence over Turkey and only increased British and French distrust of Russia's aims. In particular, they shared a joint opposition to the alarming possibility of a major Russian presence in the eastern Mediterranean. A Russian naval base here would radically upset the balance of power in the region, would pose a direct threat to French security on its Mediterranean coast and, for Britain, would give a potential enemy the ability to disrupt her important trade routes to India and the Far East. The integrity of the Ottoman Empire was regarded as vital and its preservation became a major element of British foreign policy for the rest of the nineteenth century; apart from the Crimean War, the greatest manifestation of what became known as 'the Eastern Question' was the Eastern Crisis of 1876–8.

Despite months of further diplomatic activity drawing in all the major European powers, no compromise could be reached. As a wider European war looked increasingly likely in the winter of 1853, with Austria and Prussia both closely involved in the crisis, Britain and France began preliminary moves to establish a military presence in key areas.[3] In anticipation of possible war with Russia, a combined Anglo-French fleet was moved into the Bosphorus and entered the Black Sea in January 1854. Its ostensible aim was to buttress the right flank of Turkish positions in the Balkans, support the defence of Constantinople and confine the Russian Black Sea Fleet. On 27 March 1854, Britain declared war on Russia, followed by France on 28th.

The two-year war that followed is remembered in Britain – if it is remembered at all – as 'the Crimean War'. Popular historians have concentrated on the land campaign waged on the Crimean Peninsula against the Russian Black Sea base of Sebastopol. Operating alongside French, Turkish and Sardinian land forces, Britain's army endured two years of campaigning, categorised by hard-won victories, as at the Alma and Inkermann, 'glorious defeats' like the Charge of the Light Brigade, appalling suffering in the trenches during the Russian winter and the equally appalling mismanagement of food, medical facilities, supplies and equipment. Just over 4,000 British soldiers were killed in action or died of wounds in the Crimea and over 10,000 were wounded, but it is a well-established fact that for every British soldier killed by the enemy, 3 died of disease or cold, so that by the end of the campaign over 17,500 British soldiers had been lost. The inefficiency and ineffectiveness of Britain's military system at all levels not only led to caustic comment in the press – where the first real 'war correspondents' brought home the terrible reality of the war – but also in the highest levels of politics. Universal condemnation of the army system and the government led in the end to the resignation of the Prime Minister Lord Aberdeen in February 1855, the fall of his government and the accession on 6 February of a new, dynamic leader in the form of Henry John Temple, Viscount Palmerston. Finally, after two years of gruelling effort on land and at sea, the combined allied forces finally managed to seize the southern half of Sebastopol and its dockyards in September 1855.[4] Following intense diplomatic activity and the threat of possible Austrian,[5] Prussian and Swedish intervention, the new Tsar of Russia, Alexander II, agreed to peace terms in February 1856 and the war was formally ended by the Peace of Paris on 30 March. This removed any Russian gains from her land campaigns against Turkey and declared the Black Sea to be neutral and demilitarised; in April, Britain, France and Austria united to guarantee the integrity and independence of Turkey.

For Russia, the Crimean campaign was only one element in what was a much larger European war. Her immediate concern – the full-scale campaigns in the Danube basin and the Caucasus – has been rather neglected but the great sieges of Silistria and Kars,[6] the defence of which was aided by a few British officers, were famous events in their day. In the Balkans the Turks, somewhat un-expectedly, won a series of notable victories, eventually forcing the Russians back to their own borders. But apart from the fighting in these theatres, Russia also had to allow for possible Austrian intervention in the Balkans, had to consider the alarming possibility of a Polish and/or a Finnish uprising and needed to keep large forces around the shores of the Black Sea and Baltic in case of major allied land operations there.[7] This meant that significant Russian forces had to be held back, to be deployed beyond the actual war zones in readiness for potential action in a number of other areas if required. In addition, she faced allied attacks at a multiplicity of points wherever naval power could be brought to bear on her coasts.

Equally, Britain's contribution in the Crimea was only part of her total war effort. The fact of the matter is that the campaign fought in the Crimea would not and could not defeat Russia – a fact quite apparent at the time. Even the Russians regarded the fall of Sebastopol as something of a forgone conclusion, accepting the potential destruction of their major naval base in the Black Sea with some equanimity; its siege would, after all, tie down significant enemy forces and consume their resources.[8] And after the port had fallen, allied land forces would be in no better position to defeat the huge Russian Empire. The loss of Sebastopol would of course be a national embarrassment but it would hardly force the Tsar into surrender. Where would allied land forces go from Sebastopol? What could be their next target? A continued land campaign into southern Russia really seemed to be beyond the resources of France and Britain in 1856.

In fact, for Britain the war with Russia was viewed primarily as a naval concern. She entered the war as a major sea power rather than as a land power and saw naval action as her main contribution to the conflict. Her decision to commit an army to the Crimea was important, but was largely an act in support of what was intended to be a French and Turkish land campaign. After Inkermann in November 1854, her army was hardly in any shape to contribute materially to the land campaign, which really did become largely a French and Turkish affair. Initially, in considering the opening moves against Russia, the Sultan's government had proposed to the allies the possibility of 'combined operations' on the Circassian coast of the Black Sea (for example, an attack on Anapa) and the raising of the Circassian population against Russia, combined with operations in the Caucasus. However, both London and Paris considered that the crippling of Russia's Black Sea base at Sebastopol was of greater strategic concern than a land campaign further east. In addition, it was obvious from the start that if Britain and France were to have any chance of defeating the Russian Empire, or at least forcing her into a negotiated settlement, they would have to attack the Empire at any accessible point to maximise their influence and this meant naval or combined operations on an extensive scale. By destroying Russian naval power wherever it was based, harassing her commerce, blockading her ports and attacking Russian establishments around the world, Britain and France might so seriously damage Russian interests that they would force the Russians into negotiation to end the war. The result was a series of allied naval campaigns waged largely by British warships, supported by French vessels to a greater or lesser degree, in the Baltic, the Pacific, the White Sea, the Black Sea and the Sea of Azoff. These largely successful exploits have been rather neglected by popular historians of the war but form a vital part of it and deserve to be considered as crucial to its successful conclusion in March 1856. The war against the Russian Empire was won by Anglo-French naval action and by European diplomacy – not just by the fighting in the Crimea.

Chapter 1

The Battle Fleets, 1854

The war of 1854–6 brought into action the three largest warship fleets in the world at that time: the British, the French and the Russian. Although it is traditional in terms of naval history to regard the period after 1815 as one of continued British naval domination, with the newly industrialising country controlling a powerful warship fleet which made her invincible at sea, the story is actually not that simple. Unsurprisingly, as great military powers both Russia and France maintained battle fleets of considerable size and strength and the Ottoman Empire naturally aspired to a significant naval presence in the eastern Mediterranean and Black Sea. The Italian state of Piedmont-Sardinia, which entered the war for political and opportunist reasons under Count Cavour in January 1855, also made a small naval contribution.[1]

The period 1854–6 which saw these great powers putting their fleets into action was one of transition in terms of naval warfare, with scientific and technological development in many fields, borne on the back of industrialisation. Whilst the old 'wooden wall' sailing ships that would have been familiar generations earlier were still very much in evidence, new types of warship had appeared over the past thirty years. In particular, the use of steam as a form of propulsion[2] was coming to the forefront of naval design and the experience of the naval campaigns in the Russian War was to establish firmly the dominance of steam over wind power in all the leading navies of the world. After 1856, sail may not have been dead but its day was clearly drawing to a close. The main forms of steam propulsion adopted by the navies of the great powers were side-paddle wheels and propeller or 'screw' drives. Both developed almost side by side in the 1830s and 1840s and ships equipped with either type were used to great effect during the war, but it was the steam 'screw' warship that established its supremacy. Technological and industrial advances also aided the development of new types of powerful weaponry, from the small to the large-scale – from the highly regarded Minié rifle to new types of artillery. Not the least of these was the invention and adoption of the explosive shell, destined, it was said, to put an end to wooden warships.[3] Experiments were also going on at this time with the use of iron in the actual construction of warships[4] and with the possibility of armour-plating wooden ships. Neither had come to any useable stage of development by 1854,[5] though the French employment of three armoured 'floating batteries' in the Black Sea in 1855 (see below, p. 136ff.) again showed that a new era in warship design was approaching.

Of the combatant navies of 1854–6, that of the Ottoman Empire was the weakest. The Ottoman navy had of course been a formidable fighting force in earlier times, dominating the eastern Mediterranean. A great reform of the fleet, begun in 1770 after defeat at the hands of the Russians, bore some fruit in the construction of more modern naval dockyards, training schools and new, lighter ships, their principal naval bases being Constantinople, Sinope (on their northern Black Sea coast) and Rhodes in the eastern Mediterranean. Much of their organisation was modelled on the fleets of France and Sweden and the process of reform and improvement continued well into the nineteenth century. But the Turks were not highly regarded for their gunnery training nor the quality of their naval weaponry and although they maintained a fleet of over forty warships by the 1820s, they began to suffer from financial neglect, lack of modernisation and occasionally from actual battle damage; a significant part of their navy was destroyed by a combined British, French, Russian and Austrian fleet at Navarino in 1827, the last major battle to be fought by sailing ships alone.

The Ottoman navy had last seen significant action (quite creditably) during the Eastern Crisis of 1839–40 as part of the allied naval force operating off Syria. On the heels of further modernisation, by 1853 Sultan Adbul Medjid II commanded an impressive-looking fleet of 4 powerful 3-deck sailing ships, 10 sailing frigates, 36 smaller sailing vessels and gunboats, 6 new steam frigates and 12 smaller steam warships. In all, the Ottoman fleet comprised around 70 vessels with about 34,000 men and 4,000 marines, the Sultan's best ships and crews being those derived from Egypt, then still a Turkish province. However, there were those who believed that the Turkish navy had 'hardly recovered materially or morally from the overwhelming defeat it had sustained at Navarino. New ships had been built and seamen conscripted but the force was ill-organised and the majority of officers had no great energy or experience'.[6] Turkey was not a naval force to be ignored, but her entry into a naval war with Russia in 1853 was not a happy experience, starting with a major defeat at the hands of Russia's Black Sea Fleet at Sinope in November (see below, p. 44). In truth, after Sinope the allied naval command showed little interest in the Turkish fleet and, apart from helping to wage Turkey's own war to the east of the Black Sea[7] her ships were largely relegated to transport and escort duties, though a few played a small part in operations like the bombardments of Sebastopol and actions in defence of Eupatoria, which became an important Turkish base in the Crimea.

The Imperial Russian navy was also very much in transition. Since the days of its radical moderniser, Peter the Great[8] the Russian Empire had sought not only the defence of its shores and maritime trade but a prestige force that would put Russia amongst the principal naval powers of Europe.[9] By the early nineteenth century, the administrative centre of the Imperial Russian Navy was the magnificent Admiralty Building in St Petersburg, built between 1806 and 1823. The Russian navy then consisted of about 40 battleships, 15 frigates, 24 corvettes and brigs and 16 other vessels, with combined complements of around 91,000 'people'. But the main strength of the Imperial Russian Navy by 1854 lay in its two major fleets – the Black Sea Fleet based at Sebastopol and the larger Baltic Fleet at Cronstadt, with elements at Sveaborg and Reval. Since the island-fortress of Cronstadt was vital to the defence of the capital St Petersburg the Imperial Russian government always regarded the Baltic Fleet as its principal naval arm. And needless to say, the mere existence of both fleets, even though their natural areas of operation would largely be limited to the Baltic and the Black Sea, could be used as a valuable lever in any diplomatic dispute with Britain or other European powers. There is no doubt that because of the proximity of the Baltic Fleet to British waters and the potential danger to her eastern Mediterranean trade routes posed by the Black Sea Fleet, Britain regarded the Russian navy as a threat of some magnitude and was quite ready to neutralise Russian sea power; the war of 1854–6 gave her exactly that opportunity.

Emperor Nicholas I[10] initially took a personal interest in his navy but found it under strength and in poor condition, with many warships (especially in the Baltic) simply not fit for war service. He initiated radical reforms under Admiral Prince Menshikov in the 1830s, so that both the Baltic and Black Sea Fleets were greatly expanded – causing considerable alarm in British naval circles at the time. However, neglect and lack of use diminished their real strength and further reforms under Prince Constantine after 1850 were not completed by 1854 and had little effect. Much of the Russian navy's organisation and drill was modelled on British methods but despite the fleet's intended prestige value, by 1854 the Imperial navy was again starved of funds, the victim of corruption and inefficient administration, badly manned and poorly equipped. The fleets were crewed largely by conscripts, their gunnery in particular was regarded as poor and their guns of less range and power than those employed by the British or French fleets.

In an attempt to keep up to date with modern naval developments, Russia began to experiment with the use of auxiliary steam power. In 1826, they built their first armed steamboat the *Izhora*, mounting eight guns and in 1836 constructed the first paddle-steam-frigate of the Russian navy the 1,300-ton *Bogatyr*. This process continued into the 1850s with the construction, for example, of the paddle-steamers *Vladimir* and the smaller 4-gun *Odessa*, *Krym* and *Khersones*, all of which were based at Sebastopol in the Black Sea. Others destined for the Baltic, to be serviced by a new steam depot at Cronstadt, were the 10-gun *Olaf* and the *Diana*. Since Russia did not develop much of a supporting industry, most of her steam ships and their machinery were actually built abroad, often produced by British companies and yards.[11] In terms of modern screw vessels they were weakly equipped; by 1855 they had the converted *Vyborg*, the *Orel* and the aged *Retvizan*, a Swedish vessel of 1789 largely rebuilt in the winter of 1855. A few new screw vessels were under construction in 1854–5, including the 46-gun frigate *Maria* but most were completed too late to be employed during the war, so that to any real extent, Russia had no significant screw warship fleet and comparatively few steamers by the time of the war with Britain and France. Effectively, she continued to rely on the old wooden sailing warship at a time when both Britain and France were developing and using radically new types of vessel. Not until the 1860s did the Russian fleet significantly replace its sailing warships with steamers.

Nevertheless, the Russian fleet certainly could not be underestimated; in 1854 it comprised about 60 sailing 'ships-of-the-line', each mounting something between 70 and 120 guns, with over 100 sailing frigates and smaller ships and perhaps 40 paddle-steamers. Their whole fleet mounted 9,000 guns and was manned by over 40,000 sailors. At the outset of the war Russia divided its fleet into 5 'divisions'. Each would notionally comprise about 20 ships of varying size and firepower, with 2 divisions based at Sebastopol and 3 in the Baltic – 2 at Cronstadt itself and 1 divided between Reval and Sveaborg, guarding the approaches to Cronstadt. Smaller squadrons were based in the White Sea (at Archangel), in the Pacific (the Okhotsk flotilla) and at Kertch, guarding the approaches to the Sea of Azoff. Effectively handled, the Russian navy would have been a dangerous enemy, as the Turks discovered at Sinope in November 1853. In the event, it was never tested against the fleets of Britain and France.

Whatever fears the British had about the potential threat posed by the Russian fleets, it was the increasingly powerful French navy that gave Britain most concern and against whom British developments and strategic planning were largely directed. The French royal navy of the *Ancien Régime* had of course been a formidable weapon but was more or less ruined by the French Revolution and had to be rebuilt by Napoleon I into a world-class fighting force. But after Trafalgar in 1805 and in the wake of Anglo-French naval engagements around the world, Britain contained the threat posed by France's renewed naval power and reigned supreme at sea. This was the fact of the situation in 1815 when the long French wars ended and during the years of the restored monarchy little was done to develop or expand the French navy. Only the accession of Louis Napoleon as President in 1848 and then as the Emperor Napoleon III in 1852 brought about a radical change. Napoleon sought to expand and strengthen the French fleet for many reasons – to defend France's two vulnerable coastlines along the English Channel and in the Mediterranean, to protect France's growing overseas and imperial commerce and not least as a pure matter of personal and national prestige. Napoleon III wanted to recreate a 'Great Power' battle fleet and as far as the British Admiralty was concerned, there was only one possible goal for French ambitions – a naval confrontation with Britain. After 1850 there was something of a naval arms race between Britain and France, very often with the French making the running[12] and by 1854 the French had indeed produced a powerful battle fleet with 290 sailing warships, the largest mounting between 80 and 120 guns, and 117 steamers of various types and sizes, mounting between them over 13,000 guns.

Ultimately, however, for all her design flair and determined effort France lacked the industrial development and capacity to produce a modern warship fleet that would really challenge British maritime supremacy – their production of iron, machinery and weapons, for example, could not match that of Britain in either quantity or quality.[13] It is nevertheless true that throughout the Russian War, when Britain and France acted as naval allies – and with great cordiality between their naval forces – both were developing their navies with an eye to the other and to possible Anglo-French conflict in the future. Following the humiliation of French foreign policy in 1839–40[14] and growing antagonism with Britain, British naval strategy in the 1840s was concerned to counter a possible French challenge and developed detailed plans for attacks on French naval bases, especially Cherbourg, with its first-class deepwater harbour and dockyards, which was considered to be potentially the most dangerous threat to Britain. British ships built for deployment in Russian seas and for use against Russian fortifications, whether at Sebastopol, Sveaborg, Cronstadt or Kinburn, could equally be used against Cherbourg or other French bases; experimenting with new types of warship and armaments and creating large battle fleets in 1854–5 was not solely related to the needs of the current war with Russia.

Britain's Royal Navy was the largest of the combatant fleets in 1854. As an island, with an extensive maritime trade and a growing overseas empire, Britain simply had to maintain a naval preponderance in the face of her potential European enemies, especially France and Russia. There were still many ships in service in 1850 that would have been familiar to Nelson and his men – the old 'wooden walls' or sailing line-of-battle ships that dominated the seas by 1815, though these were increasingly larger and more powerfully armed than those known to Nelson. Edward Seymour commented that 'Admiral Benbow [d. 1702] might have taken command of a sailing line-of-battle ship in 1853 and only remarked that it was larger and the guns heavier than he had been used to'.[15] But it is unsound to think of the British navy as simply an old-fashioned force, sticking to its traditional styles and resting on its hard-earned laurels.[16] Although Britain continued to build wooden sailing warships, they were not simply copies of older types; newer types were greatly improved – larger, stronger and better armed. New ships like the 121-gun 3-decker *Royal Albert* launched in 1854 – the largest warship of its day – were immense floating fortresses and represented the most powerful weapons available at that time and the greatest development of the wooden-hulled sailing ship. There were many others in the Royal Navy. Britain did indeed 'downsize' its fleet and naval manpower after 1815, largely on the grounds of expense[17] but even though the era after 1815 was one without a major European war, there were plenty of opportunities for naval intervention. British squadrons played their part in the Portuguese and Spanish crises of the 1820s and 1830s, in the Greek War of Independence in the 1820s, in the great Eastern Crisis of 1839–40 and in China and South America. And this is not to mention anti-slaving, surveying, mapping and hydrographical work carried out by British naval vessels around the world.

The period 1815–54 was also one of great technological and industrial progress in Britain. The Admiralty, often considered to be a conservative force reluctant to contemplate or impose radical change, was in fact at the forefront in the testing and development of new technologies. It was a case of establishing the effectiveness of new systems rather than adopting them without thought and whilst steam power and iron construction developed rapidly from the 1820s in the merchant service, the Admiralty was more circumspect. The use of steam, new machinery and improved weaponry were all gradually adopted by and absorbed into Admiralty planning, so that the British battle fleet of 1854 was one very much in transition – the old and familiar ranged alongside the most up-to-date designs. The most important new development after 1820 was the adoption of steam power. Using engines controlled by steam power allowed finer control of the steering and manoeuvring of the vessel than did reliance on the vagaries of the wind, enabling steam ships to get closer to the shore, or to control their passage through harbours or narrow channels. In 1853, *The Times* commented:

> When the nature of this modern agent [steam] is considered, and its adaptability for the purposes of naval warfare, the contrast which it illustrates becomes still more formidable. For giving certainty and rapidity to the movements of a fleet, and for all the attendant advantages which are thus secured, the steam-engine far exceeds the standard by which its capabilities are measured ... [we have] the sublime idea fully realized of man controlling the sea and subjecting the winds by a mechanical power developed by the patient

observation of natural forces and the happy application of them to our wants.[18]

It is true that the Admiralty waited for years after the successful and extensive use of steam power in the merchant service before wholeheartedly introducing the new systems into the warship fleet, but once the machinery and manufacturing processes were tried and tested, the Royal Navy adopted steam power with a will, though initially only in smaller vessels. The earliest steam-powered ships were of course side-paddle-steamers, extensively adopted by commercial lines after 1812, whose steam engines propelled the vessel via large wheels mounted to port and starboard. The first Royal Navy paddle-steamers, like the *Monkey* of 1821 and the *Comet* of 1822, were not fitted out as warships, but were given more mundane roles as dispatch vessels, tugs or dredgers. The first steamers to feature in the *Navy List* were the *Lightning* class – *Lightning*,[19] *Echo* and *Meteor* of 1827–8 – and the first 'serious' steam warships the 6-gun paddle-wheeler *Gorgon* and her sisters built from 1836. The use of steam spread through the 1830s and 1840s and the size and power of the ships increased accordingly, from vessels like the *Cyclops* of 1839 to the powerful frigate *Terrible* of 1845. HMS *Terrible* is a fine example of one of the new steam paddle-wheel frigates that played such a major role in the Russian War. Laid down at Deptford in 1845, she was 'always the finest paddle-wheel man-of-war in our navy'.[20] At 1,847 tons, with an 800 nominal horsepower, she could reach a full speed of 13 knots under steam – regarded as remarkable for its day. Her 7 68-pounder guns were the heaviest in service anywhere and she also mounted 4 10-inch and 10 8-inch guns. When built, she was the most powerful steam warship afloat. By this time, paddle-steamer warships of the East India Company[21] had served in the 'Opium War' with China between 1840 and 1842 and in Burma in 1852 and powerful frigates like *Terrible* dominated the naval campaigns of 1854–6.

Paddle-steamers could be fast and heavily armed and were highly manoeuvrable, technically capable of turning on their own axis – a considerable feat in those days. But the problems with side-paddle-steamers were easily apparent. Their great paddle wheels were highly vulnerable in action and prevented the deployment of a full broadside of guns, limiting the ship's firepower in conventional terms even when the ships were lengthened. The weight of coal the ships had to carry restricted their range and their sailing powers were not good in rough seas, which reduced the efficiency of their paddle wheels. Nevertheless, as gunboats, they were fast and manoeuvrable, packed a heavy punch and could be deployed in shallower water; they could also be used to carry troops and stores to the theatre of war and to tow sailing ships and transports.[22]

The more advanced siblings of these newer types of vessel were the 'screw' warships – those powered by steam-driven propellers[23] – which developed from the late 1830s side by side with paddle-steamers. Screw warships proved to be faster and much more powerful[24] and had clear advantages over paddle-steamers; their machinery was protected below decks, so less vulnerable in action and their gun decks were not obstructed by paddle wheels. The first screw warship in the Royal Navy was the converted sailing sloop *Rattler* (re-launched as a screw conversion in 1843), followed by the *Dauntless*, laid down in 1844. It was partly because of fear of a coming war with France and her growing naval strength (for example, with her construction of *Le Napoléon* and the development of her base at Cherbourg) that after 1845 the Royal Navy began the conversion of older sailing ships to screw power – *Nile* being an early example. Several old 74-gun sailing ships-of-the-line were converted into powerful 60-gun screw 'blockships'.[25] This conversion of existing sailing warships (and many others followed after 1849) was the first systematic attempt to apply screw propulsion to major warships. The 'blockships' were originally conceived as relatively immobile steam batteries intended solely for harbour defence but were soon given a reduced sailing rig rather than none at all to make them into sea-going ships. They served essentially as 'floating batteries', especially intended for coastal bombardment. Such conversions were a cost-effective experiment of great value and the ships subsequently gave good service in the Russian War. Many more conversions to steam followed, like *Sans Pareil* in 1851,[26] before the first ship to be completely designed from scratch as a screw steamer was built in the form of the 91-gun *Agamemnon*, originally laid down in 1849. She was a direct response to the construction of large French screw battleships, like the 90-gun *Le Napoléon* and her sister-ships, which caused something of an Anglo-French naval arms race. Screw warships rapidly became a familiar element in the British fleet and they gave Britain's navy a formidable edge. A fine example of the type was the massive *Duke of Wellington*, which became the flagship of the Baltic Fleet in 1854. Laid down in Pembroke as the *Windsor Castle*, her launch date coincided with the death of the Duke of Wellington in 1852 and Queen Victoria ordered her to be re-named in his memory. At 3,759 tons and the first screw 3-decker in the world, she mounted 131 guns and carried a complement of 1,100 'people'.[27] This huge ship was to be *the* centre of attraction at the Spithead Review in August 1853 (see below, p. 10), a commentator noting that 'by its floating batteries of the heaviest description, and by the power of steam to move them rapidly into any position that may be required, the British navy has now become the grandest concentration of force for destructive purposes that can well be conceived'.

One further consideration as a 'modern development' was the potential for the use of iron in warship construction – partly considered because of the development of exploding shells which, many feared, would make wooden ships obsolete. Henri-Joseph Paixhans (1783–1854), a French military officer who had served in the Napoleonic Wars, developed between 1823 and 1827 the first guns to fire explosive shells, filled with gunpowder. These 'Paixhans' guns' were widely adopted.[28] They became the first naval guns to combine explosive shells and a flat trajectory, thereby – it is often stated – triggering both the demise of wooden ships and the iron or armoured hull revolution in boat building.[29] Iron warships – that is, ships whose hulls were actually constructed of iron, rather than wooden ships armoured with iron plates which developed after the Crimean War – appeared in the Royal Navy in 1840[30] with the packet *Dover*; this was followed in 1843 by the *Trident* and from 1846–9 with the first sizeable iron paddle-frigates *Birkenhead*, *Simoom* and *Megaera*. However, the use of metal-hulled warships found little favour[31] – in particular, tests showed that their sides were vulnerable to shell fire and their armour, once hit, liable to splinter and fragment, potentially causing serious casualties on board the ship. The earliest iron-hulled vessels, like the *Megaera*, were not a success and were quickly converted to troopships.[32] The Royal Navy only turned to full iron construction after the Crimean War (and again largely under pressure from French designs) when in 1860 it produced the revolutionary HMS *Warrior*.[33]

The Admiralty was equally unconvinced by trials with simple armour plate, so that the Royal Navy did not resort to armouring its wooden ships until after the Russian War; the British fleet of 1854–6 was still one of 'wooden walls'. Nevertheless, the Russian War may be said to have set the last nail in the coffin of the large wooden warship. The last and largest of the old unarmoured type to be laid down, although powered by steam screw, were the three-deck *Victoria* and the two-deck *Duncan* of 1858–60; their construction ended a very long tradition. 'Ironclads' became the standard after 1860.

Despite reductions and fluctuations in the size of the fleet, its armament and complements during the long years of peace, by 1853 the Royal Navy could still list a fleet mounting over 15,000 guns and comprising 300 sailing warships, reinforced by 77 new screw steamers and 113 paddle-steamers, crewed, notionally at least, by approximately 33,000 sailors and 12,500 marines. In addition, 14 new sailing ships and 21 steamers were under construction at the beginning of 1854.[34]

At least part of Britain's potential naval might was arrayed for the world to see on 11 August 1853, just after the Russian invasion of the Danubian Provinces, when a great Naval Review conducted by Queen Victoria was held at Spithead. Interestingly enough, the Tsar's two eldest daughters, visiting

Britain at the time, were present as guests and watched the great display and its 'sham fight' (see Appendix 1). One observer commented on the sight of 'twenty-five ships-of-war, thirteen of which are screw steamers, nine paddle-wheel, and three sailing ships-of-the-line. The total steam-power employed, being stated at about half its actual value, probably represents a larger horse-power than all the cavalry regiments in the service put together.' The report continued:

> In the present state of Europe, we are satisfied that the maintenance of a considerable force afloat is one of the chief guarantees of our security, and of the tranquility of the world. In other countries you may see an array of troops, horse and foot, far outnumbering [those we can assemble]; but the evolutions of a steam fleet of line-of-battle ships, manned and manoeuvred by British seamen, can happily be seen in England alone ... With these elements of naval power, and with the natural energy of Englishmen upon the sea, we cannot for a moment doubt that, whatever be the progress of other States in their marine, we shall remain ahead of them, as we are already and as we have been of old ... The spectacle of to-day is not a mere summer's pastime among the yachts of Cowes, but a political occurrence the significance of which will be understood in every Cabinet of Europe; and among the spectators of this scene there are some, at least, who may learn, that if foreign Governments imagined the martial spirit of this country to have declined, they were egregiously mistaken.[35]

Chapter 2

The Baltic Campaign, 1854

As war between Turkey and Russia spread into the Danubian Provinces in 1853, high-level diplomatic discussions to resolve the Balkan crisis continued. Nevertheless, Britain and France prepared for a war that looked increasingly likely. Apart from military aid to Turkey in the Balkans, the most obvious point of attack for the British was the Baltic and preparations duly went ahead over the winter of 1853–4 to assemble a major Baltic Fleet.[1] The area had of course been known to British merchants since at least the mid-sixteenth century and was for Britain a highly important source of naval stores like timber (not least for masts and spars), pitch, tar, rope and the like. But as the base of a major Russian warship fleet, it was also a potential threat to Britain and an obvious target for naval action.

The man appointed to command the Baltic enterprise in February 1854 was Vice Admiral Sir Charles John Napier (1786–1860). Napier was nearly 68 years old but came to the appointment as a highly popular choice on the back of a distinguished naval and political career. Possibly the best-known naval commander of the day, 'Charlie Napier' had served since 1799 and had a wealth of active sea experience behind him from the Napoleonic Wars, through service with the Portuguese navy in the 1820s and most recently in the Mediterranean during the Eastern Crisis of 1839–40. Also known as 'Mad Charlie' because of his eccentric and occasionally wayward habits, which frequently found him at odds with the Admiralty, he was a popular reformer who had worked to improve sailors' conditions and terms of service and had been an enthusiastic advocate of new steam technology from its first appearance in the 1820s.[2] At the time of the Russian crisis, Napier had recently retired as commander of the Channel Fleet but was the obvious choice to lead what was to be the largest warship fleet assembled by Britain since 1815.

Napier hoisted his flag in February 1854 aboard the new screw warship *Duke of Wellington*[3] at Spithead, his subordinates being Rear Admirals Armar Lowry Corry[4] as second in command, Henry Ducie Chads[5] as third in command and James Hanway Plumridge,[6] who was to command an independent squadron. A French contingent under Admiral Alexandre Parseval-Deschênes[7] of nine line-of-battle ships,[8] with a few frigates and smaller vessels, was only slowly assembled, but some joined Napier in the Baltic in June. Napier's eventual fleet

The Baltic,
1854–5

was to be the biggest in number of ships assembled in Britain since the Napoleonic Wars and the most powerful in terms of armament that had ever sailed from British ports. It was a fleet notable for the preponderance of steam warships, especially screw vessels and was eventually to comprise Napier's flagship, *Duke of Wellington*, the *Royal George*, *St Jean d'Acre*, *Princess Royal*, the 91-gun *James Watt*, *Nile* and *Caesar*, the 80-gun *Cressy* and *Majestic*, four blockships, *Edinburgh*, *Blenheim*, *Ajax* and *Hogue*, as well as six sailing battle-ships, smaller steam frigates and others. But the fleet, impressive as it was, was not all that it seemed, especially in comparison with the fleet that Britain put into action in the Black Sea, which was largely based upon the existing Mediterranean Fleet from Malta. Although the latter was to have only two steam battleships, *Agamemnon* and *Sans Pareil*,[9] the Mediterranean Fleet was ready for war, maintained in good order, already fully equipped, fully manned and under discipline. Napier's new Baltic Fleet was very different.

Napier was to be hauled over the coals by the British press (especially *The Times*), in Parliament and by elements of public opinion during and after his command of the Baltic Fleet in 1854. It is indeed still true that today he is remembered on the basis of contemporary criticism launched against him as an aged, timorous commander: Napier's appointment 'has shown the unwisdom of entrusting officers over threescore with the conduct of warlike operations' who missed obvious chances, declined to engage his enemy on land or sea and achieved nothing significant with the powerful and impressive fleet under his command.[10] But his own vehement defence of his actions[11] paints a very different story and is surely borne out by the evidence. Napier faced a multitude of serious problems. Initially, his fleet was scattered and had to be rapidly concentrated for war service in the Baltic. More importantly, many ships were chronically undermanned – a constant and very apposite criticism leveled by Napier and some of his captains.[12] The gradual abolition after 1815 of the hated press gangs and the system of impressment led to an all-volunteer force but this in itself left the navy regularly short of experienced seamen.[13] The Royal Navy was still not necessarily seen as a lifetime 'profession' for its 'people' – the men of the lower decks. Some, of course, as they completed their time on one ship would immediately re-engage for another voyage, but equally many might not and the navy regularly lost experienced sailors as some returned to mercantile, fishing or land service. A re-commissioning warship taking on a new crew might attract a hotch-potch of men, from highly trained and experienced seamen returning to service, to men of the merchant or fishing fleets who may have had some expertise, to 'landsmen' who had never served at sea – complete novices who would need training 'on the job'.[14] Despite recent reforms to naval service, including continuous service, better rations, pay and general conditions,[15] 1854 was no exception; Napier rattled off lists of ships that were hardly fit (in terms of their complement) to take to the seas on active service. The Admiralty could only suggest – but did little to implement – a policy of recruiting seamen in Sweden, Norway 'and even Denmark'.[16] But this did not work. Neither were there enough charts of the region nor pilots and navigators with a knowledge of the complicated Baltic seas, currents and coastline and no one in authority seemed to consider recruiting extensively from the pool of experienced merchant-service commanders and pilots who had regularly plied the Baltic.[17] Instead, some additional strength was found by recruiting ex-sailors serving in the Coast Guard and naval pensioners – the only real 'reserves' of the Royal Navy.[18] Added to all this – the basic problem of simply getting large warships into a theatre of war – was the fact that Napier's fleet in the spring of 1854 comprised mainly large, deep-draught vessels, powerful gun batteries but not always suitable, as it transpired, for close coastal operations in stormy waters and along unfamiliar rocky coastlines.

Nevertheless, by one means or another, Napier's formidable fleet was readied for war and cheered away from Portsmouth by huge crowds and to wild public enthusiasm. The Queen and Prince Albert aboard the tiny steam yacht *Fairy* led out the fleet:

> In order to give *éclat* to a scene in which the whole nation felt the deepest interest, Her Majesty had announced her intention of lead-ing the squadron to sea and as a preparatory formality had received the Admiral and his Captains aboard her yacht by way of farewell. The enthusiasm of the fleet as well as of the multitude assembled to witness a scene unique even in the naval annals of England was without bound and high hopes were raised for the success of an expedition thus Royally inaugurated.[19]

There were indeed great expectations of this powerful force, the Baltic becoming at that moment 'a centre of breathless interest'.[20] Napier's famous signal to his men as the fleet set sail was less succinct than Nelson's 'England expects ...' and though greeted with ridicule by many of his officers,[21] was really addressed to the men of the lower decks, amongst whom Napier was immensely popular:

> Lads! War is declared with a numerous and bold enemy. Should they meet us and offer battle, you know how to dispose of them. Should they remain in port, we must try to get at them. Success depends upon the quickness and precision of your firing.[22] Also, lads, sharpen your cutlasses and the day is your own!

The initial squadron comprised 4 line-of-battle ships, 4 blockships, 4 steam frigates and 3 paddle-steamers.[23] They were later joined by other warships of all kinds. But although Napier did indeed have a number of new screw warships and steam paddle-frigates, no steps had yet been taken to produce an adequate fleet of smaller gunboats and mortar vessels which might be useful for the bombardment of coastal positions at safe ranges. Only in 1856, following 'The Great Armament' (see below, p. 107) and based on the experiences of 1854 and 1855, was a large fleet of light gun and mortar boats actually created ready for a major campaign in the Baltic in that year – but too late as it turned out.[24]

Undermanned and inexperienced or not, there really was need for haste in getting the Baltic Fleet into position. Rumours had already been received that the Russian fleet in the Baltic had been increased to 27 battleships, with 8 to 10 frigates, 9 paddle-streamers and a host of other vessels, including – according to the British Minister at St Petersburg – an alarming 180 gunboats.[25] This enemy force would have to be bottled up in the Baltic as quickly as possible. Leaving on 11 March 1854 – a fortnight before Britain declared war on Russia – the fleet's immediate goal was the deepwater harbour at Kiel[26] but Napier quickly settled on Kioge Bay near Copenhagen as a better placed base for a future blockade. Practical problems of manning, training and fitting out the fleet were not all that Napier faced. The initial instructions he received from the Admiralty via the First Lord, Sir James Graham, seemed clear enough and Napier surely succeeded in carrying them out. As they are critical to understanding Napier's tactics in the Baltic, they are worth looking at in detail. At the end of March, the Admiralty instructed Napier that his main aims should be to prevent the Russian fleet leaving the Baltic, to bring that fleet to action if he could, to establish 'a strict blockade' of the Gulf of Finland and to dominate the main sea lanes to destroy Russian trade. He was specifically instructed to examine the Åland Islands and the defences of Bomarsund and to report on the feasibility of an attack. Operations against any other 'fortified places' were left to his discretion.[27] One commentator noted:

> the state of the Baltic Fleet, the communications between Sir Charles Napier and the Board of Admiralty at home, together with their refusal to furnish him with the requisite auxiliaries of gun-boats and troops, would almost tend to throw doubts as to whether it were ever the intention of our Government to strike an important blow in the Baltic; it would rather appear that their object was merely to establish a blockade of the Russian fleet in order to prevent any attack on the coasts of England in her then unprotected state.[28]

No sensible naval commander of those days was at all keen to try wooden walls against solid stone defences, especially of the quality of some of the Russian fortifications in the Baltic, and it was implicit in Napier's orders that he was 'on no account to knock his head against stone walls' in attacking strongly fortified positions like Cronstadt and Sveaborg.[29] These requirements were repeatedly emphasised; on 2 April Sir James Graham again reminded Napier of the vital need to block the exit from the Baltic, and continued:

> when you are sure . . . that you have the whole of the enemy's forces in front of you and within the Gulf of Finland, the first object is to keep them shut up there and to see if they are disposed to measure their strength with you. I am afraid that they will avoid an action in the open sea and will await your attack under cover of their fortifications. I doubt the prudence of commencing any such operations.[30]

Sir James later told Napier:

> I have a great respect for stone walls and have no fancy for running
> even screw line of battle ships against them, because the public here
> may be impatient; you must not be rash because they at a distance
> from danger are foolhardy – you must not risk the fleet in an
> impossible enterprise. I believe both Sweaborg and Cronstadt to be
> all but impregnable from the sea[31]

In carrying out what he could practically achieve, Napier succeeded very
well. But he was to be constantly criticised by the authorities and others for not
taking the risks his orders specifically forbad and for not risking his ships and
men in actions that would have jeopardised the fleet. He was of course assailed
by younger officers, especially some of the commanders of the newer steam
frigates, who often come across as dynamic young men, anxious to write up
their every action as a major naval triumph and eager to get their next promotion and the Order of the Bath at the cannon's mouth. To many of them,
Napier seemed too reluctant to take aggressive action, too eager to take the
simple path of blockade rather than risk strenuous assault.[32] For example, in
April 1854, it was reported that the Russian Baltic division based at Sveaborg
was actually stuck in the ice *outside* the line of defences, but Napier took no
action. It is easy to understand the frustration of some of the steamer captains,
like Lord George Paget in *Princess Royal* and George Giffard in *Leopard* when
they blamed Napier for lack of enterprise in failing to attack the Russian ships
there and then. Privately, in their journals and letters, and sometimes publicly
in the British press, such officers railed against Napier's lack of drive. They
clearly thought him something of an 'old women', half-hearted, nervous of loss
and anxious to explain away chances of attacking the Russians – blaming, for
example, the lack of pilots and coastal charts. But equally, it is easy to see why
Napier failed to seize what appeared to be obvious opportunities. He seriously
regarded his fleet as inexperienced and undermanned, genuinely lacking charts
and pilots, and did not have the type of ships or armament which could take on
well-built and well-armed stone defences like those at Cronstadt and Sveaborg.
And anyway, Napier was fulfilling perfectly well the instructions he was given.
The Aberdeen government did not expect – and had not provided for – major
military action in the Baltic in the spring of 1854; if Napier were to attack
Sveaborg and/or Cronstadt he would need different types of ship and considerable land forces, to deploy ashore far beyond the naval and marine
contingents carried on the allied fleet. Although the French later sent a large
military force to take Bomarsund in the Åland Islands, even they were unwilling to commit them to further action and they rapidly returned to France.

Napier was left without adequate military forces and as the campaign in the Crimea developed, it was unlikely that he would get them.

Nevertheless, in 1854 Napier carried out his main brief, blockading the Baltic and the Gulfs of Bothnia, Riga and Finland, preventing the movement of enemy merchant shipping,[33] blockading all of Russia's Baltic ports and so intimidating the Russian fleet that it never moved from its moorings to offer battle or respond to allied coastal raids. Napier's ships operated as far as the northernmost point of the Gulf of Bothnia, bombarding towns and burning shipping and stores ashore and actually destroyed the Russian fortifications at Bomarsund in the Åland Islands. Only occasionally did they meet with minor setbacks (for example, at Gamla Karleby; see below, pp. 20–1) but in general they easily demonstrated the allies' complete domination of the Baltic and the Russian government's inability to respond at sea. And it was estimated that even the mere presence of Napier's squadrons, with the implied threat to Cronstadt, Helsingfors and a range of other ports, was at least occupying the attention of significant Russian forces which might otherwise have been dispatched to the Crimea.[34]

Early in April, a report that Russian warships had been seen in the heart of the Baltic pushed Napier into action and he led the fleet eastwards from Kioge Bay. If any such Russian squadron had put to sea, however, it must have returned to port in good time for its own safety: the allies saw nothing. By the time that Napier, with Admirals Corry, Plumridge and Chads, began to move eastward, the British fleet had accumulated nearly forty ships, of which more than half were modern steamers. They carried between them something like 1,700 guns and 18,000 men. But they were rarely assembled for long in one spot since detached squadrons were deployed to scour the Baltic – to reconnoitre the coasts, stop and search vessels and watch the numerous enemy ports. A 'flying squadron' under Hanway Plumridge with *Leopard*, *Odin*, *Valorous* and *Vulture* was detached from the main fleet to patrol the Gulfs of Bothnia and Finland, as far as the ice would allow. This squadron really became a 'raiding party', destroying stores in quantity or burning shipping (forty-six vessels in one month) along the Finnish coast (see below).

The first point that attracted Napier's attention early in May was Hängo Head.[35] At the point of the peninsula that separates the Gulfs of Bothnia and Finland, it guarded the entrance to the Gulf of Finland and had been fortified by the Russians. Napier had detached single warships to reconnoitre to the north and east of the headland and here on 19 May the first naval action in the Baltic took place. Captain Hastings Yelverton in the *Arrogant* with Captain William H. Hall in the *Hecla* – both steamers – entered the bay east of the Hängo Peninsula, whose entrance was dominated by the town of Ekness. Yelverton and Hall aimed to capture at least one of three merchant vessels known to be anchored in the bay but the coastline seemed to be alive with defenders and defences, including three batteries of artillery, infantry armed with rifles and a troop of horse artillery. Both ships soon found themselves under heavy shot and rifle fire, *Hecla* receiving several hits to her funnel, steam pipe and hull and both vessels being studded with rifle balls. Nevertheless, despite the unexpectedly severe opposition, Captain Hall steamed into Ekness, cut out a barque and towed her away, much to the shock of the inhabitants. The 46-gun *Arrogant* was too heavy to approach the shallow water as closely as Yelverton wished so that the fight was really carried on by *Hecla*, with the Russian infantry, cavalry and artillery moving along the coast parallel with the steamer, dodging its fire and returning fire themselves. This was the first of many instances in the developing war that demonstrated that vessels of shallower draught were better fitted than the larger men-of-war for service in coastal waters and close into the shore.

Another subsidiary expedition was carried out by Captain Cooper Key, with the screw steamers *Amphion* and *Conflict*. Their goal was the coast of what was then Courland,[36] close to the frontier with Prussia. Arriving off Libau,[37] Key learned that several Russian merchant vessels lay in the port and that the place was defended by 500 or 600 soldiers. Nevertheless, he decided to attempt the capture of some or all of the vessels. Steaming within gunshot of the town on the 17 May, Key summoned the governor to surrender; his refusal led to the manning of all the boats belonging to both ships, those of *Amphion* being commanded by Captain Key and of *Conflict* by Captain Arthur Cumming. The boats had to pull 1½ miles up a small creek to reach Libau and as the river was only 50 yards wide, they were lucky that Russian soldiers did not man the banks, or the boat expedition might have fared badly. The boats could land only 130 men in all, against a population of up to 10,000 aided by perhaps 600 soldiers. Nevertheless, so well did Captain Cumming manage a conference with the port authorities that they agreed to his terms – to save damage to the town – and all the Russian ships were given up without a shot being fired on either side. Before nightfall *Amphion* and *Conflict* were able to steam away with eight new Russian merchant vessels in tow, having destroyed other government property ashore.

Similar success was had by Captain James Willcox in the 6-gun paddle-steamer *Dragon*. Whilst cruising in the Gulf of Finland, he reconnoitred the port of Reval,[38] on the coast of Estonia opposite Sveaborg. Seeing two vessels at anchor there, he made a dash at them. Regardless of the shot poured towards his little steamer from the land batteries, he ran in close ashore, captured both of the ships and towed them into Hängo Bay on the following morning. Incidents like these were widely reported and enthusiastically greeted in Britian.

These and similar raids aside, for the whole month of May Sir Charles with the bulk of the fleet remained in the region between Gotland and Hängo, ready to attack the Russians if they emerged from the Gulf of Finland, but reluctant to undertake anything that might appear to be rash – as ordered. He knew that a large Russian fleet remained safely masked behind the fortified islands of Sveaborg, guarding Helsingfors, and that a much larger force was at Cronstadt. If the ships at Sveaborg could be tempted out and drawn into action there remained the possibility that the larger Cronstadt fleet might then sally forth and take the allies at a disadvantage. It was deeply hurtful to Napier and his officers and men to know that the British press was already impatient for action and demanding to know why some great naval victory had not been achieved.

During most of May and into the first week of June, Admiral J.H. Plumridge was engaged in 'special service' with a 'flying squadron' whose main object was to examine the maze of intricate channels between the scattered Åland Islands, which form something of a barrier to the Gulf of Bothnia, and which as Russian possessions gave her virtually the command of that sea. However, as it turned out, the expedition largely involved the mass destruction of shipping and property. Plumridge's squadron was certainly impressive – *Leopard*, *Vulture*, *Odin* and *Valorous*, all new paddle-steamers, mounting fifty-six heavy guns between them. After establishing that the maze of Åland Islands really could not be navigated without experienced pilots or local knowledge, he carried on up the east coast of the Gulf of Bothnia to its extreme northern limits. It was late in May before Plumridge reached these areas but within days his ships had wrought havoc on the coastal trade of the region. The usual practice was for the warships to moor at a distance from the shore whilst their boats rowed in to search local ports, like the small coastal towns of Brahestad, Uleaborg and Tornea,[39] all near the northern end of the gulf. On 30 May, for example, fourteen vessels and a huge quantity of stores were destroyed at Brahestad, which had a small Russian dockyard. When the authorities refused to surrender government property, a landing party under Lieutenant B.P. Priest of *Leopard* was sent in to destroy the shipping and stores, an operation that lasted seven hours.[40] Surgeon Edward Cree aboard *Odin* noted that there was 'great destruction of property but it was in order to assist in crippling the enemy. The unfortunate people fled to the country, for there was no resistance. The blaze was tremendous and an awful and cruel sight, but such is war.'[41] Uleaborg, one of the largest and most important ports in northern Finland and a major exporter of wood and tar, was attacked on 1 and 2 of June, twenty-three vessels being destroyed there, along with quantities of tar, hemp and timber whose burning 'illuminated the country for many miles around ... crippling [the Emperor's] shipbuilding in the Baltic'.[42] Over the next few days eight vessels were burned nearby and another on 8 June on the Komi River near

Tornea. In all, on the Finnish shore of the gulf between the 5 May and 10 June, Plumridge's ships destroyed no fewer than 40 merchant vessels, afloat or on the stocks, amounting to 11,000 tons, along with 40,000 barrels of pitch and tar, 60,000 square yards of rough pitch and a huge quantity of timber, spars, planks, deal, sails, ropes and other naval stores estimated to be worth £400,000.[43] He did not lose a man during this process but it did not seem to occur – yet – that these stores might have been taken for allied use rather than simply destroyed.

Not surprisingly, there was considerable criticism of these actions in sections of the British press, both because of the sheer waste of useable supplies and on humanitarian grounds. At Uleaborg, for example, local merchants had gone out under a flag of truce to meet Plumridge personally and begged him to spare their town. He told them that private property would be left untouched and that only government buildings and stores would he destroyed; but at the same time, he warned them of the dire consequences if the locals showed any sign of resistance. At Tornea, near the Swedish frontier, the inhabitants themselves destroyed the barracks and government warehouses before the British squadron arrived, thus avoiding further damage; they were followed by the inhabitants of the nearby frontier town of Haparanda, where after a search the warships left after inflicting only minor damage. It was only because government ships and stores were kept at these places that the attacks were made and the destruction was undoubtedly meant to be restricted to actual government property but it was an unfortunate fact that overshooting and the force of the wind often led to private property being burned or destroyed along with that which really belonged to the Russian government. When news of these raids was published in Britain a few weeks later, an attempt was made in the Commons to show that the rules of 'honourable warfare' had been breached; the MP Thomas Gibson, for example, demanded in the House that the First Lord of the Admiralty explain 'a system which carried on a great war by plundering and destroying the property of defenceless villagers', but the issue was not pursued. The Russian and some European journals made similar claims that Britain was waging an uncharacteristically uncivilised and un-worthy form of warfare against largely defenceless civil communities.[44]

But the loss was not all one way. Plumridge's activities were closed by an embarrassing incident. On the shore of Finland south of Brahestad is the small town of Gamla (Old) Karleby,[45] once one of the richest towns in Finland, noted for its export of tar and its ship-building. *Odin* and *Vulture* arrived off Gamla Karleby on the 7 June and sent out several boats late in the evening, when there was still some daylight at those high latitudes.[46] When a summons to surrender government stores was refused, the ships' boats were sent in to attempt a landing – two paddle-box boats,[47] a pinnace, a cutter and a gig. To their considerable surprise they found, as 'our poor foolish Jacks and Marines were taking it easy, smoking their pipes, their muskets and carronades not even loaded',[48] that the village was well defended and not at all prepared simply to stand by and watch the destruction of their property. Concealed in the town, there were in fact two field guns and two companies of infantry who suddenly opened fire on the shore party at close range. For an hour, there was a brisk firefight but the boats were ultimately forced to retire, carrying away a few dead and wounded and leaving some of their men as prisoners of the Russians. From the *Odin*, Lieutenant Carrington, Midshipman Athorpe, Mate Montagu and three men were killed and fifteen others wounded. One of the paddle-box boats of HMS *Vulture* was fouled by a sunken vessel and trapped and all her men were seized and taken ashore,[49] twenty-eight being captured in all. Since the water along the coast at that point was very shallow, the steam frigates could not safely come within miles of the shore and were prevented from assisting their own boats at close range. However, Plumridge clearly thought that the insignificant town was not worth further effort or loss and simply withdrew, leaving the Finns and Russians to claim a great victory; highly coloured accounts duly appeared locally and in major Russian newspapers like the *Journal de St Petersburg*.[50]

Soon after these opening actions in the Gulf of Bothnia, a French fleet of twenty-four vessels under Vice Admiral Parseval-Deschênes joined the British, reaching Hängo on 13 June. Their commander hoisted his flag on the *Inflexible*, whilst his second-in-command, Rear Admiral Penaud, sailed in the *Duguesclin*. On the 15th Parseval-Deschênes made a formal visit to his British counterparts on board the *Duke of Wellington* on what was a novel occasion – never before had British and French fleets met in amity in the Baltic. It is interesting to note that unlike the British fleet which simply relied on its own sailors or the complements of Royal Marines borne aboard the ships, the French fleet carried a force of both infantry and artillery, ready for service ashore. A friendly relationship quickly developed between the Anglo-French officers and crews and both cooperated well throughout the campaign.

The blockade of all the Russian ports in the Gulfs of Livonia, Finland and Bothnia had been formally effected by Sir Charles Napier before the French arrived and was officially notified in the *London Gazette* on 16 June. Napier had delayed his advance up the Gulf of Finland partly to await the arrival of the French contingent and partly because of major difficulties placed in his way – not the least of which were the dense fogs lasting days on end[51] and the Russian removal of the channel buoys, beacons and lights which had served as land-marks along dangerous coastlines.

With the French acting in concert, Napier took up a position in Baro Sound just within the entrance to the Gulf of Finland, about 12 miles from Sveaborg[52] and 15 from Reval. By the end of June there was a combined fleet of no less than 51 warships, comprising 28 ships-of-the-line, 5 first-class frigates and 18 steamers anchored in the sound; such a fleet, carrying about 2,700 large-calibre guns and 30,000 seamen and marines, had never been seen in the Baltic.

Apart from a 'simple' blockade of the outlets of the Baltic north of Denmark, to cripple Russia's import and export trade and to prevent the Russian Baltic Fleet from operating against the British and French coasts, there were several obvious targets for Anglo-French naval attacks – if the right forces had been available. Any number of towns, ports and coastal fortifications could have been hit – Viborg, Abo, Pernau,[53] Nystad and others were open to attack and some indeed were 'visited' in 1854 and 1855. But the main focuses of serious operations were easily identified – Reval, Sveaborg, Cronstadt and Bomarsund. Reval on the coast of what was then Courland and Sveaborg (once known as 'the Gibraltar of the north') both served as 'flank defences' to the approaches to Cronstadt and were home to ships of the Russian Baltic Fleet. There were hopes that they could be 'neutralised' by direct attack and no doubt public opinion in Britain expected news of an early assault on at least some of these enemy bases. In fact, three major targets, Reval, Sveaborg and Cronstadt, though frequently reconnoitred and 'watched', were protected by such formidable defences that Napier in the end simply could not contemplate a serious attack on any one of them with the fleet under his command, lacking the sort of mortar and gunboats he would need for coastal operations and almost entirely without adequate military force to follow up any successful naval attack.

Nevertheless, some major action had at least to be considered. During the last week in June the allied commanders decided on an advance in strength into the Gulf of Finland towards Cronstadt. A massively fortified island that constituted the main defence of St Petersburg and its approaches, Cronstadt was the main base of the Russian Baltic Fleet. This famous stronghold – island, town, harbour and fortress – lies in the Bay of Constadt, 31 miles from St Petersburg and was surrounded by a series of heavily fortified outcrops and islets apart from those defences actually sited on the island itself. Cronstadt was not only the main station of the Baltic Fleet but was also the outer harbour of St Petersburg and all vessels en route to the capital were searched here, their cargoes sealed and trans-shipment made to vessels intending to ascend the Neva. Cronstadt had three harbours – an outer one for warships, an inner one for merchant shipping and a large dockyard for fitting and repairing vessels. The town looked more like a military depot and arsenal than a commercial port, dominated by buildings and fortifications belonging to the Imperial navy. A range of fortresses, such as Fort Alexander and Fort Constantine, dominated the southern side of the island, whilst the northern side was equally defended by forts and redoubts, in addition to six or seven batteries on the mole. These works were begun by Peter the Great but had been constantly added to and strengthened over succeeding generations. Not only were the town and harbour defended by massive granite batteries, but every islet and passage was equally covered so that any enemy vessel attempting to sail up to St Petersburg from the north or south of the island would have to pass within range of at least two arrays of batteries. Furthermore, the 6 miles between the island and the mainland were so broken up by inlets, shoals and mud banks that the navigable channels were narrow and any approach difficult. The Russians had converted some of the small islets into strong gun positions and had even built forts on piles driven into the mud, defending the approaches from all directions. It was believed that up to 1,500 large-calibre guns, besides those carried on the Russian fleet, protected the island ands its seaways.

When the fleet was within 10 miles of the island, three small paddle-frigates, *Lightning*, *Bulldog* and *Magicienne*, were sent ahead to sound and reconnoitre more closely, and especially to search for any mines ('infernal machines') or submarine explosives, which reports (correctly) claimed the Russians had planted in the approaches.[54] Following at a short distance to offer protection were three larger warships, *Impérieuse*, *Arrogant* and *Desperate*. No 'infernal machines' were encountered on this occasion but the reconnoitring vessels approached Cronstadt near enough to see its formidable array of granite batteries and pick out the large fleet sheltered within the harbour. The Baltic Fleet's Surveying Officer, Captain Bartholomew James Sulivan[55] in the lightly armed survey vessel *Lightning*, had orders from the hydrographer Sir Francis Beaufort 'to assist with the important operations of the Baltic Fleet by making such skilful and rapid reconnaissance as well as by occasional hydrographic surveys wherever it may be considered necessary', and – interestingly – to make everything 'more or less subservient to the great object of improving our charts'.[56] He reported that Cronstadt was too well protected to risk attacking without, as Sulivan said, the use of a significant number of mortar vessels, which Napier's fleet did not possess. He counted no less than 17 'sail-of-the-line' warships 'moored outside the basin', with 3 smaller vessels and 6 steamers nearby and a host of other armed ships around the island.[57]

Although the main element of the Russian fleet within the harbour caused no problems and made no attempt to sally out and offer battle, it was simply not possible for allied ships to approach near enough to carry out a thorough examination, let alone actually try to force a passage. Napier and his subordinates rapidly agreed that to take on Cronstadt or attempt to bypass its defences was quite beyond their powers[58] – no matter what uninformed opinion in the British press might claim, already growing critical of the lack of a major victory. Admiral Napier, as the man on the spot and responsible to the nation for the safety of his fleet, wisely declined to take on Cronstadt[59] and the Admiralty concurred in his decision.[60]

After an examination of the area the allied fleet returned to Baro Sound early in July 1854, remaining at anchor for some days whilst the commanders discussed the probabilities for and against the success of any great enterprise. Whilst they worried over the possibility of attacks against major targets like Cronstadt or Sveaborg, detached squadrons continued to carry out the rest of Napier's brief in the Gulfs of Finland, Riga and Bothnia – to 'watch' enemy ports in case Russian warships emerged to offer battle, to stop, search and if necessary seize enemy merchant ships breaching the blockade and, where possible, to harass enemy positions ashore.

If Cronstadt, Sveaborg and Reval were deemed to be beyond reach, attention had to fall on the capture of Bomarsund on the Åland Islands as at least a potentially achievable goal and one suggested in Napier's original orders. In contrast to the other three Russian bases, Bomarsund, a fortress complex guarding an impressive potential harbour, was vulnerable; as it was still under construction it was likely to be incomplete and undermanned and did not have any element of the Russian fleet nearby to support its defence.

Åland, 'the land of waters', is a scattered archipelago of more than 250 large islands and up to 6,000 smaller islets and rocky outcrops scattered across the entrance to the Gulf of Bothnia. Its one large island gives its name to the group but no less than eighty of the islands were inhabited in 1854, with a total population estimated at about 15,000. The largest island, Fasta Åland, is about 18 miles long by 14 miles wide. Historically part of Sweden, at various times during the eighteenth century the Ålands were taken by the Russians but each time were returned to Sweden. The Ålanders defeated another Russian attack in 1807 but by the Treaty of Frederickshamn in 1809 the island chain was formally ceded to Russia and along with Finland itself became part of the semi-autonomous Grand Duchy of Finland within the Russian Empire.

There was some hope in 1809 that the islands would remain unfortified, since a strong Russian military and naval presence there was not acceptable to Sweden and the British government was equally unwilling for reasons of both trade and security to see a powerful Russian naval base established in the middle of the Baltic. However, since Tsar Nicholas I's aim was the defence of western Finland and Russia's important maritime post and trade route from Stockholm to St Petersburg, the Russians worked from the beginning to develop a significant military and naval base. The major work was undertaken between 1830 and 1832 with the construction of a series of fortifications more or less in the centre of the Åland Islands, to the renewed concern of the Swedish and British authorities.

Although the multitude of islands is fragmented by a maze of channels and waterways making access difficult, it was decided to erect the main fortress just about in the centre of the dispersed group on Fasta Åland, overlooking Bomar Sound. This separates Fasta Åland from the smaller island of Prästö and covers the approaches to the islands of Michelsö and Lumpar on Lumparfjord. The chosen site offered a deep, largely ice-free, defendable harbour intended to be the foundation of a major Russian naval base. The defences were extensive – though never completed to anything like their planned extent – and a large workforce, including convicts, was drawn from all over the Russian Empire to do the work. To house the influx of new administrators, officers and labourers, the nearby village of Skarpans was expanded and a 'New Skarpans' built within the defensive perimeters of the fortifications.[61] As it stood in 1854, the main fort was a huge semicircular structure, a quarter of a mile in length and two storeys high, its two 'arms' connected by long barrack blocks. It mounted 120 guns, facing Lumpar Bay and covering the southern entrance to Bomar Sound. Protecting this on high ground to its north was a tower known as Fort Notvik[62] and on the landward side to the west lay another tower-fort known as Bränklint.[63] A small fort to the southwest was incomplete and there was a 7-gun earthwork battery near Tranvik Point. The works continued across the narrow straits onto Prästö Island, where another 14-gun tower-fort covered the approach to the north side of the Sound; several other planned towers, linking curtain walls and emplacements were never built. The completed forts were massively constructed of solid granite blocks backed with brick and were formidable structures. However, although designed to house a total garrison of 5,000 men and 500 guns, by the time of the allied attack in 1854 the incomplete fortifications housed less than half that number of men and guns.[64]

Needless to say, the Admiralty had been aware of developments at Bomarsund as they occurred over the years, but in the early days of the Baltic operations a thorough reconnaissance was clearly needed. An initial survey of the approach routes to Bomarsund was carried out by the indefatigable Captain B.J. Sulivan in the lightly armed survey vessel *Lightning*.[65] In the middle of June 1854, whilst the main allied fleet remained at anchor in Baro Sound, an audacious raid on Bomarsund was carried out by Captain Hall with the paddle-frigates *Hecla*, *Odin* and *Valorous*. *Valorous* and *Odin* were part of the squadron under Admiral Plumridge blockading the Gulf of Bothnia and Hall, commanding HMS *Hecla*, took them under command in Plumridge's absence. Anxious to make a significant (and hopefully well-publicised) gesture,[66] Hall led the three warships into the labyrinth of channels leading to Lumpar Bay and Bomarsund on 21 June. With the aid of a local pilot, taken from a fishing boat that *Hecla* had stopped, and by the more extensive survey of the islands and channels that Sulivan had carried out early in June with *Lightning* and

Driver, the three ships threaded their way towards the Russian defences. Taking up position about 2,000 yards from the main fort, they opened fire. The fortress was of course heavily armed and was also defended by two companies of riflemen on the shore and by supporting batteries. A firefight was maintained for hours, with the ships occasionally changing position to improve their range and aim and with the forts replying equally briskly. Surgeon Cree recalled that 'with our long guns our shot would search the fort pretty well. They soon returned our fire but their balls fell short. A small fort or Martello tower[67] soon joined in with her guns which had greater range because it was on a hill, but fortunately the shot went over us.'[68] A masked shore battery and riflemen in the woods also opened up on the ships as they passed and all were frequently hit, though none seriously damaged. It was during this action that Mate Charles Lucas[69] of the *Hecla* performed the act that was to win the first Victoria Cross; when a Russian shell hit the deck of the *Hecla*, Lucas immediately picked it up 'whilst the fusee was still burning',[70] and threw it into the sea where it exploded, thereby undoubtedly saving many lives and much damage. Apart from the burning of a storehouse near the main fort, little significant damage was actually caused to the defences or to the ships, which kept too far out of range to do much against the granite walls. The frigates withdrew after midnight having used up most of their ammunition and carefully wound their way back out of the island maze.[71]

This action by Captains Hall, Buckle and Scott was widely praised in the British press and in the Commons as a fine example of the sort of dynamic and successful exploit that the British public expected from their naval forces in the Baltic, but many of their colleagues were less impressed. Napier, amongst others, openly praised their bravery but thought it had been a reckless act, putting at risk three important vessels for no possible gain, since they could not have reduced the Bomarsund forts by themselves but had in the meantime left Admiral Plumridge's squadron dangerously under-armed until the ships could be re-supplied.[72]

Napier intended to do much more with Bomarsund when he finally sailed westward from Baro Sound on 18 July. Admiral Hanway Plumridge's squadron, including *Merlin*, *Leopard* and *Pigmy*, watching the Gulf of Bothnia, was ordered to blockade the north of Bomar Sound to deal with any possible Russian reinforcements that might be directed from the Finnish coast, and Commodore Martin with nine ships was detailed to watch the movements of the Russians at Sveaborg and Cronstadt in case they decided to sally out against the allies whilst they were entangled in the Ålands. Napier reached Ledo Sound,[73] south of the Åland Islands, on 21 July. The larger line-of-battle ships were left there, partly to be available to Commodore Martin if the Russian fleet did appear and partly because they would be difficult to navigate through the narrow, convoluted channels. On the 22nd, the survey vessel *Lightning*, escorted by *Alban* and *Amphion*, led the 60-gun blockships *Edinburgh*, *Blenheim*, *Ajax* and *Hogue* in advance of the other ships through the islands via the Angö passage into Lumpar Bay, following a route previously explored and marked by Sulivan. The French squadron arrived in Ledo Sound on the same day.

As the ships had to sail close to the land and it was expected that Russian troops and guns would be hidden in the woods on shore, ready to oppose their passage, preparations were made to guard against a sudden attack; shot and shell were brought up on deck ready to use, men were placed on station at the guns, some guns were loaded with canister and a protective screen of hammocks was rigged up. These were wise precautions, since the Russians soon began to fire on the ships and Napier had to order them to withdraw beyond reach of the guns at Bomarsund whilst he waited for the French military contingent to arrive. In the meantime, he ordered a further survey of the intricate channels between the islands, during which two or three vessels went on shore in the narrow passages and were only freed with difficulty. From the masts of the moored ships, it was possible to make out the great fort at Bomarsund, its bomb-proof roof covered by a layer of sand 4 feet deep and with a double range of granite casemates, commanding the Sound and the bay.

When the British and French admirals had established the formidable nature of the granite batteries at Cronstadt, Sveaborg and Bomarsund and had reported their conclusions to the home authorities, the British and French governments accepted the possible need for military action ashore to back up any bombardment from the sea. As the greater land power, it was agreed that France should provide an army for service in the Baltic, in addition to the body of troops originally sent with their fleet and that Britain would provide the ships that would carry the French troops to the Baltic. During the second week of July 1854, a French expeditionary force with all its stores, ammunition and artillery was assembled at Boulogne and Calais and passed to transports and other ships anchored in Calais roads. Under their commander General Achille Baraguay d'Hilliers,[74] the French force comprised two infantry brigades, led by Generals Hugues and Gres, with General Niel in command of the engineers. By 15 July, all were ready to embark on board the transports and over the next few days two French and four British sailing battleships, filled with troops and towed by British steamers,[75] led the convoy up the Channel and towards the Baltic. Napier watched the arrival of the first French contingent at Ledo Sound on 30 July from his flagship *Duke of Wellington* and the usual round of ceremonial and visits took place; a second group with artillery and siege materiel did not arrive until 5 August.[76] Part of the allied fleet was detached to form a cordon round the islands, to remain at signal distance to watch for the possible movement of the troops on shore and to cut off all supplies of provisions and ammunition; the rest entered the straits leading directly up to Lumparfjord opposite Bomarsund.

Ignoring minor or incomplete batteries and redoubts, there were four main forts in the Bomarsund complex as it stood in August 1854; four others, all to be linked by a curtain wall, were planned but never built. The large fort on the shore facing the approaches to Bomar Sound commanded the harbour with its formidable double-storeyed convex frontage, casemated for 180 guns; with its curved face and wooden roof, according to B.J. Sulivan, 'it exactly resembles a new terrace in a fashionable watering-place'.[77] It was afterwards found that this work was defended from the land as well as the sea, with a wide moat on its western side but it had no land-facing gun emplacements. The casemates, bomb-proof chambers immediately behind and around each gun for the protection of the artillerymen, gave great additional strength to the work. The western fort (Fort Bränklint) was a tower made up of two storeys of casemated batteries, one above the other, pierced for fourteen guns.[78] The diameter of the fort was about 100 feet. Above its main bomb-proof roof was another roof of zinc plate, pierced with holes, through which riflemen could command a great sweep of country around the fort. Like the main fort, Bränklint was constructed of pentagonal blocks of granite, interlinked with great skill and backed with brick. The northern fort, Notvik, usually referred to as Nottich in British accounts, was much like the western tower, differing only in slight details; it commanded the northern entrance to Bomar Sound and could offer covering fire to the main fort and to Bränklint. Both towers also defended the landward approaches to the main fortress and were clearly capable of offering a stubborn resistance. A key point is that the towers were built on rocky outcrops with commanding views in all directions and each was surrounded by a ditch. At the foot of one was a barrack block and another low casemated battery. Another line of batteries had been started under the second tower, but had not been completed by the summer of 1854. The fourth fort – known as Fort 'Z' and much the same as the others in design and armament – lay across the Sound on the small island of Prästö, on a peninsula directly opposite Notvik, covering the northern and eastern side of Bomar Sound. Finally, a single earthwork battery of five cannon was placed under the cover of trees at Grinkarudden about a mile southwest of the main fort.

With his fleet in position off Lumpar Bay, Napier's operations were delayed for some days by the non-arrival of the siege guns from France, but he used the time to survey and map possible landing grounds, again using the ubiquitous *Lightning*. A whole coterie of the great and good of the Baltic expedition was taken aboard the survey ship on 2 August to get a close look at Bomarsund fort – Napier, Parseval-Deschênes, Baraguay d'Hilliers, General Harry Jones and a

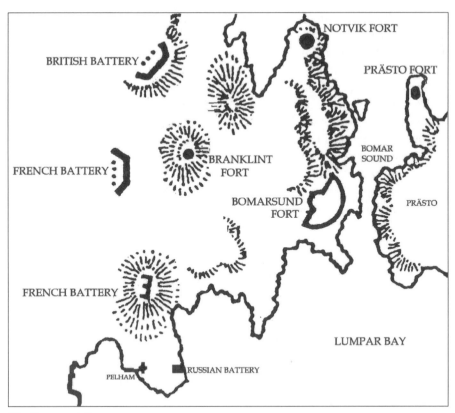

The Bomarsund Forts.

host of other senior staff officers and unit commanders – and were lucky that the fort never got their range. The French transports finally arrived with the siege guns on 5 August. In the meantime, the ships' carpenters had constructed strong wooden platforms ready to carry and move the heavy brass siege guns. The actual landings on Fasta Åland took place on 8 August at two points on the island, the troops coming ashore in the paddle-box boats and ships' cutters well away from the range of the forts, with nearly every allied ship furnishing a contingent of boats. From 4.00am to 9.00am on the 8th, the disembarkation was completed without any opposition and the troops began their preparations for a march inland towards the forts. The main French column under Baraguay d'Hilliers, 9,000 men in 5 regiments with support troops, landed to the south near the coastal village of Tranvik, to approach the landward side of Fort Bränklint. A smaller, second column under Brigadier General Harry Jones, RE with 2,000 French infantry, 100 men of No. 2 Company Sappers and Miners and 700 Royal Marines of the Plymouth Division under Colonel F. Graham,[79] with 4 field guns and rockets, landed to the north near the village of Hulta. This column, led to its landing place by *Lightning*, *Driver* and the French vessel *Fulton*, and protected by Admiral Plumridge's screen of ships,[80] was originally to join the French in a combined attack on the western fort, Bränklint, but the rapid French success in reducing Bränklint meant that Jones could only turn his attention to the northern fort, Notvik.

The preliminary operations lasted a full nine days, from 8–16 August inclusive. As each French regiment landed on the morning of the 8th, it fell into line and marched through dense pine forest and over high ground, taking up a position for the night close to the western fort, which commanded the country around it. Small 'expeditions' were sent out to destroy nearby telegraph and signal stations and for their part, the Russian defenders burned anything in the way of stores and buildings outside the defensive perimeters of the forts. The 'northern column' under Brigadier General Jones had a rather more demanding task in that it had to cross very difficult terrain, both rocky and marshy. Taking up a position about 2 miles from Bomarsund fort, they too set up their camp. Once they had reached their respective siege positions, the besiegers began to build sandbag and earth redoubts and gun emplacements, all the time coming under sporadic fire from the forts. At the same time, a force of French marines landed on Prästö Island to cover the fort on that side of Bomar Sound.

As military forces of up to 12,000 men landed, brought up their supplies and guns and took up their positions, the warships were not idle. The smaller steamers carried ammunition and provisions to the shore, whilst the larger vessels prepared to bring their broadsides to bear upon any assailable point, some firing canister into the woodlands to disperse or repel possible Russian defenders. Because of the restrictions of the anchorage, only a limited number of the allied warships could open fire on the fortifications of Bomarsund,[81] so that the military arrangements had to bear in mind the possibly restricted use of the fleet, which would control the southern and eastern side of the Russian positions. As a preliminary, *Amphion* and the French ship *Phlégethon* shelled the isolated earthwork gun emplacement which could have been a serious danger to the troops during the landing, but it was found to have been abandoned already by its Russian garrison. They then passed close to the formidable granite fort, drawing a heavy fire, and during the day the other ships fired to distract as far as possible the attention of the forts, so that the infantry would be unmolested. The blockships *Edinburgh*, *Blenheim*, *Ajax* and *Hogue* covered the landing of the troops before returning to anchor out of range with the rest of the fleet and prepared for action as soon as the military arrangements were completed. With the landing columns in their initial camps, work to land stores and ammunition continued all through 9 August. The shores were lined with small boats, ferrying ammunition and provisions, along

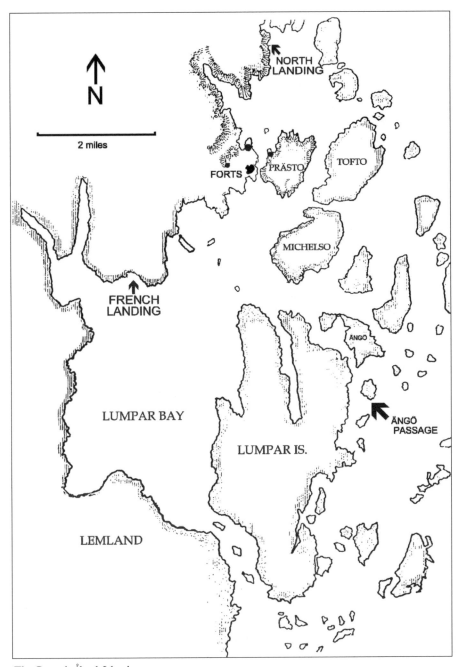

The Central Åland Islands.

with guns, carriages and the myriad supplies required by the troops. The main encampment of the French for the night had been near the village of Old Skarpans, close to Fort Bränklint, whilst the smaller force under Brigadier General Harry Jones was encamped close by, between Forts Notvik and Bränklint. The fleets were kept alert by constant reports that the Russians were about to send reinforcements from Finland, but a line of ships and boats, including the gunboat *Cuckoo*, blocked any possible access.[82]

On the 10th, some of the sailors were employed ashore. It was decided to land six naval 32-pounders carried on HMS *Belleisle* (then serving as a hospital ship) to enable General Harry Jones to construct a breaching battery. The carpenters of the ships belonging to Admiral Chads' squadron made 8 sledges, 6 for the guns and 2 for the carriages and gear. On the 10th, 3 of the guns were safely landed and sledges manned by 150 seamen each, under the command of Captain Hewlett of *Edinburgh*, dragged the guns over exceptionally difficult terrain for 4½ miles inland to the battery site – a major achievement.[83] The exhausted men reached the camp at 1.00pm and, just as they were about to have some food, immediately received orders to return to their ships, as HMS *Penelope* had run aground under the fire of the enemy and their ships might be needed. This grounding was one consequence of the narrowness of the channels through which the vessels had to steer and a number of allied ships went aground during the course of the operations. As *Penelope* had grounded on rocks dangerously close to Bomarsund, the great fort opened up on the sitting target and for two hours poured a fierce fire into her; for a while she was on fire. *Gladiator*, *Pygmy* and *Hecla* immediately went to her assistance, together with boats from *Trident* and *Duperré*. *Hecla* and *Gladiator* tried to tow her free, but she was stuck fast and taking many hits, as were the ships trying to get her off the rocks. *Edinburgh* and *Valorous* returned the fort's fire, trying to create a diversion, until Admiral Napier ordered the guns of the *Penelope* to be thrown overboard to lighten the ship.[84] This finally had the desired effect – *Penelope* floated free and could be towed away, though not before she had been hit over a hundred times in her hull or rigging. Remarkably, she lost only two men killed during the incident.[85]

On 11 August and through the 12th, as work continued to finish landing and moving into position all the necessary stores and armaments, the troops made gabions (large cylinders of light wickerwork filled with earth), filled sandbags to form breastworks for the siege batteries and carried into place wooden planks to make platforms for the guns. Captain Hewlett completed his work of bringing ashore and to the British camp the remaining three naval guns with their carriages and equipment. This time, having learned from the last attempt, he put 200 sailors to drag each gun, with the ships' bands playing them away to raise their spirits. As on other days, the Russians fired as and when targets were available to them and the day saw some initial skirmishing between the French *Chasseurs de Vincennes* and the Russian defenders.

As approached from the west, the two round forts or towers – Notvik and Bränklint – would be encountered before the great shore fort and it was necessary to deal with them before the main fortress could be attacked from the landward side. The principal batteries finally brought to bear upon them were a French Battery ('No. 1') of four 16-pounders and four mortars, stationed about 600 yards west of Bränklint, to dislodge the zinc roof and riflemen and to damage the embrasures below; a British Battery ('No. 2') mounting the naval 32-pounders, erected only 300 yards away from Bränklint and another French battery ('No. 3') of 32-pounders only 200 yards from the same fort.

Fort Bränklint was going to be the first to experience the full weight of the allied attack. Just after daybreak on the morning of 13 August, the French No. 1 battery opened fire, continuing throughout the day. The effect was truly impressive at that range, the shells bursting in the embrasures and on the roof and shattering the fort's stone-work facing. The fort of course returned fire and the firefight became very severe as night approached. On the one hand, the French *chasseurs*, clambering upon the rocks, poured a destructive fire of rifle bullets into the embrasures of the fort, hitting the Russian gunners where they stood, whilst on the other hand, Fort Notvik supported Bränklint, sending shells completely over it into the French camp and battery.

The fort fell on 14 August. The firing of the mortars and the rifle fire of the *chasseurs* (which hit or at least distracted the gunners) told so severely on Bränklint that it surrendered in the morning, with about fifty men becoming prisoners. By then, most of the Russian garrison had in fact already been evacuated to the main fort. Since the captured tower would threaten the main fort if the French occupied it intact, a rearguard under Captain Tesche had been left behind and was on the point of blowing it up when the French *chasseurs* assaulted the tower and took possession. Nevertheless, soon after its capture, Bränklint blew up, whether by the mines set by Tesche being fired by burning debris or by deliberate fire from the main fort was never established. Captain B.J. Sulivan was one of a number of over inquisitive officers, anxious to see the Russian defences close up, who narrowly escaped death when the fort suddenly erupted.[86]

General Jones's No. 2 battery was not finished by the 14th despite the Herculean efforts of the sailors and Graham's Royal Marines and could do nothing to support the French attack on Bränklint. But as the great fort and Notvik tower maintained a heavy fire throughout the attack, it quickly became necessary to complete the British battery, which was manned by seamen and marine artillery from the *Hogue*, *Edinburgh*, *Ajax* and *Blenheim*, under Captain Ramsay of the *Hogue*. By the 15th, the British were ready for action and their guns were turned against the more distant fort Notvik, 750 yards away. For over fourteen hours the fort took a real pounding from Jones's battery manned by its sailors and men of the Royal Marine Artillery. It replied equally well, but suffered heavy casualties and major structural damage and since there was no hope of relief there was nothing left to its garrison but to surrender, which it did at 6.00pm, having disabled the remaining guns.

For many hours on the 15th, the French, having taken Bränklint, were busily engaged in erecting another battery to pound the main fort itself, the great semicircular structure dominating the southern end of Bomar Sound. This was now to receive all the attention of the land batteries from the west and from the warships themselves, ranged to the southeast. On the 16th a powerful array of British and French ships anchored at a range of about 2,000 yards in one shallow crescent stretching from the west coast of Michelsö Island to the opposite coast – *Asmodée, Darien, Phlégethon, Arrogant, Amphion, Valorous, Driver, Bulldog, Hecla, Trident, Duperré, Edinburgh* and *Ajax*.[87] In reserve in a line about 1,000 yards behind the bombarding ships were the French vessels *Tilsit, Breslau, Fulton, St Louis, La Cléopâtre*[88] and HMS *Blenheim*. Other ships anchored out of range, the transports sheltering behind smaller islands masked from the main fort's line of fire. In an audacious and much-lauded action, Captain Pelham of the *Blenheim* landed a 10-inch gun and set it up on the earth battery to the southwest of the fort, which had been abandoned by the Russians a few days before and later shelled by *Amphion* and *Phlégethon*. He kept up a steady fire[89] with his single gun and despite heavy counter-fire, Pelham and his sailors maintained their position all day without loss.

From dawn on the 16th, the warships poured in a well-directed fire of shells, battering the granite fortification, causing significant damage to the structure and heavy casualties amongst the defenders. This naval bombardment called for considerable care; overshooting might hit the French and British land batteries and the limited space in the anchorage before Bomarsund and the intricacy of the navigation prevented the ships from manoeuvring and coming as near as could be wished. The fort, of course, replied to the ships and to the land-batteries. All day, the batteries and warships kept up a ceaseless fire. Inevitably, the constant battering from both sides, with no hope of relief, was too much to stand for long and a white flag appeared at 1.00pm. It was the opinion of Sir Charles Napier, as expressed in his dispatch,[90] that if the fort had not surrendered when it did, the whole place would have been reduced to rubble next day, so effective was the power of the main breaching battery (which General Niel had placed within 400 yards of the fort) and the weight of metal poured in from the ships.

When the flag of truce appeared at the great fort, Napier sent Captain Hall ashore and he, with an officer from Admiral Parseval-Deschênes's staff and two officers from the staff of General Baraguay d'Hilliers, entered the fort and arranged its surrender. The three commanders themselves, Napier, Parseval-Deschênes and Baraguay d'Hilliers, then went in person to meet the fortress governor, Major General J.A. Bodisco, to receive his submission. General Bodisco had initially requested a ceasefire to allow negotiations but only unconditional surrender was acceptable to the allies and there was little he could do but give up his sword; he and the survivors of his 2,300-strong garrison became prisoners.[91] The fort was entered and occupied by French troops, its magazine secured and the prisoners taken aboard allied ships. The stage was now set for the looting of all the sites by the various land and sea forces, French and British, by hordes of local islanders and intriguingly by scores of 'tourists' who had turned up in yachts and small boats to watch the fun.[92]

Later on the same day, the tower on Prästö was attacked by French marines and bombarded for three hours by ships from Plumridge's squadron, *Leopard* and *Hecla* with the French steamer *Cocyte*. Their original aim had been to shell the Bomarsund forts from the north, but since they would then risk over-shooting and hitting the land batteries, they had turned their attention to Prästö. By the time of the attack, the other forts had already fallen and as resistance was clearly futile the defenders – 3 officers and 149 men under Lieutenant Chatelain – could do little but surrender, having first disabled their guns.

The end of the siege gave the engineers and gunners, naval and military, a chance to examine at close hand the structure of the forts and the effect of iron shot and shell on solid stone defences – a matter of considerable interest, given the importance of the similar defences of Sebastopol, Cronstadt and Sveaborg and the desire of public opinion to see something done against them. They seem to have been generally surprised at the extent of the damage done, especially by the land batteries at the close ranges of less than 800 yards; further than that, at the range of some of the warships, the bombardment had much less effect.[93] For a short while, part of the great fort was left standing, so that Captain Henry Chads, a leading gunnery expert (and formerly commander of the naval gunnery school HMS *Excellent*), could test the power of his guns against granite walls and embrasures at different ranges. The *Edinburgh* was brought up to about 500 yards, at which range its shot easily breached the solid wall, knocking several embrasures into one and completely splintering the granite; when the ship retired to ranges of 1,000 yards and more, the effect was much less damaging.[94] The final demolition of all the forts in the Bomarsund complex was quickly completed. All were to be levelled and about two weeks after their capture the work of wholesale demolition began. The three main forts had already suffered severe damage and were finally destroyed in a succession of spectacular explosions. The isolated Fort Prästö, which had had little influence on the main action and was assaulted by French marines and ships under Admiral Plumridge on the 16th, was also blown up by a large charge of gunpowder.

The destruction of Bomarsund really was a major achievement, not only in terms of the immediate war and the Baltic campaign but on a wider strategic level; as an important Russian naval base it could have been a serious threat to Sweden and possibly to Britain. After its fall in 1854, the works were never rebuilt – the attention of subsequent Tsars was drawn elsewhere – so at least that potential danger was actually removed in 1854.[95] King Oscar of Sweden was offered possession of the Ålands, and put under very strong and sustained diplomatic pressure by Britain, but refused. After all, Sweden would have to live as Russia's neighbour once the war was over and the allies had departed. The British and French governments decided that the Åland Islands would not be occupied and they were quickly abandoned by them after the complete destruction of the defences;[96] they were eventually re-occupied by the Russians but not re-fortified.[97]

News of the fall of Bomarsund, transmitted by fast steamer and telegraph to London, was greeted with wild enthusiasm in Britain and Napier, all too briefly, became the hero of the hour.[98] Hopes were expressed for similar success against Sveaborg and Cronstadt. The arrival in Britain of most of the 2,235 Russian and Finnish prisoners taken at Bomarsund[99] equally excited great interest; 323 were shipped in the *Hannibal*, 420 in the *Algiers*, 764 in the *Royal William*, 207 in the *Termagant* and 521 in the *St Vincent*. They were initially held in the prison hulks *Devonshire* and *Benbow* off Sheerness until preparations had been completed for their reception, some in converted military barracks and over 350 in the former county gaol in Lewes in Sussex. All were released on the conclusion of the war in 1856.[100]

When the work of destruction and salvage was completed, the soldiers embarked in various transports and troopships to return to the rendezvous at Ledo Sound, though not before a serious epidemic of cholera had swept through the French ranks, killing up to 700 soldiers – far more than had been lost in the attack. A few allied warships remained briefly off Bomarsund, but for the rest the round of events now turned again to routine blockade duties and patrols. One such duty fell to Captain Francis Scott of the *Odin*, who received orders on 18 August to cruise around the Åland Islands to obtain information on possible Russian troop and gunboat movements from the Finnish shore.[101] Taking under his command the *Odin*, *Alban*, *Gorgon* and *Driver*, he quickly had real experience of the difficulties of navigating through the dispersed Åland chain; when cruising near Kunlinge, Asterholm and other small islands all his ships ran on shore, some of them more than once, and were only towed free by their boats with great difficulty. Scott could learn nothing about any enemy troops or gunboats in that area, but was told that a small steam boat from Abo was somewhere in the vicinity. Abo, a significant port and the capital of Finland before Russian rule in 1809, lies 70 miles east of Bomarsund on the Finnish coast near the point that separates the Gulfs of Bothnia and Finland. The warships, at last freeing themselves from the narrow channels, headed for the town, where Scott saw a small steamer and a body of troops in several gunboats. The ships approached within 3,000 yards and the *Alban*, moving in more closely to take soundings, found the harbour closed by a chain laid on a floating platform. Within the harbour were nearly twenty small gunboats and four steamers under shelter of the headlands. All Scott's ships opened fire, which was returned by the gunboats and by well-hidden shore batteries which had not been detected. However, since the object was to make a reconnaissance rather than attack Abo and take on Russian gun vessels, Captain Scott halted the action and returned to Napier to report his findings.[102]

With the success of Bomarsund behind them, the allies' attention could turn again to the fortress of Sveaborg, guarding the approach to Helsingfors, the capital of Russian Finland and another base of the Imperial Russian Baltic Fleet. The allied fleet at this date still carried the French army which had successfully captured Bomarsund and some felt that it was equally capable of taking on Sveaborg or Helsingfors. Many of the allied ships had passed and re-passed Sveaborg during the summer, partly to examine its fortifications and partly to tempt the Russian fleet to emerge and offer battle. At the time of the siege of Bomarsund, Rear Admiral Martin, with an Anglo-French squadron of twelve to fourteen ships, was doing a double duty: his larger ships had been sent into the Gulf of Finland to blockade Reval, whilst his smaller steamers were cruising between Reval and Sveaborg, hopefully offering a tempting bait to draw out the Russian ships. But it did not happen. Later in the month, Martin took a 'flying squadron' into the Gulf of Bothnia, whilst Hanway Plumridge brought a large reinforcement to the blockading squadron in the Gulf of Finland. After the fall of Bomarsund, General Baraguay d'Hilliers, Brigadier General Harry Jones and the two admirals-in-chief went in *Driver* to examine for themselves the Finnish coast around Abo and the forts at Sveaborg. They found Abo, as Captain Scott had reported, well defended by small gunboats and shore batteries and whilst the allied ships were powerful enough to destroy or take the town, they could not bring the larger ships-of-the-line close in. The channel for deep-draught shipping into Abo was simply too narrow to allow entry by large warships. As the *Driver* rounded Hängo Head, on the way to Sveaborg, the allied commanders found that the Russians had destroyed the main fortifications there, three forts which defended Hängo, the entire garrison and many local people having been employed in the demolition. The commanders then continued towards Sveaborg, nearly coming to grief on rocks during their long and careful reconnaissance, well aware that if they failed to attack the fortress their actions and reasons would be closely scrutinised at home by a host of 'armchair admirals'. The Surveying Officer Captain B.J. Sulivan soon afterwards drew up a detailed plan on the possibility of an attack on both Sveaborg and Cronstadt, but which would require mortar boats or floating batteries not yet available to the allies.[103]

The famous stronghold of Sveaborg – or one which became famous in 1854 – was actually a group of islands[104] guarding the approach to Helsingfors, the capital of the Russian Grand Duchy of Finland. It lies at the mouth of the River Vannft or Wanna, on the north coast of the Gulf of Finland, about one-third of the distance from Hängo to Cronstadt. When Finland was ceded to Russia in 1809, Helsingfors was selected as the new capital and the site for a powerful naval base, part of the defended approaches to St Petersburg, and underwent a major remodeling in 1815. The fortifications on the island chain were formidable and were augmented by two forts on the mainland at Braborg and Ulrieaborg, the whole defending and partly enclosing a port in which sixty warships could be moored. The outer works were built on a series of islands carrying the collective name of Sveaborg – 'the fortress of the Swedes'[105] – and were all fortified in immense strength, some of the islands connected by bridges or causeways. They together mounted nearly 1,000 guns and could accommodate a garrison of at least 12,000 men. The close examination of Sveaborg and its approaches by the allied commanders quickly led to the realisation that, as at Cronstadt, the stronghold could not be attacked with any hope of success with the fleet constituted as it was.[106]

It seemed to the allied commanders that an attack by a powerful army, landed a short distance from Helsingfors, might draw off much of the defensive power in that direction and enable the fleet to succeed in a seaward attack. But to what purpose? And that sort of military manpower simply was not available; without it, any attack on Sveaborg, perhaps followed by an attempt on Helsingfors, was a dangerous waste of time and material. On 4 September the *Electra, Driver, Gladiator* and *Asmodée*, with five troop transports, reached Baro Sound from Bomarsund, carrying part of the French army, the steamers towing the transports. General Baraguay d'Hilliers had indeed come from France with an army for the Baltic (and had earned himself a field marshal's baton for the taking of Bomarsund) but his orders were now simply to return to France; no other land operations were considered by the Emperor, who increasingly came to see the Baltic as a sideshow. About 1,000 men reached Cherbourg on the 14th and the others followed within a few days – ending the purely military expedition to the Baltic and any real hope of further military action that year. As a result, although there was some dissension amongst the high command, the weight of opinion suggested the abandonment of plans to attack Sveaborg or Cronstadt.[107] Once the Admiralty had accepted this view,[108] there was little to do as the winter season advanced other than to wind down operations in the Baltic.

During the whole of August nine British and two French ships had been anchored at Nargen, blockading Reval and guarding the entry to the Gulf of Finland, but without seeing any action, whilst the steamers *Impérieuse*, *Euryalus*, *Arrogant*, *Magicienne* and *Rosamond* had cruised the gulf, watching for any signs of the enemy in the shape either of merchantmen or warships. When the last of the French troops had gone, Admirals Napier and Parseval-Deschênes decided to concentrate their main naval forces at Baro Sound and Nargen Island. The whole of September passed as August had done, with this large fleet stationary near Nargen, facing increasingly severe winds and weather and it became likely, as winter drew on, that many of the ships must soon leave Baltic waters for Britain or France; decreasing numbers would remain, cruising and watching, until ice, storms and wind made further operations in these seas too dangerous.

October opened with real dissatisfaction in the fleet that more had not achieved and there was even more complaining in Britain that other Russian fortresses had not been attacked or destroyed.[109] But gradually, as October passed, the fleets simply withdrew. Admiral Plumridge's squadron, which had been at Nargen for seven weeks, had already left for Britain, whilst the other ships remaining in the Gulf of Finland began to experience indications of a severe winter, with biting winds and driving sleet. Napier received a dispatch at that time ordering him to send the bulk of his remaining ships to Kiel, en route to Britain; as most of the departing allied ships stopped there, by the middle of the month a formidable fleet lay at anchor. On 19 October the *Duke of Wellington*, *St Jean d'Acre*, *James Watt*, *Princess Royal*, *Blenheim*, *Hogue*, *Edinburgh*, *Royal George*, *Nile*, *Majestic* and *Cressy* weighed anchor and began their westward journey. During several days, the weather was rough and the returning ships were scattered, each captain steering towards Kiel without waiting for the others so that it was not until the 28th that all were assembled in the rendezvous. A squadron of steamers, including the *Impérieuse*, *Euryalus*, *Arrogant*, *Magicienne*, *Desperate*, *Basilisk*, *Bulldog* and *Dragon*, under Captain Watson, was left to maintain the blockade in the Gulf of Finland down to the latest date the weather and ice would permit. As regards the Gulf of Bothnia, the blockade was formally raised during the last week in October.

As November arrived, a severe winter set in, with heavy ice spreading further and more rapidly than usual. By the third week of the month 13 ships still remained off Kiel, mounting more than 1,100 guns, and carrying 10,000 men, to continue the general blockade of the entry to and exit from the Baltic and 7 steamers under Captain Watson still blockaded the Gulf of Finland. But they did nothing and from time to time telegraphic dispatches arrived from Britain ordering the departure of the larger ships, two or three at a time, destined for home waters.

The last month of 1854 saw the final separation and departure of the great Baltic Fleet. On 1 December, Napier himself was ordered home and later that week Captain Watson announced that the ice in the Gulf of Finland was so extensive that he needed to leave the area, in accordance with his orders, and set off for Kiel. Others simply awaited orders to return home, which soon came and by Christmas nearly all the ships and crews were back in Britain. Sir Charles Napier landed at Portsmouth on 18 December, where he was well received by the authorities and inhabitants. By the last day of the year, the *Duke of Wellington, James Watt, Hogue, Blenheim, Impérieuse, Arrogant, Penelope* and *Locust* were back at Portsmouth; the *St Jean d'Acre, Princess Royal, Nile, Caesar* and *Euryalus* were at Devonport; the *Edinburgh, Cruiser, Archer* and *Magicienne* at Leith; the *Odin* at Woolwich; the *Cressy, Majestic, Royal George* and *Amphion* at Sheerness; the *Conflict* and *Desperate* at Hull; the *Bulldog* at North Shields; the *Dragon, Rosamond, Basilisk* and *Vulture* at Cromarty; and the *Driver* at Harwich. This wide dispersal of the returned fleet was necessary on the purely practical ground of finding enough yards with facilities for repairing and refurbishing so many large ships at one time, especially at a time when many yards were busy at work on new commissions for the campaigning season of 1855. The new year was to see the dominance of steam fleets in both the major theatres of naval warfare – the Baltic and the Black Sea.

Thus ended the 1854 Baltic campaign – operations that had involved, at huge cost, large military and naval forces and that had called into use a larger fleet than had ever before entered the Baltic. They had carried with them the highest hopes and expectations of the British public but the campaign ended only in general disappointment to the nation, many of the officers and most of the men.[110]

When the allies decided to abandon the Åland Islands and began to withdraw from the Baltic, the Russians lost no time in retaking possession. Equally, there was time before the ice really set in to restart some of the lost mercantile trade and import merchandise from Sweden and elsewhere into Finland after a blockage of all trade for months; it was widely believed that the blockade had been raised too early and the Russians and Finns made full use of the advantage. At Reval, where the allies had done little harm to the town and port, except for the long stagnation of trade, the people were amazed to find the allied warships suddenly gone. All around the Baltic, merchant ships were soon back in operation plying their trade, bringing cargoes of tar, firewood, salt, herrings and other commodities. The Russian fleets at Helsingfors and Cronstadt emerged cautiously from behind their granite defences as soon as the allies had departed, to reconnoitre and possibly pick off a few of the enemy's smaller cruisers; but some of these vessels – untouched by the allied armada – were considerably damaged by the severe weather in the Gulf of Finland and all quickly returned to harbour to lie up for the winter. All around the Finnish coast, large numbers of labourers were set to work in repairing coastal defences and the main road between Abo, Helsingfors and St Petersburg, to facilitate the movement of troops and heavy stores ready for what would obviously be a renewed campaign in 1855. Russian military and naval commanders were summoned to the capital to report on all that had occurred and to receive instructions concerning new defensive works at Cronstadt, Sveaborg, Helsingfors, Abo, Reval and Riga. In short, except for the destruction of Bomarsund,[111] the damage to smaller Finnish towns and the interruption to trade, the Russians had not suffered very greatly from allied operations in the Baltic.

There was huge and publicly expressed disappointment in Britain that if Sveaborg and Cronstadt had proved to be too formidable, the allies could have taken or bombarded Riga or Reval or Abo. On the other hand, some commentators argued that the advantages resulting from the campaign should not be ignored. Many contended that the force placed at Napier's disposal was both too strong and too weak – too strong to tempt the Russian fleet to emerge and risk an open engagement but too weak to capture or destroy Cronstadt or Sveaborg. During the campaign, Napier felt he was hampered by contradictions in the Admiralty's instructions and especially by the attitude of the First Lord, Sir James Graham. In fact some of the Naval Lords seemed to react more to adverse coverage in the British press than to Napier's assessments on the spot and relations between them deteriorated badly. Not one to mince words or submit to what he felt to be unwonted criticism, Napier sealed his professional fate by frequently adopting what was called a 'disrespectful' tone in some of his dispatches, which the Admiralty disliked. On his return in December 1854, 'where disappointment was loudly expressed at the small results of the naval campaign',[112] he was ordered to haul down his flag, told that his command was terminated and placed on half-pay. It is noticeable that none of Napier's flag officers of the 1854 campaign was allowed to return to the Baltic in 1855, the new fleet being given to Admiral the Hon. Richard Saunders Dundas, then the Second Sea Lord.

The Admiralty attempted to make Napier a scapegoat for what British public and press opinion perceived to be the failure of the campaign but it is interesting that although there were many who *had* criticised and carped at Napier's actions, some of the leading officers of the Baltic Fleet maintained that his strategy had been wise and that the faults lay with the Admiralty themselves.[113] In the end, though lacking any major dramatic action apart from the capture of Bomarsund, Napier had achieved something. His ships had effectively neutralised (though not destroyed) the Imperial Baltic Fleet, preventing the deployment of additional warships outside the Baltic and perhaps even to the Black Sea. He had maintained through all weathers a successful blockade which had disrupted Russian trade, fishing and supply routes and had demonstrated the allies' ability to attack at will targets like ports, shipyards and stores and the corresponding inability of the Russians to defend their own coastlines. In addition, Russian land forces in their thousands had been held along the Baltic shores in anticipation of allied landings and were thus prevented from reinforcing the Russian Army in the Crimea or elsewhere.[114] Also, Napier's constant emphasis on training had welded the fleet's personnel into a much more competent force for the coming campaign and not a single ship had been lost. One result of all this was that even Sir James Graham, who really had become Sir Charles Napier's enemy, recognised that new types of warship were needed for the planned Baltic campaign of 1855. In October 1854, a programme of construction was put into action which would produce five new blockships and no less than twenty new gunboats. These would enable Napier's successor, Admiral Richard Dundas, to contemplate an attack on the fortresses of the Baltic in 1855 with some hope of success.

Chapter 3

Opening Moves in the Black Sea, Summer 1854

In the early days of the Russo-Turkish war, as the fighting in the Danubian Provinces settled down into something of a stalemate, the opening moves of a naval war began to take shape. British and French naval forces began to assemble in Besika Bay,[1] south of the Dardanelles, initially to offer protection to Constantinople and the flanks of Turkish land forces in the Balkans. Russian warships from the fleet at Sebastopol, ranging over the Black Sea and patrolling its southern and eastern coasts, struck at the Turkish coastal town of Batum in November 1853, bombarding the port and capturing two Turkish paddle-steamers. In response, as a means of supporting their garrisons along the coast and their land operations east of the Black Sea, the Turks decided, against British advice, to send naval patrols into the Black Sea. One of these, a larger squadron of ten sailing ships, corvettes and paddle-streamers under the command of the British-trained Osman Pasha, sailed eastwards along the northern Turkish coast. On 13 November, in the face of worsening weather, the ships sought refuge in the port of Sinope, where they met the *Taif* and the *Kaid Zafer* which had already taken shelter there. Somewhat inevitably, since they spent all of seventeen days in the confines of Sinope harbour, the Turkish ships were spotted by a Russian naval patrol from Sebastopol. On 30 November 1853, part of the Russian Black Sea Fleet under its commander Admiral Pavel Nahkimov – 11 ships mounting over 700 guns – attacked the Turks and, in part thanks to the first use in action of the new Paixhans exploding shells (see above p. 9), destroyed the Turkish squadron within two hours.[2] Four coastal batteries were also bombarded and destroyed. No Russian ships were lost and the only Turkish warship capable of escape, the battle-damaged paddle-steamer *Taif*, fled to Constantinople where her arrival on 2 December with news of the disaster spread something akin to panic in the city. The victorious Russian squadron arrived back in Sebastopol on the same day.[3]

Although Britain and France were not at war with Russia, the action was denounced in Britain as something of a massacre and public opinion seems to have swung violently in favour of war.[4] The attack was, of course, a perfectly legitimate action and demonstrated the alarming fact of Russia's complete

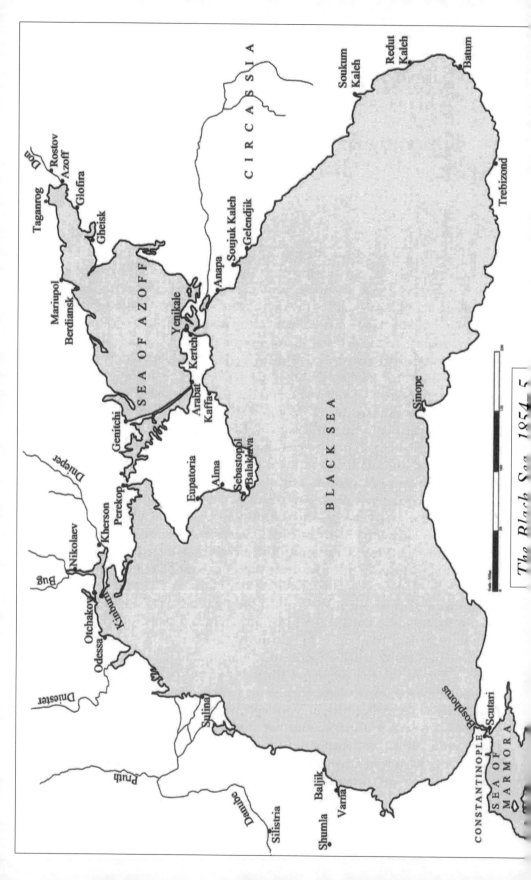

The Black Sea 1854–5

control of the Black Sea. It was Russia's first and only significant naval success in the long war that followed and initially spread shockwaves across Europe, triggering a major Anglo-French response. In what was clearly meant to be a warning to Russia and a spur to further diplomatic efforts, British troops were moved to Malta and immediate naval action was taken by the powers. The paddle-steamer *Fury* and a French ship were sent to Varna in Bulgaria to withdraw the British Consul and allied warships, the British element drawn from the Mediterranean Fleet at Malta, were ordered from the Bosphorus[5] into the Black Sea on 24 December. As a result of these orders, on 3 January 1854, thirty-one ships, of which twelve were paddle-steamers, moved into the Black Sea as 'a very definite demonstration of our intention to support Turkey',[6] an intention formally notified to the Russians on 12 January by the British and French governments. This was, incidentally, the first time that foreign (i.e. not Russian or Turkish) warships had entered the Black Sea since the Treaty of Unkiar Skelessi in 1833 and the Straits Convention of 1841.[7] Soon afterwards, no less than 18 sailing warships and 12 steam frigates were dispatched to Sinope, including the *Tiger*, *Highflyer*, *Vesuvius* and *Banshee* and 5 Turkish steam frigates.

The Russian government was formally notified that allied warships would protect Turkish vessels and immediately four French steamships, the five Turkish frigates and the British warships *Agamemnon*, *Sans Pareil*, *Terrible* and *Sampson*, all under Rear Admiral Edmund Lyons, were deployed to escort Turkish transports to the eastern Black Sea coast, in support of Turkish operations in the Caucasus. Lyons was ordered to 'warn off' all Russian vessels 'and to take them if they should persist in blockading or otherwise inflicting injury on the Ottoman territory or flag' – a strange situation given that no state of war existed between France, Britain and Russia.[8] This duty was performed with no interference from the Russians, as was a similar voyage on 7 February, when 7,000 Turkish troops were landed at Batum and Trebizonde[9] and allied ships reconnoitred the coast of as far as Redut Kaleh, a large town garrisoned by the Russians.[10] Lyons returned to Sinope and, having made a pointed gesture, all the allied ships were back in the Bosphorus by 22 January 1854.

Plans were already being laid in the Admiralty for operations in the Baltic and for the neutralisation of the Russian base at Sebastopol. HMS *Retribution* had visited Sebastopol in January formally to notify the Russians of British intentions to defend Turkish vessels and property and her officers had made sketches of the port defences. Whilst his ship lay off the port, her Captain counted 350 guns bearing on him, not including those available on the Russian warships.[11] With European diplomacy apparently not forcing Russian compliance, on 27 February 1854 the British and French governments formally demanded the withdrawal of Russian forces from the Danubian Provinces – a demand that was ignored by the Tsar. After a further month of delay, amidst a last-minute flurry of international diplomatic activity to avert an escalation of the war, an Anglo–French fleet entered the Black Sea on 24 March 1854, heading for Kavarna Bay; they remained off Baljik until a formal declaration of war was received. When diplomacy finally failed, Britain declared war on Russia on 27 March, although the British commanders of the Black Sea Fleet only heard about the declaration on 9 April.[12] France declared war the next day, 28 March, and a formal treaty of alliance was signed by Britain and France on 10 April, joined by the Ottoman Empire on the 15th. The Russian War had begun – finally sparked off by a Turkish naval defeat, by fears of Russia's naval power in the Baltic and Black Sea and by the perceived strategic need of Britain and France to destroy the potential threat of Russian power in the eastern Mediterranean.

The commander of British naval forces to be deployed in the Black Sea was Vice Admiral James Dundas, commander of the Mediterranean Fleet since 1852.[13] Dundas had had a most distinguished career, but like so many of those in high command during the Russian War, he was considered by many of his subordinates to be too old for the job and lacking the drive, decisiveness and tactical skill his war command required. Nevertheless, as the commander of Britain's Mediterranean Fleet when the war began, he was the man of the moment.[14] His orders from the Admiralty on 29 March were clear: having entered the Black Sea, he was to be

> guided by the movements of the Russian fleet and army and [according to the movements of Russian forces in the Balkans] to bring his fleet or a portion of it to bear on the left flank of that army, for the purpose of upholding the fortress and town of Varna, of cutting off supplies by sea to the Russian forces and of opening communications with Omar Pasha, the Commander of Turkish forces in Bulgaria.[15]

If the Russian armies did not continue their advance in the Balkans, Dundas was to maintain

> a careful watch upon the harbour of Sebastopol and [prevent] the Russian ships from slipping out in his rear towards the Bosphorus, sweep around the coasts ... as far as the Asiatic boundary of Russia near Batoum and attack and destroy the various batteries and forts which he may find to be assailable and at the same time worthy of attack.[16]

On the same day, 29 March 1854, the government asked the Admiralty to instruct all naval commanders 'on all stations' that they were 'to commence and execute all such hostile measures against Russia and against all ships belonging to the Emperor of Russia or to his subjects or others inhabiting within any of his countries, territories or dominions'.[17]

As the original allied plan centred on defending the right flank of Turkey's positions in the Balkans and offering protection to Adrianople and Constantinople, an allied landing on the Gallipoli Peninsula was initially planned. Parts of the peninsula could be fortified against Russian counter-attack and from there allied land forces could be deployed into the Balkans if needed. As the initial war planning worked on this basis a Royal Engineer group under Captain F. Chapman was sent to Gallipoli on HMS *Banshee* in February 1854 – the first allied soldiers to set foot on Turkish soil in preparation for the coming war.[18] Their task was to develop potential landing sites and they were quickly followed by companies of sappers and miners to construct defences and jetties near Bulair; work continued into May. The occupation and fortification of the Dardanelles by allied naval forces was also seen as a vital precursor, sealing Russian naval forces in the Black Sea. But in the event the speed of the Russian collapse, with their failure at the siege of Silistria (19 May–22 June) followed by a string of Turkish victories, placed a new light on the allies' contribution. With the Russians eventually forced back towards their own frontier, Anglo-French military intervention in the Balkans was unlikely to be required. Instead, the focus of allied interest switched more fully towards the Black Sea. The destruction of Russia's Black Sea Fleet and its great naval base at Sebastopol were obvious goals – and all the more so since they fitted both British and French strategic ambitions beyond the immediate needs of the war.

By May 1854, 18,000 British troops under Lord Raglan and 32,000 French under Marshal St Arnaud had already been landed at Gallipoli. But despite all the work to prepare sites there, it was decided to abandon Gallipoli as a potential base and to move the centre of operations into the Black Sea . The site chosen for the main allied naval base was the port of Varna in Bulgaria. An ancient walled town of 12,000 people located 180 miles north of Constantinople on Kavarna Bay, it had nothing greatly to recommend it apart from the location nearby of long sandy beaches which would aid the disembarkation of men and materials and decent nearby anchorages for the fleet and transports at Baljik Bay.[19] It soon became the busy centre of the allied armies and their multitude of stores, armaments and equipment coming up from Gallipoli and Scutari and large tented camps sprang up for miles around the town. Escorting the armies and their stores and landing them at and near Varna was the first important work of the allied navies.

The build up of allied land forces and supplies at Varna and in Kavarna Bay continued throughout the spring and summer of 1854, with naval officers naturally playing a major role in supervising the landing, movement and collection of troops and equipment.[20] The Anglo–French fleet adopted Baljik Bay just north of Varna as its principal anchorage, where it was eventually joined by the main Ottoman naval squadron, twenty-two ships led by the powerful 124-gun *Mahmoudie*. This fleet left Constantinople on 4 May to enter the Black Sea, ostensibly to operate with the allies against Russian bases on the eastern and Circassian coasts of the sea. But it was never put to effective use by the allies and languished in harbour at Baljik Bay for months as its crews starved or died of disease. More worryingly, cholera began to appear and spread through the ships and camps.

Up until the formal declaration of war in March 1854, the allied fleets did little but reconnoitre the Black Sea's eastern coast, the area around Odessa and the coast of the Crimea.[21] However, once the news of the state of war was received things moved up a gear. April witnessed the allies' first serious naval engagement of the war – the attack on the city of Odessa, 150 miles northeast of Varna. A modern city with over 100,000 inhabitants, Odessa lay in a small bay between the estuaries of the Dnieper and the Dniester and offered a large, deep and safe anchorage. It was a major port (especially for grain) and regarded as an architectural showpiece, once called 'the Florence of Russia'. The reporter for *The Times*, William Howard Russell, thought it a delightful place:

> an extensive city built on the curve of a high sea shore, with descending terraces and broad flights of steps to the beach, which was enclosed by broad quays and the walls of ports and casemated batteries, all shining brightly in the morning sun. Broad esplanades or boulevards lined with trees towards the sea front ran along the top of the bank, with a background of stately mansions worthy of the best 'Rows' near Regent's Park ... Behind, and in continuation of this esplanade are splendid residences with pillared porticoes and ornamented peristyles, magnificent public institutions ... barracks, palaces, governor's house, prisons rising in front of a confused but graceful mass of domes, columns, steeples and spires[22]

Once Vice Admiral Dundas had received official notice of a British declaration of war on Russia on 9 April, he was given his first task – to remove the British Consul from Odessa. HMS *Retribution* and *Niger* were already off Odessa, 'watching' the port but HMS *Furious* under Captain William Loring was deputed to do the job and, anchoring off Odessa, Loring sent in a boat under flag of truce to arrange the evacuation. When no answer was returned to the request to allow the Consul to leave, the ship's boat began her return journey to *Furious*, but was fired on as she left, though without sustaining any damage. Captain Loring took no immediate action and returned to Baljik Bay to report to Dundas.

Such an insult to the usual international conventions could not go unpunished and on 17 April, a combined Anglo–French squadron set off to Odessa.[23] The French contingent was led by Admiral Ferdinand Alphonse Hamelin, the British by Admiral Dundas in *Britannia*, with Rear Admiral Sir Edmund Lyons as second-in-command[24] in the new 91-gun auxiliary screw line-of-battle ship *Agamemnon*. Lyons, 63 years old was, like his contemporary naval commanders, a man of many years' experience, having spent over forty years in the service, but nearly twenty of those years had been spent as British Ambassador to Greece and in Sweden. Dundas's fleet for Odessa comprised 10 sailing line-of-battle ships, 11 frigates (2 of which were screws), 4 paddle-steamers and 9 paddle-sloops. Anchoring off the port on 20 April 1854, an explanation was demanded of the city's governor, General Dmitry Osten-Sachen.[25] His reply, that he had fired on the warship itself, since it had entered the harbour without formal permission, and not on the cutter flying a flag of truce, was rejected. Dundas demanded the surrender of all Russian shipping in the port, failing which the city would be bombarded next day by the squadron. At that time, the harbour and docks of this major port were filled with merchant shipping not only from Russia but of many other nations, including American, Spanish, Swedish and Norwegian vessels. Most of these lay off the Quarantine Mole, separated from the Russian ships, and strict orders were given that the allied warships were not to fire on this area and risk damaging neutral vessels nor on the private houses and other buildings.

Inevitably, there was no compliance, though a few neutral ships wisely decided to flee the port, and on the 22nd the Anglo–French squadron took up position and opened fire on the harbour works and on the Russian ships lying within their protection. The firing began at 6.40am and was concentrated on the Imperial Mole, defended by over seventy guns, on nearby Russian shipping and on the large storehouses and barracks on the shore – deemed fit targets as government property. As far as was possible, the intention was not to damage the rest of the city.

The attack force comprised the British warships *Tiger*,[26] *Retribution*, *Sampson*,[27] *Terrible* and *Furious* all under Captain Jones and the French ships *Mogador*, *Vauban*, *Descartes* and *Caton*. A squadron of rocket boats armed with powerful 24-pound rockets, many supplied by larger warships not engaged in the actual bombardment, under Commodore Dixon would be deployed against the naval dockyards in advance of the attack and the larger vessels *Highflyer*, *Arethusa*[28] and *Sans Pareil*[29] lay further off, in reserve.

The squadron was led into action by *Sampson* and *Tiger*, followed by the others, engaging in pairs and delivering their broadsides in succession and then, in the classic manoeuvre of the old days of sail, completing a full circle, to bring their guns to bear again and again. The Russian defenders, of course, made a sturdy reply and since Odessa was well defended, caused considerable damage to some of the allied ships. The French *Vauban* in particular was badly holed and set alight by red-hot shot, though she soon got this under control and rejoined the bombardment. At 1.30pm, the main magazine on the mole blew up with a tremendous roar and by 2.00pm, Russian counter-fire had all but ceased, with a number of buildings ashore now in flames. Red-hot shot from *Terrible*, which approached her targets more closely than any other allied ship, caused most of the damage to the merchant shipping (which burned for forty-eight hours), to a Russian frigate and to wooden buildings ashore. Eventually, the staunchest resistance came from a single Russian horse-artillery battery, which galloped onto the beach and opened fire on the rocket boats – though without doing any damage. This brave battery now became the centre of attention, receiving the fire of the rocket boats and steam warships until the gun crews wisely took the decision to limber up and flee into the town. Firing continued throughout the afternoon until it was deemed that honour had been satisfied and the insult to a flag of truce avenged.

Dundas recalled the attacking force at 5.00pm, though *Arethusa* engaged the outer batteries late in the day, destroyed a barrack block near Odessa and blew up its magazine.[30] The whole attack was reported as 'very skillfully and bravely carried out. The rocket boats were adroitly managed under a galling fire from an enemy very well prepared, but nothing could surpass the determination of the united steam squadron'.[31]

In what was effectively the first demonstration of the power of steam warships, the allies did not escape without some damage. A total of 3 British sailors were killed and 5 wounded on *Terrible* and 8 men wounded aboard *Retribution* and *Sampson*. Apart from the fire on the *Vauban*, many of the steamers were more or less damaged; *Terrible* had her paddle-wheel boxes badly shot up and her hull holed in twelve places.

This was the first time that a naval bombardment had been launched against a major city since Lord Exmouth's attack on Algiers, the base of the Barbary Pirates, in 1816[32] and gave a good impression of what modern, powerful warships could do. This early attack on a defended port was to set the seal on a type of naval action that was repeated in all the theatres of war – in the White Sea, in the Baltic, in the Sea of Azoff, in the Black Sea and in the Pacific. Time and again as the war progressed, allied squadrons or individual ships attacked enemy ports and towns, destroyed military installations and huge amounts of shipping, food and stores, escaping with relative impunity. The absolute dominance of Britain and France at sea was to render Russian coastlines anywhere in the world open targets for aggressive naval action and almost wanton destruction.

After the bombardment of Odessa, the allied fleet headed towards Sebastopol, to reconnoitre the port and area, leaving *Tiger*, *Vesuvius* and *Niger* on station off Odessa,[33] where the population rapidly repaired the damage done to their defences. Here an unfortunate accident befell the *Tiger*, resulting in one of the few losses of an allied warship during the whole campaign.[34] On 12 May, the 17-gun paddle-steamer under Captain Henry W. Giffard[35] approached too close to the rocky coastline near Odessa in a heavy fog and ran aground under high cliffs. She became stuck fast and inevitably offered a sitting target to the Russians on the shore, who fired on the ship with rifles until field guns were brought up. The crew fought back, but without much chance of any success, until Captain Giffard was seriously wounded and others of the crew wounded or killed. Giffard could do nothing but strike his flag and join his men in surrender. The *Tiger*'s escorts, *Niger* and *Vesuvius*, came up just too late to be of any assistance and had the mortification of seeing the *Tiger*'s crew marched off into captivity. The 225 members of the crew were taken into Odessa where they were treated very well by the Russians (though Captain Giffard died of his wounds in captivity) and were exchanged for Russian prisoners held by the allies in July.[36] The ship itself proved to be beyond salvage and was burned, though the Russians managed to remove some of its guns. On 13 July, *Furious* visited the site and opened fire on the wreck to destroy what was left of *Tiger* before the Russians could remove any more of her machinery; this action took place under the fire of Russian field guns and played out before a large and interested crowd of locals who gathered on the cliffs to watch.[37]

Meanwhile, Dundas had arrived off Sebastopol on 28 April and found the Russian Black Sea Fleet penned within its harbour – thirteen battle ships, five frigates and a number of smaller vessels. Edward Seymour aboard *Terrible* later recalled:

> It was a very pretty sight to arrive off Sevastopol [*sic*] early on a lovely summer's morning and see the white town girt as to its sea shores with massive grey granite forts and beyond the town on the south side the ground sloping upwards and often covered with many white tents where the allied armies' lines and batteries were soon to be made. The harbour displaying a fine fleet all ready for sea and all as it were smiling in the sunny morning and as little foretelling the really awful destruction of life and property and the frightful human suffering which a few months was to witness here.[38]

The fleet remained off Sebastopol until 5 May, when it returned to Varna, with one squadron under Lyons detached to cruise the coast to the eastern shores of the Black Sea as far as Batum. It comprised *Agamemnon, Sampson, Retribution, Highflyer, Firebrand* and *Niger* with the French ships *Mogador, Vauban* and *Charlemagne*. Their job was to locate a possible landing place and harbour, closer than Varna, which the fleet could use[39] and to fire upon Russian shore defences en route but not to attack undefended towns. One further aim was to try to contact Circassian leaders who might be encouraged to rise in revolt against Russia. The entry to the Strait of Kertch was reconnoitred by *Highflyer* before the squadron visited Anapa – deemed to be too large to tackle[40] – and examined a series of coastal forts. All the smaller coastal defences were found abandoned and destroyed, the Russians clearly having decided that such remote outposts could not be properly defended. The town of Soukum Kaleh was equally found to have been abandoned by its Russian garrison, but Lyons learned that Redut Kaleh was still occupied. Determined to seize the town and cut off the garrison, Lyons picked up a Turkish infantry force near Batum and arrived off Redut Kaleh on 19 May. Nearby, 800 Turkish troops were landed and *Charlemagne* and *Agamemnon* opened fire on the town's defences. The garrison put up only a brief resistance, setting fire to their magazines before retreating inland; a Turkish garrison was left in control of the town, initially defended by *Sampson* which remained on station off the coast. Having examined the Circassian coast, but failing to raise the Circassian chiefs, the rest of Lyons' squadron rejoined the allied fleet anchored at Baljik Bay on 28 May.

It had of course been clear for some time that Sebastopol would have to be tackled; the First Lord of the Admiralty Sir James Graham always regarded Sebastopol as *the* vital target: 'my fixed purpose from which I have never swerved is the capture of Sebastopol and the destruction of the enemy's fleet'[41] – not only for the immediate reasons of the security of the allies in the Black Sea but equally for the greater strategic interests of France and Britain in destroying the base of the Russian Black Sea Fleet. On 15 June, six Russian steam warships did sally forth from Sebastopol to challenge *Furious* and *Terrible*, which were cruising close to the coast to reconnoitre the port and shots were exchanged at long range for two hours before the Russians withdrew.[42] But Odessa aside, little was done by the combined fleets in the early days of the war apart from patrols to reconnoitre the Black Sea, the Danube estuary, the eastern coast and the Crimean Peninsula, varied with stays off Baljik in Kavarna Bay.

The first important strategic naval action was the blockade of the mouths of the Danube, begun on 1 June. In support of Turkish operations along the Danube, and as the Russians began a withdrawal from the area, allied warships patrolled the mouth of the river near the town of Sulina,[43] occasionally shelling Russian positions but one other 'mishap' occurred here. In one of these actions, involving boats from *Vesuvius* and *Firebrand*, a serious loss occurred. On 7 July, the boats landed sailors and marines to destroy shore works near Sulina but came under unexpectedly heavy fire from well-defended Russian positions and a fairly severe action took place, with the ship's boats firing shot and rockets and a sizeable force being landed to storm the defence works. During the fighting, the well-regarded Captain Hyde Parker of *Firebrand*, leading one of the boat parties as it landed, was mortally wounded.

> A strong party of boats from the *Vesuvius* and the *Firebrand*, led by Capt. Parker in his gig [proceeded ashore] . . . A heavy fire from some houses and a strong stockade on the right bank was soon directed on Captain Parker's boat, which was riddled and some of his men wounded. He then directed a detachment of seamen and marines to land and storm the place. As they advanced, led by Captain Parker, they encountered a tremendous fire and their gallant leader, who by his eagerness was much exposed, fell shot through the heart.[44]

Although the marines and sailors comprising the landing party eventually drove off the Russians and burned some of the defence works and nearby houses, it was regarded as a small return for the loss of so popular an officer. Some of the suburbs of Sulina were burned during the raid but on 17 July boats from *Vesuvius* and *Spitfire* returned to the scene and completed the destruction of the town, sparing only the church.

In the meantime, the Russo-Turkish land campaign in the Balkans continued. The fighting here, as with the campaign in 'Asiatic Turkey', to the east of the Black Sea, has received scant attention, though both involved some British participation. The initial Russian invasion plan in the Balkans called for the seizure of the fortress-town of Silistria, defending both the lower Danube and the Turkish garrison-town of Shulma. Silistria became the scene of a once-famous siege, which reduced parts of the town to rubble, but at which the Russians were ultimately unsuccessful and from which they withdrew on 22 June. The focus of Russian attacks then switched to the autonomous Turkish province of Bulgaria. The Russians established themselves near Giurgevo on the Danube 100 miles west of Silistria, opposite the Turkish base at Routschouk. The Turks already had a bridgehead on the 'Russian' side of the Danube but the Russian withdrawal from Silistria freed Russian forces under Prince Gortshakoff for a major attack on Routschouk, planned for 10 July 1854.

There was some British involvement on the margins of all this activity. The Turks, planning a pre-emptive strike against Russian forces, requested British and French assistance in their offensive from Routschouk and as a result, thirty British sappers and miners under Captain G. Bent, RE and a party of French *pontoniers*, bridging specialists, were posted to Routschouk in mid-July. They were to construct a pontoon bridge across the Danube (more than 650 yards wide at that point) to enable the Turks to cross in force and take the offensive. To augment this engineer party, Lord Raglan forwarded on 5 July a Turkish request to Vice Admiral Dundas asking for a party of sailors to man gunboats on the Danube near Routschouk and to assist with the pontoon work. Dundas, flying his flag aboard *Britannia*, chose his First Lieutenant Henry Carr Glyn to command the party, seconded by Midshipman HSH Prince Ernest of Leiningen, half-brother of Queen Victoria. Thirty sailors for 'the Danube Party' were hand-picked from *Britannia*, *Queen*, *Trafalgar*, *Albion*, *London*, *Agamemnon*, *Bellerophon*, *Rodney* and *Vengeance*, anchored at Baljik, and left for Varna on HMS *Caradoc* on 6 July. Mounted on horseback – an unusual mode of transport for sailors! – they rode the 130 miles to Routschouk, arriving on 13 July, six days after Turkish forces had crossed the Danube to concentrate for an attack on Giurgevo. Whilst the engineers helped with bridging and the construction of earthwork defences in the bridgehead, the sailors served aboard Turkish gunboats operating between Slobenizie and Giurgevo before joining in with the demanding pontoon work, which involved securing fifty-five heavy boats 'carried out under a ceaseless fire of field artillery'.[45] The bridge was only completed on 10 August 1854 but the Turkish forces that crossed towards Giurgevo effectively thwarted any planned Russian offensive and the Russians began to withdraw northwards, under Turkish pressure, back towards their own frontier.

On 11 August, the sailors, with some of the sappers and miners, sailed down the Danube aboard a Turkish gunboat via Silistria for Varna and rejoined their ships 'in high health and high good humour'.[46] The sailors seem to have suffered considerably from exhaustion and sickness, as well as the occasional harassing fire of the enemy, but no deaths are recorded in what was a most unusual 'naval operation' in the midst of a major land campaign.

And whilst all this was going on, the British government had ordered a full-scale invasion of the Crimean Peninsula – another land campaign was soon to get well and truly underway.

Chapter 4

'The Invasion of the Crimea':
the Navy Ashore

The British government ordered a full-scale invasion of the Crimea – 'the Garden of Russia' – on 29 June 1854, the orders being received by Lord Raglan on 16 July. Admiral Dundas, who received the news on the same day, disliked the plan: though he agreed that he could land an army on the shores of the peninsula, he was not convinced that the navy could undertake to supply it during a long campaign.[1] Nevertheless, it *was* to go ahead and the organisation of the naval arrangements and transport was put into the hands of Admiral Dundas' second-in-command Sir Edmund Lyons and his Flag Captain W.R. Mends, formerly captain of *Arethusa*.[2] Their immediate job was to scour the Constantinople area and Malta for transport, light boats, timber and other materials. A naval reconnaissance of the Sebastopol area and possible landing sites towards Eupatoria[3] was carried out by *Agamemnon*, *Fury* and *Cacique* between 21 and 25 July and the work of assembling the naval armada, loaded with troops and supplies, continued through July and August, only interrupted by a severe outbreak of cholera which swept through the fleet.[4] Lord Raglan heartily complimented the officers and men of the Royal Navy for their tireless efforts in embarking the soldiers, guns and a multitude of supplies;[5] Sir Edmund Lyons recorded:

> It was indeed a work of great magnitude and difficulty, this embarkation of a complete force of infantry, cavalry and artillery with all their stores, food, ammunition and siege appliances, in addition to food for man and beast, an operation moreover not effected in a home port with all the resources of a Portsmouth or Southampton, but on a foreign shore with no facilities but such as were created on the spot.[6]

The warships and transports that set sail in five long columns on 5–6 September were a magnificent sight: 'the sea was studded for miles with line-of-battle ships, with frigates, with war steamers, with transports – 412 vessels ... the embodiment of aggressive strength'.[7] The various elements, Turkish, French and British, rendezvoused on the 8th off Cape Tarkan, the most westerly point of the Crimean Peninsula, to form one great armada. It was widely felt that the Russians missed a major opportunity to strike against this huge fleet whilst it was at sea and some must have expected that the battleships and frigates of the much-vaunted Russian Black Sea Fleet at Sebastopol would sally out of to attack the mass of transports. The safety of the whole fleet largely depended on the Royal Navy, since the transports were unarmed and the twenty-seven French and eleven Turkish warships, most towing transports, were said to be so closely packed with troops that they could not work their guns.[8] Nevertheless, no Russian attack was made.[9] After much complex discussion amongst the allied commanders on potential landing points – even now not finalised – and with consideration given to the bay of the Katcha, the Yetsa or even Kaffa, the actual site for the allied landing was chosen as the long shingle beach near 'the Old Fort' on Kalamita Bay, about 14 miles south of Eupatoria. The army of 63,000 men (26,000 of them British), 4,000 horses, 128 guns (54 British) and a wealth of stores was eventually landed without loss or opposition between 14 and 18 September. Over 350 small boats had to be found or made to land this force and every form of ship's boat and improvised pontoon was used to get the army ashore.

Russian forces in the Crimea, at that time up to 60,000 men under Prince Menshikov, had not disputed the initial allied landings, but on 20 September, only 2 days after the invasion force came ashore, they took up a strong position on the heights of the River Alma to block the allies' southward advance towards Sebastopol. Here, after heavy fighting, they were forced to withdraw and the allies were left to continue their advance.[10] Part of the allied fleet had kept abreast of the advancing army, but naval involvement in the battle was minimal, although some French warships bombarded Russian positions at long range.[11] British naval forces were not employed in the actual fighting – apart from a few detached officers on Raglan's staff, the crews in the warships anchored off the mouth of the River Alma were nothing more than spectators of the action ashore. The young George Tryon, then Acting Mate aboard *Vengeance* which 'anchored close to the shore in full view of everything', reported:

> The next day at about eleven the army was seen to advance; the French and Turks, close to the shore, climbed up a very steep road, which the Russians were unable to prevent, as our guns would have been able to knock them over. The French rushed up most gallantly; the artillery had a tremendous drag to get up at all; twice we saw the French shelter under the brow of the hill, making a short retreat from the murderous fire, whilst their forces were increasing; when collected they rushed on, carrying everything before them.

Now, for our part of the field. Our men advanced, first coming to a village in flames, filled with sharpshooters, who were driven out by the Rifles, and were assailed by a storm of shot, shell, and grape. Now they came to a brook about 300 yards from the main Russian battery: it had very steep banks, and part of the men were up to their armpits; but nothing stopped them. They shoved each other up the opposite bank, and rushed on right in the face of a battery of twenty-four guns. Took it, guns and all, killing or driving out of the redoubt all the Russians, when some one hailed, 'You are firing on the French.' A bugler heard it, sounded cease firing, which was repeated down the line and obeyed. The 23rd leapt out of the battery; the Russians rallied, returned, retook their guns, and carried them off. In a few minutes the mistake was found out, but too late to save the lives of hundreds of brave men, who huddled together, afforded a fearful opportunity to the Russians to pour in a murderous fire ... but our own men rushed up again as soon as the mistake was found out, captured two guns, and routed the Russians, who, like a flock of goats, now fled towards Sevastopol.[12]

Tryon was one of many who could do no more than simply watch the fighting from a distance, in his case through a telescope from the main-top.[13] Having relayed its principal events to the deck below as they happened, he then went ashore to help the wounded. Nevertheless, over the next 2 days 600 sailors and marines were landed to help remove and treat the wounded,[14] British, French and Russian, who were eventually transported to hospitals like Scutari or Therapia in the Bosphorus. *Vesuvius, Albion* and the transport *Avon* carried over 500 Russian wounded, landing them at Odessa.[15]

The warships then proceeded along the coast towards Sebastopol, shadowing the army. Sebastopol boasts one of the finest deepwater harbours in the world. The inlet on which the city stands runs for nearly 4 miles inland and in 1854 had water deep enough for the largest warships along its entire length. Running southwards from this outer harbour or 'roads' was an inner bay, often referred to as 'the man of war harbour', which offered shelter from rough seas and high winds and was the main anchorage of Russia's Black Sea Fleet. At its widest, the entrance to the whole inlet was only 1,000 yards, making it easier to defend and more difficult for a hostile fleet to manoeuvre. Naturally enough, the entire approach was dominated by powerful defences, some of them very recently constructed. The massive stone forts protecting Sebastopol's harbour, especially Fort Constantine, Fort Alexander and the Quarantine Fort, were built in solid granite and very well armed, these forts alone mounting 198 heavy guns defending both the roads and the seaward approaches. Typical of the greatest defence works was the horseshoe-shaped Fort Constantine, with walls 6 feet thick and 30 feet high, mounting 97 guns; one side faced the outer harbour and the other, mounting 50 guns, looked out to sea. Fort Alexander and Fort Michael were similar but smaller. These major forts were supported by numerous 'lesser' batteries and earthworks, like the 'Wasp' and 'Telegraph' redoubts. The sea defences were formidable but they were, after all, designed to protect one of Russia's greatest naval bases.

It was widely believed that a rapid advance and an attack on the *north* side of Sebastopol should have been launched immediately, with the allied navy descending on the harbour of Sebastopol and its warships. Russian forces were relatively weak and the defences of Sebastopol at that time were hardly in a position to withstand an assault. But no such action occurred. The French thought that this plan was too rash until heavier siege guns and ammunition could be brought up, to provide an adequate preliminary bombardment prior to an infantry assault.[16] In the meantime, on 23 September, the Russians, under the view of HMS *Sampson* and *Highflyer*, which were watching the port, scuttled seven warships across the mouth of Sebastopol harbour, effectively blocking it and preventing in one simple move any possibility of a sudden naval raid into the bay.[17] The action equally sealed the Russian fleet within the harbour, where it would remain bottled up, so that it was immediately apparent that 'there would be no naval engagement in the Black Sea during the war; no great victory afloat [to] add a fresh jewel to the naval crown'.[18]

As the allied army slowly moved to the *south* of Sebastopol[19] in the famous 'flank march' to begin the close siege of the city and port, the fleets moved into nearby harbours – the British into Balaklava and Kazatch Creek and the French off the River Katcha and later into Kamiesch Bay. Admiral Dundas accepted Sir Edmund Lyons' suggestion that the British 'inshore squadron'[20] should centre its attention on the narrow but deep harbour of Balaklava as a convenient and sheltered base near enough to the proposed British siege lines. British warships led by Lyons in *Agamemnon* entered the bay on 26 September[21] and the demanding process of landing stores and equipment of all kinds, not least the siege guns and their ammunition, began immediately. The harbour (whose crowded scenes were later captured so evocatively in the photographs of Roger Fenton and James Robertson) was to become the principal landing point for stores and equipment for the British army in the Crimea[22] but it was so small that the larger ships could not be accommodated and were forced to anchor outside the bay; equally the French warship squadron under Rear Admiral Charnier, which soon joined Lyons, could find no room there so the French established their principal naval bases off the Katcha and at Kamiesch Bay, to the west of Sebastopol, which became further depots and landing points for the allies.

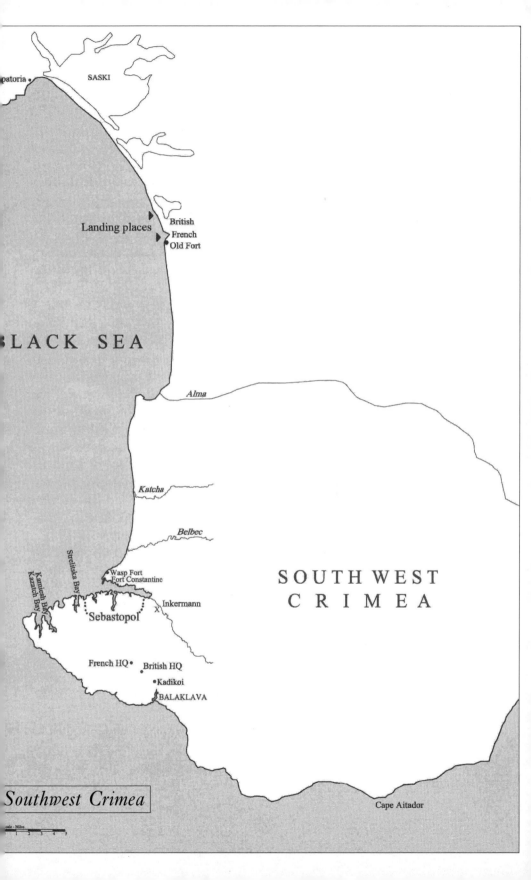

Southwest Crimea

Something of an 'all over by Christmas' attitude seems to have prevailed, with little talk of a possible winter campaign and bets being laid amongst the men as to how many days or weeks it would all last. But as the allies slowly lumbered into their chosen siege positions, the Russians very rapidly put Sebastopol into a state of defence. They were lucky with their senior commanders. The effective command of the city's military forces was placed under the experienced Admiral Pavel S. Nakhimov[23] assisted by the equally impressive Vice Admiral V.A. Korniloff,[24] whilst the brilliant engineer Count Franz Todleben[25] was put in charge of the defences. Making excellent use of the terrain, he constructed a series of linked redoubts and forts around the city perimeters, such as the soon-to-be-famous Quarantine and Flagstaff batteries, the Malakoff and the Great Redan.

It was evident from the earliest days of the allied landing in the Crimea and the beginnings of the active siege of Sebastopol that the Royal Navy might have a greater role to play than simply transport duties, blockade and occasional coastal bombardment. Such was the shortage of adequate siege equipment and gun crews that the use of heavy guns landed from the fleet, supported by naval and marine contingents, was soon suggested. One factor that supported the denuding of the fleet to support land operations was that Sebastopol was no longer deemed vulnerable to an immediate naval attack and, since the Russian fleet was bottled up, the allied fleet was not needed for much in the way of actual operations at sea. The allied naval command had hoped that a swift descent on Sebastopol might find its harbour open and undefended, but the Russians had responded too quickly to the allied advance. They had initially blocked the approaches to Sebastopol harbour with a simple line of seven linked ships and, as related above on the night of 22–3 September following the allied advance from the Alma, had scuttled these ships, effectively blocking the mouth of the harbour and sealing inside it the rest of their Black Sea Fleet. The Russian naval commanders were said to have been angry and bitterly disappointed that their ships were not ordered out to fight the allies and, if unsuccessful, at least to go down fighting. However, many of the allied naval commanders thought the move was wise under the circumstances – the Russian fleet had not shown itself to be very dynamic when offered the chance to attack the allied convoy as it was crossing the Black Sea or in emerging to oppose the landings. Paradoxically, the bottling-up of the Russian fleet actually helped the Russians, since it rendered impossible a sudden allied naval raid into the heart of Sebastopol[26] and against the anchored Russian fleet and, just as importantly given their role throughout the siege, it freed thousands of otherwise redundant Russian sailors and their guns to play a vital part in the defence of the city.[27]

With no major naval operations against Sebastopol in view for the moment, Dundas and his French counterpart, Admiral Hamelin, suggested as early as 28 September – only a fortnight after the initial landings – that a Naval Brigade should be formed for shore service. In the British fleet, the 5 largest warships would each contribute 200 men, the smaller ones in proportion, along with most of the ships' gun crews and all their marines, with the necessary equipment and spares. This eventually produced a British force of over 2,400 sailors, 2,000 marines and nearly 160 guns. A total of 25 officers and 988 men of the Royal Marines under Lieutenant Colonel Thomas Hurdle, RM were immediately landed at Balaklava, followed over the next few days by a further 10 officers and 212 men. The marines ashore were formed into two battalions, most being based on the heights above the port, and immediately set to work constructing batteries and building perimeter defences over 2 miles long, centred on the village of Kadikoi.[28] Slightly later, two companies of marines served for some months 'at the front' with the batteries, being engaged at Inkermann, and a detachment of Royal Marine Artillery under Major Alexander manned guns in the forward positions during the summer.

The British siege positions were divided into what were called the 'Right Attack' (more or less covering the Russian defences between the Redan and the Flagstaff Bastion) and the 'Left Attack', covering the line from the Redan via the Malakoff to the Little Redan. The two 'attacks' were separated by the Worontzoff Ravine. To add to the allied firepower before Sebastopol the navy manned 17 guns in Chapman's Battery and 7 (out of 26) in Gordon's Battery.[29] Six of the new 68-pounder Lancaster guns were set up in two other batteries on the Victoria Ridge and others were located along with more conventional guns in various positions. But the navy's main work ashore consisted in supporting the allied artillery pounding the Russian defences or in counter-battery work. Placed under Captain Stephen Lushington, commander of *Albion*, seconded by Captain William Peel of the *Diamond*, the Naval Brigade was initially camped on the Victoria Ridge, near the Woronzoff Road, just over 2 miles south of Sebastopol harbour. Its first job was simply to employ teams of 'bluejackets' to manhandle from the busy harbour of Balaklava the heavy siege guns and ammunition and the timber and materials necessary to construct gun emplacements.[30] The distance was 6–8 miles, depending on the point in the front line and the men worked ceaselessly from 5.30am until after 6.30pm, often under fire. To increase the allies' firepower 'before Sebastopol' heavy guns were removed from the major battleships: the powerful 8-inch guns of *Albion* and *Retribution* along with 32- and 68-pounders from *Britannia*, *Agamemnon*, *Queen*, *Rodney*, *Diamond*, *Trafalgar*, *Bellerophon*, *Terrible*, *Vengeance* and *London*; *Beagle* landed two of her new Lancaster guns. Some ships, like *Diamond* which provided the first of the naval batteries under Captain Peel and immediately lost twenty 32-pounder guns, were just about stripped of their main armament.[31] For each naval gun, the sailors brought ashore 150 rounds of shot and 30 of common shell and an appropriate supply of gunpowder. It was, as Lyons recorded, a 'Herculean' task to get all this ordnance and ammunition ashore.[32] George Tryon recalled:

> We were sent off the other day with fifty siege guns to assist the siege train and more are landing now. We have from a hundred to a hundred and fifty men from each line-of-battle ship on shore – a merry party, as long as the fine weather lasts . . . We run our guns by hand, landed from the ships, much faster than the artillery. Everyone seems to be delighted with the progress we have made, but there is an immense deal to be done.[33]

There is no doubt that, like the land forces alongside whom they served, the Naval Brigade was to have a difficult and challenging time over the long eighteen months of siege operations, assaults and counter-attacks which followed. It is, however, frequently claimed that 'the navy ashore' suffered less from the general rigours of the siege and climate because the Naval Brigade camp was generally better equipped and fed than the army equivalent, supplied from its own ships or the depot ship in Balaklava harbour and weathered the terrible winter of 1854–5 better than did the army. It had good wells, better sanitary arrangements, decent food and better accommodation. Sailors in the front-line batteries were regularly supplied with hot coffee, hot chocolate and soup and those returning to camp, coming from an often cold and wet stint in the muddy trenches and batteries, were given hot drinks. Quinine and lime juice were freely available to those on duty, so that all in all there was proportionally less disease and fewer deaths amongst the naval contingent.[34] George Tryon even had a much-admired bivouac with real glass windows, having been 'lent' the glass plates by Captain George Bowyear of *Vengeance*.[35]

Apart from the strenuous effort of assisting with the manhandling of stores, guns and equipment from Balaklava to the siege lines and the transporting of the wounded, reinforcements and supplies back and forth across the Black Sea, the Royal Navy felt rather underused in terms of prosecuting the war. In the winter of 1854, as the allies settled down to what was already looking like the long siege of a well-defended port, it was felt that the combined navies could do something to bring their impressive firepower to bear against Sebastopol. The French high command equally believed that, since the navy had not yet been engaged in any significant action and considering the allied inferiority in gun power compared with that of the Russian defenders, the navy should do more to aid the progress of the siege. But not until 13 October did the land command feel that it was in a position actually to begin serious siege operations, the main guns and positions having at last been established. The stage was set for the 'First Bombardment' of Sebastopol on 17 October 1854 in which the navy was to be fully involved. The huge naval force would at least be given some definite and useful task and could be seen to be actively supporting the siege operations.

The allied high command agreed that the first coordinated attack on Sebastopol would take place on 17 October. Their batteries, whose construction was long delayed by the difficulties of simply getting the siege guns and their ammunition into place, would open a heavy fire from their newly constructed positions south of the city, followed by an infantry assault on the Russian defence lines. The military commanders seem to have agreed that in any general assault on Sebastopol the navies could assist. But there were long and difficult discussions between the naval and land commanders over what exactly the navy should do to assist the attack. Although the allied fleet could put into action over 1,100 guns in a single broadside against the 600 Russian harbour guns, some of the naval commanders, Dundas amongst them, were less than optimistic. Lord Raglan and the French command really wanted the allied fleets to contribute to a form of 'combined operation' in which following a preliminary bombardment from the siege guns and warships there would be an infantry assault on Sebastopol's defences. But Admiral Dundas and many of the allied naval commanders were not greatly anxious to risk the fleet in a battering match with Sebastopol's harbour forts, especially since it was likely to be only a secondary attack – really just a demonstration – against fortresses known to be extremely strong.[36] Dundas certainly agreed that some form of naval attack was feasible – perhaps a diversionary bombardment of the northern forts which might draw Russian defenders away from the south side – but he doubted the validity and the effectiveness of a sea-borne bombardment against the main harbour defences. He really believed that it could seriously damage the allied ships to no real purpose and put forward very valid reasons for not risking the ships in a shooting match. However, Rear Admiral Edmund Lyons, who commanded the 'inshore squadron' based at Balaklava and very much had Raglan's ear, was an enthusiastic supporter of the whole project. Under pressure from a government in London anxious to see some success against Sebastopol and eager to support Lord Raglan[37] Dundas reluctantly fell in line with the allied plan and agreed to give the navy's support to an assault on the city. Had the plan succeeded it *might* have taken Sebastopol in one short, sharp action. However, some naval commanders felt that to have any effect the warships would have to go in so close that they would be seriously endangered by the Russian forts. As a result, although the combined fleet could bring to bear an impressive broadside, to reduce the damage to ships simply sitting offshore in range of the forts, they would engage at long range – which really meant that they were likely to have little effect. French warships would attack

Fort Alexander and the Quarantine Fort, whilst British ships would attack the northern sector of the sea defences, including the mighty Fort Constantine and the heavily armed earth redoubt nicknamed 'the Wasp' battery.

It seems that the land commanders Raglan and Canrobert expected the naval bombardment to coincide with that from the land batteries, to begin at 6.30am on 17 October, in what was said to be the greatest artillery bombardment ever attempted. But although 126 guns in the land batteries opened on time, the warships were not in place by then and the fleet did not move into position until 10.30am or begin to open fire until after 12.30pm – six hours later. At the last minute the French naval commander Admiral Hamelin altered the timing of the naval attack so that it would coincide with the land assault, not the preliminary artillery bombardment. It appears that Hamelin, like Dundas, had little faith in the plan and because of a shortage of ammunition on the allied ships – only 70 rounds per gun were available – did not want to use up all his ammunition in an early bombardment, leaving the allied ships with no role during the later infantry attack.[38] Overall, the allied naval commanders considered that it was better, with their limited ammunition, to support the actual assault and to open fire only when that had begun. However, even by 10.30am the fire of the Russian defenders had put out of action many of the French siege batteries[39] and the landward assault was actually called off. What happened from the navy's point of view was therefore a largely unsupported naval bombardment of the port's coastal and harbour defences by the allied fleet, with no infantry attack to support.

The British assembled a truly formidable array of firepower for the occasion – said to represent one-third of the total available strength of the Royal Navy at that time[40] and reflecting the last significant use of the old wooden sailing battleships, including *Albion, Arethusa, Bellerophon, Britannia, London, Queen, Rodney, Trafalgar* and *Vengeance*; they fought alongside those signs of modern times, the screw and paddle-steamers *Agamemnon, Tribune, Terrible, Sphinx, Lynx, Firebrand, Niger, Sans Pareil, Triton, Vesuvius, Furious, Retribution, Highflyer, Spiteful* and *Spitfire*. This fleet, along with no fewer than eleven French and two Turkish warships, was a most impressive force and represented the cream of the allied fleet in the Black Sea.[41]

Sir Edmund Lyons, who unlike Dundas ardently supported the idea of a massive single blow against Sebastopol, requested permission to take one squadron closer into range along a recently surveyed channel which would bring his ships to within 800 yards of Fort Constantine on the northern side of the harbour. This dangerous route had been reconnoitred on the night of the 16th by the Fleet Surveying Officer Captain T.A.B. Spratt and three ship's masters, who had personally scouted the shoals and buoyed a channel which

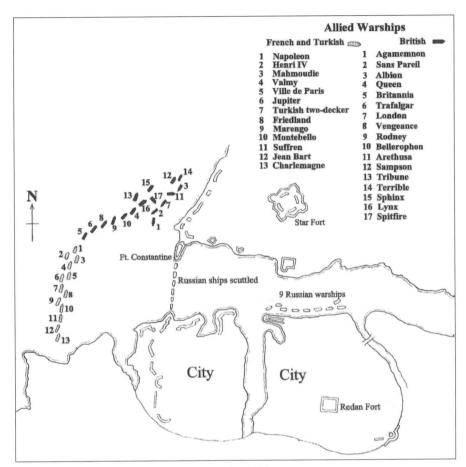

Allied Warships

French and Turkish	British
1 Napoleon	1 Agamemnon
2 Henri IV	2 Sans Pareil
3 Mahmoudie	3 Albion
4 Valmy	4 Queen
5 Ville de Paris	5 Britannia
6 Jupiter	6 Trafalgar
7 Turkish two-decker	7 London
8 Friedland	8 Vengeance
9 Marengo	9 Rodney
10 Montebello	10 Bellerophon
11 Suffren	11 Arethusa
12 Jean Bart	12 Sampson
13 Charlemagne	13 Tribune
	14 Terrible
	15 Sphinx
	16 Lynx
	17 Spitfire

The naval bombardment of Sebastopol, 17 October 1854.

ran in front of the great fortress. Permission was given to make the attempt and
during the bombardment on the 17th, the screw warships *Agamemnon* (flagship
under Lyons) and *Sans Pareil* under Captain Sydney Dacres – the only steam
battleships with the British fleet in the Black Sea – with the sailing ships
Albion, *London* and *Arethusa* were given this task. For the rest, the steam
vessels of both fleets would be lashed to the offside of the sailing battleships
and manoeuvre or tow them into their bombarding positions off Sebastopol –
an interesting comment on the old and new ships.[42] The whole would form
one single line, 2 miles long, right across the entrance to the port, at ranges
of 1,600 yards to 1,800 yards. The young Edward Seymour aboard *Terrible*
remembered adapting the ship's 68-pounder carriages to give an increased
elevation and extend their range of 4,000 yards 'which we thought extraordinary' but which he reckoned could be matched by the guns of the *Wasp*

battery.[43] Because of the confined space, the bombarding ships would not be able to wheel and manoeuvre (as they had at Odessa) but would have to remain stationary in their battle line and would not be able to move out of shot.

The Times reported on the 18th that:

> Yesterday morning, about daybreak, the English and French opened fire from their [land] batteries on the south side of Sebastopol ... The paddle-wheel and screw frigates lashed themselves alongside the sailing line-of-battle ships and all was got ready for the fight. The French were to occupy the right as you enter the harbour – that is, the southern side – and the English, the left, or northern side, in one line, about 1,500 yards off. The French got into their places about half-past twelve o'clock, and immediately commenced a heavy fire, which was vigorously returned from the batteries. The distance, however, was certainly greater than originally contemplated, and, as far as I can ascertain, was over 2,000 yards. By degrees the English ships successively took up their stations, passing in rear of the French, and anchoring to the left. The *Agamemnon*, *Sans Pareil*, and *London* ... however, took an inside station in advance – perhaps about 1,000 yards from Fort Constantine. Nothing could be more noble than the gallant way in which the *Agamemnon* and *Sans Pareil* steamed in amid a perfect hail of cannon-balls and shells, preceded by a little tug-steamer, *Circassian*.[44] ... This little bit of a cockleshell, which looked as if she might have been arrested by a fowling-piece, deliberately felt the way for the large ships till her services were no longer required.
>
> The firing soon became terrific. At the distance of 6 miles the sustained sound resembled that of a locomotive at full speed, but, of course, the roar was infinitely grander. The day was a dead calm, so that the smoke hung heavily about both ships and batteries and frequently prevented either side from seeing anything. From about two till dark (nearly six) the cannonade raged most furiously.
>
> Towards four o'clock, Fort Constantine, as well as some of the smaller batteries, slackened somewhat in their fire; but towards dusk, as some of the ships began to haul out, the Russians returned to their guns, and the fire seemed as fierce as ever ... At dark, all the ships returned to their anchorage.[45]

The whole thing (in the grand tradition of the Crimean War) was something of a farce. The allied warships continued in action against the forts, for no great reason since there was no allied land attack, and not surprisingly did some damage to the lesser and upper defence works but none at all, at such a long range, to the solid main defences. Even the ships under Lyons, closer in at only 800 yards, could do little against Fort Constantine. The Russian batteries naturally put up a good fight and some of the warships came under severe cross fire from a number of forts at once. By 1.30pm the firing was so intense that clouds of smoke enshrouded the whole scene, so that the Russian gunners could hardly pick out individual ships, some firing 'blindly into the wall of smoke at the entrance to the waterway, fearing that the enemy was about to emerge';[46] others simply sighted their guns on the gun flashes from the allied ships. And all was done at great and unjustified cost to the allied fleet. They were in effect little more than sitting targets – immobile, firing broadsides at static defence works – and suffered tremendous damage even at that range.

> On former occasions, as at Algiers and Acre, it had been seen that a heavy fire from wooden ships having a large number of guns on the broadside and engaging at close range could be very effective against sea forts. The natural disadvantages of a wooden structure exchanging fire with one of solid stone – or earth emplacements – could be compensated for by a superiority in gun power if judiciously concentrated.[47]

Perhaps they weren't 'judiciously concentrated' enough. One account relates that Russian artillery officers calmly and accurately gauged the positions of the vessels and then plied them with red-hot shot and shell. Some of the warships' decks were reportedly 'cut up like ploughed fields'[48] and fires broke out in ship after ship. It was indeed a terrible and alarming demonstration of the power of solid defences and modern shells against the wooden walls of the Royal Navy.[49]

Edward Seymour – then a very junior officer – commented:

> I have little personal to say about the action: a naval cadet hardly can have. I was stationed at the fore main deck quarters [on HMS *Terrible*] and from the bridle ports at times had a pretty good view. It was certainly the greatest noise I ever heard and when one considers that all the allied land breaching batteries and some twenty-three sail of the line besides smaller vessels were firing away as hard as they could, and that the Russians from hundreds of guns were replying, the noise may be imagined.[50]

The damage to British ships was considerable – as Dundas had feared.[51] The frigate *Arethusa*, one of those that had gone close in to Fort Constantine, had her rigging cut to pieces, many shots through her hull and twenty-three killed and wounded; her main and lower decks burst into flames and she came close to sinking. HMS *Albion* had three serious fires around her magazine and with eleven killed and seventy-one wounded was forced to abandon the fight, badly mauled and more or less out of control; *Agamemnon* – Lyons' Flagship and part of the squadron attacking Fort Constantine – was set on fire and was more exposed than any other ship because of her closeness to the forts, though she suffered far more aloft than in her hull largely because the fort's guns could not be depressed enough to hit the ship lower down. Hit 240 times, she was twice set on fire.[52] *Sans Pareil* came in to support her and, in an action much praised at the time, *Bellerophon* under Captain Lord George Paulet came to her assistance. But she was herself raked from stem to stern, burst into flames and had to be towed out of range. HMS *Queen*, having successfully targeted cliff-top batteries, was set on fire and forced out of the line, whilst *Rodney*, sailing forward to deflect fire from *Agamemnon* and *Sans Pareil*, ran aground and though she continued to fire broadsides, could do little damage. *London*, with four killed and eighteen wounded, was also forced to retire. *Britannia*, *Trafalgar*, *Queen* and *Vengeance* were much less damaged (though *Queen* caught fire, as did also the *Britannia*, which received over seventy shots in her hull). The last ship to remain in action was *Bellerophon*, which retired at 7 o'clock with five killed and sixteen wounded.

Some ships were so badly cut up that they were forced to sail back as far as Constantinople and even Malta for repair and there was significant loss of life – 44 killed and 266 wounded in the British fleet alone,[53] with HMS *Albion* and *Sans Pareil* (part of the squadron that Lyons had taken close to Fort Constantine) suffering the heaviest losses amongst their crews. The French contingent suffered equally badly. Minor damage to the lesser defences of the harbour forts of Sebastopol was in fact all that was achieved – the massive granite ramparts and gun positions were not significantly damaged and the earthwork batteries in particular had taken the pounding very well. It was reported that in some forts no guns were put out of action and the Russian casualty list, reported at just over 1,000, was reasonably light given the weight of fire directed against them.[54]

With the first great assault a decided failure, the build up of the allied positions and renewed siege operations continued. It had become brutally apparent that the Russian defences – contrary to the over optimistic expectations of any number of junior officers – could take everything that the allied guns could give out and that there was to be no rapid, easy victory. The siege was shaping up to be a long, drawn-out affair. But although fairly static as far as the allies were concerned, we perhaps tend to forget that the siege of Sebastopol did not prevent active land operations in the Crimea by Russian forces. In fact, they initially played a far from stationary role. Retaining large forces 'in the field' beyond the half-beleaguered city, they made a series of major attacks on the fixed allied positions in an attempt to raise the siege and drive off the invaders. The Russians under General Liprandi[55] made their first major attack on the allied positions near Balaklava on 25 October 1854, in an attempt to seize the port and cripple the British base of operations. During the resulting Battle of Balaklava, famous for the charges of the Light and Heavy cavalry brigades and the defence of the port by the 93rd Highlanders in their 'thin red line', the officers and men of the Naval Brigade were principally engaged with their own siege guns 'before Sebastopol' and played little part in the actual battle. A Royal Marine contingent of over 1,200 men, mainly drawn from the larger battleships and bringing many of the ships' guns ashore with them, had been landed from 29 September and was deployed on what became known as 'Marine Heights' on the defensive perimeter of the port of Balaklava, to free infantry battalions for more active service. The port's defences centred on the village of Kadikoi and had been put in the hands of Sir Colin Campbell's Highland Brigade, which included the famous 93rd Highlanders along with the marines. They saw more of the action than did the sailors at their siege guns. Manning the outer defences of Balaklava, where gun positions were still being set up by the marines along this perimeter on 23 October, they opened fire on Russian cavalry formations that were operating in the valley right in front of them and harassing the Turkish gun teams retreating from their own batteries. The Russians advanced across the valley and overwhelmed the Turkish-held redoubts on the Causeway Heights, whilst the mass of their cavalry surged into the south valley. The greater part of the Russian force halted and was attacked by the Heavy Brigade under General Scarlett, but four squadrons were detached by the Russian commander to destroy the artillery park at Kadikoi. The Turkish defenders fled, so that all that stood between the Russian cavalry and their target was Campbell's small force of 93rd Highlanders, detachments from Balaklava and the artillery. The Marine Artillery had plenty to fire at and their guns poured in 24-pound, 32-pound and 8-inch shells, the shells seen to burst amongst the Russian cavalry, and bowling over horses and riders. It was at this stage that the 93rd received a charge in line and poured rifle fire into the Russian cavalry in the incident later immortalised as 'the thin red line'. Once the Russians retreated, the Marine Artillery continued to fire into them until they passed out of range.

Only the next day did any of the Naval Brigade see any action, when on the 26th the Russians made a sortie in force from Sebastopol[56] trying again to attack the port defences and directing their efforts on the weakly defended positions held by Sir de Lacy Evan's 2nd Division on the far right of the British lines.[57] In so doing, they threatened the Right Attack positions and the naval Lancaster battery manned by Acting Mate William Hewett and seamen of the *Beagle*, which came under heavy rifle fire at close range. Rejecting a verbal order to spike his single gun and fall back, Hewett continued to defend the position, even blasting away part of his own parapet to enable the gun to be swung round and continued in action, firing grapeshot, until the Russians retired.[58] Reinforcements were landed on the same day, including 200 more Marines from HMS *Algiers*, and for the next few days the marines manned their batteries and defensive positions on the heights above Balaklava on the alert for another major attack – perhaps even at night. For several days after the Battle of Balaklava the sector was constantly on the alert for another attack and several long-range artillery duels took place. One night a Cossack patrol got close enough to pepper the marines' tents and these Russian probes showed that Balaklava – and indeed the whole British flank of the allied siege positions – was still vulnerable to a determined Russian attack. As a result, reinforcements from the Naval Brigade were sent up to Marine Heights and the steamships *Agamemnon*, *Sans Pareil*, *Wasp*, *Cyclops*, *Vesuvius* and others were ordered to stand off Balaklava in case of renewed attacks on the port. Other naval vessels – *Firebrand*, *Niger*, *Beagle* and *Arrow* – ferried the wounded and sick from Balaklava to the Katcha and returned with ammunition and stores.

The naval guns and shore contingents played only a slightly greater role in the Battle of Inkermann on 5 November 1854 – the second major Russian attack and a much larger and more dangerous affair. Russian forces available to their Commander-in-Chief Prince Menshikov had been reinforced to 100,000 men, far outnumbering the besieging army. The French siege positions lay between the coast near Sebastopol and then joined the British left flank, so that they were fairly secure, but the right-hand flank of the British position was ill-defined and hopelessly 'in the air' – a tempting target. On 5 November, through deep mist, the Russians launched a sudden and massive attack on the weak British right, seized the heights of Inkermann and set in chain one of the bloodiest and most desperate battles in British military history. After a day of fighting in a confused 'soldiers' battle', the Russians were eventually driven off, with a loss of over 11,000 men. They really should have won a great victory; had they engaged their reserves that day, they might well have inflicted a real disaster.[59]

A total of 600 sailors actually took part in the fighting at Inkermann, whilst others kept the naval guns in action from their existing positions like Gordon's and Chapman's batteries, firing into the fog at the advancing Russian columns. The battery of the now Acting Lieutenant William Hewett, comprising three 68-pounders and a Lancaster, was again assailed and hand-to-hand fighting ensued. In a famous incident, five of Hewett's sailors stood on their own parapet and fired into the attacking Russians, whilst their comrades handed up freshly loaded weapons taken from dead soldiers; two of this gallant group were killed, but the other three lived to receive the Victoria Cross.[60] The major contribution of the Naval Brigade actually during the fighting was to help defend threatened strongpoints or redoubts. It was initially drawn up in reserve behind the notorious Sandbag Battery – 'the abattoir',[61] which was lost and recaptured many times during intense fighting that day and the scene of terrible slaughter. At one stage, sailors engaged in the fighting there to support the Grenadier Guards and companies of marines were similarly drawn into the action, some serving alongside the Light Division and helping to stem the Russian advance along Kareening Ravine.

Close on the heels of the great Battle of Inkermann the navy was to suffer severe loss, but not at the hands of the Russians. On 14 November, a terrific hurricane ('the Great Storm') swept along the coast of the Crimea, wreaking havoc as it went and all the naval anchorages were more or less badly affected. At or off Balaklava, no fewer than 34 transports and over 400 lives were lost, the ships being sunk or driven onto the rocky coast, and immense damage was done to the shore establishments. Although every British steamer was damaged to some degree,[62] the warships actually within Balaklava harbour fared somewhat better in the storm; *Retribution*, her rudder unshipped, was forced to throw her guns overboard, but only *Vesuvius* and *Ardent* suffered severe damage, though remaining afloat. The story was the same at the other naval bases. Off the Katcha, the main anchorage of the French fleet,[63] nine French and five British transports were lost, and both *London* and *Sampson* were badly damaged; the latter collided with transports that had broken loose and three of her masts collapsed 'and fell aft, reminding me of the dominoes which a child sometimes puts up to knock each other over'.[64] At Eupatoria, five British transports and a Turkish warship were lost and the French *Pluton* and *Henri IV* were driven ashore. The Russians, not slow to take advantage of the disruption caused by the storm at Eupatoria, launched an attack with 10,000 men, but were driven off, partly by the gunfire of the grounded warships, which though swamped could bring their guns into action, acting almost as coastal forts.

The greatest significance of this unfortunate natural disaster was not so much the damage to warships – most of it was fairly superficial, to masts, spars and rigging and was quickly repaired – but in the loss of huge quantities of supplies, including ammunition, medicines, food, uniforms and warm clothing which might have made the terrible Russian winter of 1854 less of an ordeal for the land forces. One famous example is the loss of the transport *Prince*, which had only just arrived from England carrying the 46th Regiment and, having fortunately landed her troops, went down with all hands and a huge amount ammunition and winter clothing – a loss that would be severely felt. In the *Resolute* 4,000,000 Minié rifle cartridges were lost. One significant result was the decision to scatter or withdraw many of the transports and even warships, some being sent as far as the Bosphorus or Constantinople.

The camps of the allied forces besieging Sebastopol had never been much to look at or to live in. On the windswept 'uplands' beyond Balaklava there was neither cover nor comfort. The tented camps of both the sailors and the marines were devastated[65] by the hurricane, as were their stores and magazines, and their sites reduced to a mudbath. Medicine, food, clothing and ammunition were impossible to move in any quantity from Balaklava through deep mud, and with wagons and even mule transport immovable, only columns of weary men could manhandle the supplies from the port to the camps and trenches. Evelyn Wood, a young midshipman of HMS *Diamond*, serving with his beloved Peel, recalled that the 'storm was the beginning of a misery so intense as to defy adequate description'.[66] The daily grind of these duties continued past Christmas through the months of the harsh winter and not until January 1855 was a light railway track slowly laid by the navvies of Messrs Peto, Brassey and Company between Balaklava and the siege lines to ease the transport of supplies to the front.

The losses at Inkermann followed so soon after by the severe damage caused by the Great Storm really put back any plans for another allied assault on Sebastopol. There was even talk of raising the siege altogether, such was the shortage of ammunition of all types, but in the end it was agreed to await reinforcements and supplies and simply sit it out until they arrived. The Admiralty constantly carped about the withdrawal of guns, sailors and marines from the ships, rendering them 'inefficient' as a fleet and denuding them of their crews and guns in penny packets, but Lyons managed to persuade Their Lordships that there was a real need for the naval presence ashore and ultimately, to his relief, the Admiralty allowed Lyons to be the judge of what was needed.[67] As a dreary and hard winter set in, the fleet off Sebastopol – reduced in the face of the hurricane – carried out a round of routine duties. Allied ships ferried troops and supplies to and from the Bosphorus to the Crimea, patrolled and blockaded the coast and escorted transports and troopships. After their early involvement with the Turkish operations in the eastern Black Sea, allied ships seem to have played no part in the long campaign waged by the Turks in the Caucasus. This generally uninspiring service was only enlivened on 17 December when the Russian steamer *Vladimir* emerged from Sebastopol harbour just far enough to shell the western sector of the French siege lines. As it happened, none of the allied ships was in any state to deal with her at that moment, but *Terrible* and *Valorous* got up steam just in time to chase her back out of range.

On 20 December 1854, Vice Admiral James Dundas, his three-year tenure in command of the Mediterranean Fleet having ended, sailed home in *Furious*, his parting signal to the fleet being 'Success Attend You'. Like Napier in the Baltic, Dundas was widely believed to have been an over timid commander who missed opportunities – his opposition to the bombardment on 17 October was well known.[68] He was replaced, as expected,[69] by the 64-year-old Sir Edmund Lyons, a sailor known for his courage and dash – he had taken a squadron to within 800 yards of Fort Constantine during the naval bombardment – and for his good relations with Lord Raglan and the French. Despite his long absence from the navy as a diplomat, not least as Minister to Greece during the period 1835–49, he was considered to be 'the right man in the right place'; he had played a major role in the transport of the British force from Varna to the Crimea and was highly regarded by Lord Raglan. Lyons adopted as his flag ship the magnificent (and new) screw steamer *Royal Albert*. The change in the British high command was mirrored in the French: Admiral Hamelin was succeeded by a new French commander, Vice Admiral Bruat, who was equally considered to be a more dynamic and energetic leader.[70] By this time, more and more of the older sailing battleships had been sent home, replaced by newer screw warships, typified by Harry Keppel's command, the *St Jean d'Acre*,[71] which arrived off Balaklava on 30 January 1855.

Rear Admiral Lyons in *Terrible* carried out a personal inspection of the entrance to Sebastopol harbour on 6 February 1855. He found it still defended by its formidable (repaired) batteries, and still with a line of sunken ships whose masts rose from the water and had been connected with spars, ropes and timber to add to the barrier. Any attempt to try to break into the port was clearly not going to work so that in any real sense there was little else to do but continue with the daily grind of shelling and counter-fire. The main naval battery on the left of the British position was a regular target for Russian fire, as was a naval battery in the Right Attack and the daily shelling and sniping inevitably caused casualties for little apparent result; on one day, for example, they suffered five killed and nineteen wounded – not a high figure, but such regular losses were a steady drain on the personnel of the Naval Brigade without there being much chance of replacement.

On 6 March 1855 news of the death of the Tsar, who had died on the 2nd, reached the allies. At first, it caused little to change but in the long run it proved to be of great significance; the new Tsar Alexander II proved to be increasingly less eager to continue an expensive and apparently pointless war and was ultimately to lead Russia into the negotiations that ended the fighting. More important to the navy at this time was the virulent outbreak of smallpox which spread through the fleet, causing some ships to be dispersed to sea and others to withdraw temporarily to quarantine areas.

After Inkermann in November 1854, the Russians were less ready to tackle the allied army 'in the field' and the siege settled down into the familiar day-to-day grind of artillery fire and counter-fire, punctuated with raids and occasional assaults. Equally, having strengthened their batteries and built up their ammunition over months (with the Russians doing exactly the same), the allies were ready to attempt a second general bombardment of Sebastopol by the beginning of April 1855. As part of the preliminary preparation in the days before the attack, some British warships (for example, *Valorous* and *Gladiator*) tried the novelty of night attacks on the defences of Sebastopol harbour, aided by a light system devised by Lord Clarence Paget. Edward Seymour recalled:

> Night attacks by single ships, or two or three in company, were occasionally made on the sea batteries, in which we [*Terrible*] occasionally took part. Lights were laid down on buoys for the purpose of guiding the ships where to go and we steamed in a curve in front of the harbour, delivering one or two broadsides towards the town; and as we did so, our ships were occasionally hit by the return fire[72]
>
> It was hoped that the ships could get in close under cover of darkness and that the Russian defenders would be unable to make accurate retaliation. But the hopes were wrong; the Russian gunners proved to be just as capable in the dark, firing at the flashes from the ships' guns, so that the plan was abandoned after only a few nights.[73]

Much of the new armament that would open on Sebastopol's defences was provided by the fleet. The commander of the Naval Brigade, Stephen Lushington, listed the thirty-seven naval guns which would take part in the bombardment: Right Attack – 14 guns of which there were 9 32-pounders, 3 68-pounders and 2 Lancasters. Left Attack – 23 guns, of which 14 were 32-pounders, 1 68-pounder, 2 8-inch 65-hundredweight and 2 8-inch 50-hundredweight Lancasters; 2 24-pounder Lancasters and 2 10-inch Lancasters.[74]

The second bombardment began on Easter Monday, 9 April 1855, in heavy rain, with 123 British guns in action, 47 manned by the Naval Brigade.[75] It was not a success, with the Russians maintaining a very effective counter-fire and not enough damage deemed to have been done to the defences to warrant an infantry assault.[76] Over the course of a further week of firing, despite the naval batteries being extended and reinforced so that no fewer than forty-nine guns in the siege batteries were manned by naval personnel, no great headway was made. So little were the Russian defences affected by the bombardment – usually rebuilt and re-supplied overnight – that a land assault seemed futile and was never launched; the proposed attack was completely abandoned on 17 April. By this time, the naval guns and their platforms were showing signs of severe wear and tear, their ammunition was running short and there was a depressingly steady drip of casualties.[77]

Although further serious attempts against Sebastopol continued (for example, the successful assault on The Quarries on 7 June, in which the

Naval Brigade manned no fewer than fifty-six guns), nothing had so far pierced the main Russian defences. Nevertheless, plans for a further full-scale attack on Sebastopol took shape and as part of this plan it was arranged for a preliminary naval bombardment on the 16–17 June. By now, some of the ships from the expedition to Kertch had returned (see below, p. 124ff.), so that more war-ships were available to support the bombardment. Most of this was done by *Tribune, Highflyer, Terrible, Miranda, Niger, Arrow, Princess Royal, Viper* and *Snake*, with rocket boats, supported by French warships including *Jean Bart*. They moved inshore during the night of the 16th and opened up next day on the harbour defences. This attempt to distract at least some of the Russian defenders was met by the usual heavy return fire, the whole attempt being of little consequence except that it led to the wounding of the highly regarded Captain 'Jack' Lyons of *Miranda*, fresh from the ship's successful operations in the Sea of Azoff. He was transferred to the hospital at Therapia in the Bosphorus, confidently expected to recover since his actual wounds were not serious, but he contracted gangrene in hospital and to the universal regret of the fleet died a few days later on 23 June.[78] Although naval fire continued through the 17th, it achieved little that would aid the land forces committed to a full-scale attack on the 18th. At the same time as this naval attack, all the allied land guns had been brought to bear on the ramparts of Sebastopol – 466 French and 166 British, of which 56 were manned by the Naval Brigade – along with some of the 68-pounder guns and 13-inch mortars of the Royal Marine Artillery, brought down for the occasion from their usual positions amongst the defences on the heights above Balaklava. British efforts were largely directed, as usual, against the Redan and Malakoff forts. Surgeon Edmund Cree, wandering amongst the batteries on the 17th, recorded what must have been a typical experience at the front line during a heavy bombardment:

> Walked up to the batteries in the front. First visited the left or French attack, then crossed the ravine to No. 9 Sailors' Battery and to No. 10 where a party of the 67th Regiment were. Remained there some time looking at what I could see of the town – not much! As the firing was getting rather hot we were obliged to keep our heads low, well below the sandbags. We were about 800 yards from the Redan; shells were flying overhead and bursting beyond but we could generally see them coming and lay down close till they had burst. Rifle balls gave a sharp disagreeable ping! ping! every instant[79]

On 18 June, the great attack on the Redan was launched, only to be repulsed with heavy loss. After the artillery bombardments of 17 June, the commander of the Naval Brigade, Captain Stephen Lushington[80] had offered the services of his sailors to lead the storming parties, carrying scaling ladders and other equipment during the British attack on the Redan. Accordingly, companies of sixty sailors each accompanied the four main assaulting columns, overall command 'on the ground' being given to Captain William Peel of *Diamond*.[81] Inevitably, being in the forefront of the assault, the sailors met the full force of the Russian resistance – as determined as the attack – and suffered a high proportion of casualties, including Peel himself who was severely wounded.[82] Only two of the naval ladder parties actually made any progress, suffering 50 per cent casualties, but with the general failure of the whole operation, were forced to retreat with the others. Rear Admiral Lyons' reporting to the Admiralty, could commend 'the gallantry which had distinguished the Naval Brigade throughout this war [which] was never more distinguished than it was yesterday during the attack on the Malakoff Tower and Redan'[83] but the fact of the matter was that a major defeat had been suffered and it caused terrible dejection in the allied camp.

Fitzroy Somerset, Lord Raglan, the British commander in the Crimea died on 28 June, his death hastened, it was said, by the terrible casualties sustained in the unsuccessful assault on the Redan. Although much criticised at the time (and since), Raglan was actually quite popular with the Crimean army and with the French and his death was met with genuine sorrow and regret. His body was taken to Kazatch Bay to be sent home aboard HMS *Caradoc* and he was succeeded in command by General Sir James Simpson.[84]

From June to September 1855, the siege plodded on without any great incident to break the routine or the monotony. The arduous daily grind of siege operations, with rifle fire, shelling and counter-fire continuing daily, caused proportionally severe casualties to the Naval Brigade. Surgeon Cree recalled a typical scene:

> A good deal of firing all night from both sides. It is interesting and exciting to watch the shells after dark, but the volleys of musketry are far more deadly ... The same sort of work goes on night and day more or less continually. At present there seems to be no chance of it ceasing and the daily list of killed will be greater as we work nearer to the Russian lines[85]

Numbers of new mortar boats, capable of high-angle fire, arrived off the Crimea in July 1855 and, moored close to Sebastopol in Strelitska Bay under command of Captain George Digby of the Royal Marine Artillery, kept up a regular fire against the harbour forts, especially Alexander and Constantine, which were regularly shelling the left of the French siege positions, just within range of their guns;[86] Russian ships in the harbour at Sebastopol were also occasionally hit by mortar fire. The allied armies were gradually built up over the summer of 1855, to reach approximately 50,000 British, 120,000 French,

40,000 Turks[87]and up to 15,000 Sardinians[88] – more than enough to defend the allied positions from Russian counter-attacks. Thus it was that the last great Russian attempt to break the siege failed on 16 August, when General M.D. Gorchakov launched his forces against allied positions on the Tchernaya, an action largely fought by French and Sardinian forces, and was defeated. This, as it transpired, was the last throw of the dice by the Russian field army in the Crimea and really sealed the fate of Sebastopol: there would be no relief from the outside. That the Russians realised that this was the case is clear from the fact that after the defeat on the Tchernaya they began to construct the floating bridge that would eventually enable them to evacuate the southern (besieged) side of Sebastopol. It was completed on 26 August.[89]

The last and finally successful assault on the defences of Sebastopol took place on 8 September, the British again deputed to attack the Great Redan on the right, whilst the French concentrated on the Malakoff. In three days of heavy preliminary bombardment, 5–7 September, with British artillery now contributing no less than 200 siege guns, the Naval Brigade as usual joined the general firing against their designated targets. The mortar boats in Strelitska Bay continued their high-angle firing against harbour defences but although detailed plans were laid for the allied warships to join in, largely to engage the harbour forts like the Quarantine batteries to distract them from the land assault, in the event they could not be employed; because of severe weather and heavy seas the ships could not be manoeuvred or fire with any accuracy at fixed targets. George Tryon, writing on 11 September, recalled that 'the ships were to have cooperated but could not do so owing to the strength of the wind and today we have a gale and are knocking about very disagreeably'.[90] In the event, after terrific fighting, the French took the Malakoff but the British attack on the Redan again failed, with heavy loss of life. In the Naval Brigade alone, causalities amongst the sailors who joined the main assaulting parties were severe, with 30 killed and wounded – though they formed only a small proportion of the 2,447 British casualties.

The fall of the Malakoff convinced the Russian command that Sebastopol could no longer be held and General Gorchakov ordered the evacuation of the city to the northern side across the bay. Sebastopol was abandoned during the night, the Russians escaping across a specially constructed bridge and pontoons; magazines, drydocks, granaries and storehouses of all kinds were set on fire or blown up and the remaining ships, naval and civilian, scuttled or set alight. Sebastopol burned for two days before the allies entered the city on 10 September,[91] to find only the sick, wounded and dying crowding the Russian hospitals. One remaining Russian ship, the *Vladimir*, came under flag of truce to move some of the Russian wounded and dead to the northern shore but having done so was scuttled by her crew later the same day.

Rear Admiral Lyons reported:

> The enemy has destroyed all his steamers in the harbour. Thus
> the Russian Black Sea Fleet is annihilated ... the bottom of the
> splendid harbour is now encumbered with more than fifty sunken
> vessels, including eighteen ships-of-the-line and several frigates and
> steamers, whose menacing attitude but a short time ago materially
> contributed to bringing on the war in which we are now engaged.[92]

After a year of hardship and dedicated service, the end came very quickly
for the Royal Marine contingents and the Naval Brigade, now under Captain
Harry Keppel, who succeeded to the command on the promotion of Stephen
Lushington. As early as 11 September – only a day after the allies finally
entered Sebastopol – they were ordered to re-embark and on the 17th the
sailors marched in three divisions down to the ships in Balaklava harbour.
Amidst great cheering, flag-waving and ceremony and played away by an array
of regimental bands, the naval contingents were quickly aboard their ships and
away. The marines were equally quickly removed, gone by early October. In
the end, 4,469 officers and men, RN and RM, had been landed between
1 October 1854 and 16 September 1855. Of these, 8 officers and 95 men had
been killed, 38 officers and 437 men wounded.[93] A General Order from
Sir James Simpson at Head Quarters complimented the whole Brigade:

> The Commander-in-Chief of the Forces heartily thanks the officers,
> petty officers and seamen for the very efficient services they have
> rendered in the batteries and on all occasions when their aid against
> the enemy was required; and he has to notice the patience and
> courage with which, side by side with the soldiers of this army, they
> have endured the dangers and hardships of nearly a year's duty in the
> trenches ... General Simpson acknowledges the obligations he is
> under to Rear Admiral Sir Stephen Lushington KCB who so ably
> commanded the Brigade from its formation until his removal by
> promotion to a higher rank and to Capt. The Hon. H. Keppel who
> succeeded him and retained the command until the conclusion of
> this ever-memorable siege.[94]

A similar 'high approbation' of the conduct of the Royal Marines was
recorded, they and the Naval Brigade having 'shown the most cheerful
endurance of the hardship and fatigue of the trenches as well as the greatest
skill and gallantry in working the guns and bearing their part in the dangers of
the advanced works in the assault on the enemy's lines'. The French naval
contribution was equally acknowledged.[95]

Chapter 5

Operations in the White Sea, 1854–5

A major feature of Britain's use of global seapower was her decision to strike at the huge Russian Empire wherever it was susceptible to naval attack. This meant offensive operations at any accessible point – including the remotest corners of the Empire. One of the most remote areas, which surely felt itself far beyond the actual 'theatres of war', was Russia's Arctic coastline along the White Sea and in the Kola Inlet. It was a region that had been known to western European traders – not least British – since the mid-sixteenth century but the White Sea was under ice from early October to May, so that the ordinary trading and campaigning seasons were brief.

Now largely forgotten, allied naval exploits in that most inaccessible of regions were highly successful in the limited aims they set. As part of the policy to carry the war to Russia, the Admiralty decided as early as the spring of 1854 to send a small squadron to attack the apparently undefended ports and fishing villages of Russia's far north, though the blockade of Russia's Arctic coast was only formally announced on 12 August 1854. The area can hardly be said to have been militarily significant – most of the accessible area was the Lapland region of the Grand Duchy of Finland, technically part of the Russian Empire but hardly central to her military strategy or economic strength. The region was sparsely populated and its economic activity largely dominated by coastal trade and fishing. But it was, nevertheless, a potential target and an area where British and French warships could make a mark with relative impunity, if only on the economy of an isolated region. Initially, since the formal blockade was not declared until August, neutral shipping – Danish, Norwegian, German etc. – was allowed to continue to trade unmolested.[1]

A British 'Detached Squadron' under Captain Erasmus Ommanney of the 26-gun sailing frigate *Eurydice*, with the 15-gun *Miranda* and the steam corvette HMS *Brisk* set off early in June 1854. *Miranda* was launched at Sheerness in 1851 and was typical of the smaller steam-powered vessels that were to do so well during the Russian War. A screw sloop of 1,070 tons, she was well armed, with 10 32-pounders and 4 20-pounders in broadsides and carried a crew of approximately 230. Her commander was Captain Edmund ('Jack') Lyons, younger son of Rear Admiral Sir Edmund Lyons, second-in-command of the Mediterranean Fleet and soon to be commander in the Black Sea. This was

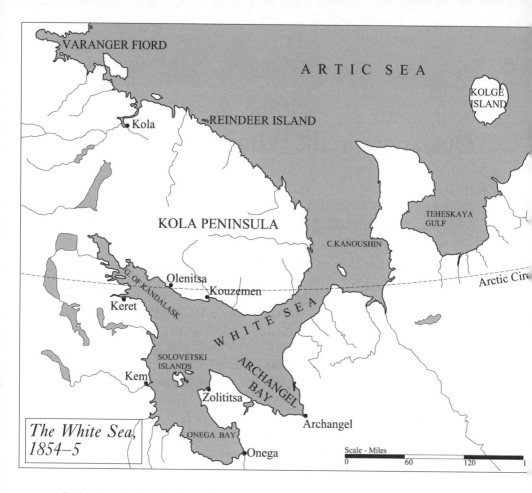

Jack Lyons' first independent command and he obviously meant to make it tell.[2]

Given the distance, the remoteness of the area and the notoriously dangerous waters,[3] their orders seem remarkable – they were to sail around Norway and into Arctic regions to enforce a blockade, stopping trade, capturing or destroying any and all Russian and Finnish vessels and attacking Russia's northernmost ports. It was a dangerous and audacious plan and succeeded spectacularly well in is limited objectives. Joined by two French ships under Captain Pierre Guilbert, the flotilla successfully rounded the western coastline of Norway and anchored for a few days off the Norwegian port of Hammerfest, the most northerly town in Europe, before heading into the White Sea.

One possible major target was the ancient city and major port of Archangel[4] which sheltered part of a division of Russian warships. The allied squadron found that Russia had few warships in the region, other than these ships at Archangel,[5] estimated as 1 gun-brig, 2 schooners, 2 steamers and 19 small gunboats. But these never attempted to leave the shelter of Archangel and offered no opposition to the free movement of the allied warships. The allied reconnaissance also found a large number of merchant vessels, primarily Dutch, sheltering in the port. The city itself, reconnoitred as one of the first tasks of the squadron, was deemed to be too strongly defended to risk attack and the waters of the Dvina too shallow for the warships to enter. Although some larger towns like Linsli and the Imperial dockyards at Strombol were known to be well defended and beyond reach, there was little in the way of local coastal defence around the White Sea, for the fairly obvious reason that the authorities did not anticipate an attack on this coast. Nevertheless, what happened over the next three months was truly staggering; a continuous process of chasing, stopping, searching and (having established ownership) usually burning 'enemy' merchant vessels and their cargoes, along with shore installations, including stocks of timber, foodstuffs, hay, fish and anything else deemed to be a legitimate target. On some occasions, the allied squadron was divided, with one or two ships operating almost in a 'commerce raider' role and it was quickly reported that 'the Russian coast [of the White Sea] is completely at our mercy, except Archangel for the present'.[6] Not surprisingly, the Russian press expressed intense outrage at attacks by a naval power on defenceless fishing boats and coastal luggers.

Finding that Archangel and its immediate neighbours were effectively beyond attack, the squadron approached the Solovetski Islands in the Gulf of Onega. Here, what may be considered the first 'major' action of the White Sea campaign took place. The islands were famous as the location of a wealthy and influential monastery, founded in the fifteenth century. Gradually becoming involved in all sorts of economic activity over generations – fishing, maritime trade, saltworks, fur trapping, ironworking etc., the settlement had become an economic and political powerhouse in the White Sea region. The abbots of the monastery were appointed by the Patriarch and the Tsar himself and Peter the Great had stayed there in 1694. Needless to say, it was also an important spiritual and cultural centre and a famous repository of manuscripts and books. Because of its wealth and local power, the monastery and islands were heavily defended and with its Sumskoy and Kemsky stockades, Solovetski Monastery became an important frontier fortress with a strong garrison.[7]

Having withdrawn from the reconnaissance of Archangel by 7 July, *Miranda* and *Brisk* approached the Solovetski Monastery a few days later and exchanged shots with a Russian battery in woodland nearby. Under a flag of truce, a landing party was sent to the superior of the monastery, the Archimandrite Alexander, to demand its unconditional surrender, which was unsurprisingly refused. Firing between the two ships and Russian shore batteries recommenced until nightfall ended the duel. Anchoring offshore over the night of the 18th, the two warships renewed the engagement next day and a hot fire passed between them and the shore batteries, the Russians eventually withdrawing their guns inland in the face of red-hot shot from *Miranda*. The heavily defended monastery – from which an equally heavy fire was directed at the ships – was itself shelled for over nine hours but its walls had withstood much more than this in the past and little damage was done by the time the ships ceased firing. Over the next few days, landing parties went ashore to destroy what was deemed to be 'government property' nearby, but for a cost of six casualties it cannot be said that much was achieved by the time the ships withdrew to continue their scouring of the White Sea and headed into the Gulf of Onega.

The local Russian, Lapp and Finnish coastal traders and fishermen cannot have felt a close connection with Russia's war against Britain and France – if indeed they knew much about it. They nevertheless took the full brunt of a relentless onslaught. One example was the port of Novitska, shelled and burned to the ground by *Brisk* and *Miranda* on 23 July. The figures seem incredible; over a period of eighty days, *Miranda* alone 'anchored forty-eight times [to land search parties] and whilst underway boarded 375 ships'.[8] Most of the enemy ships, mainly local merchant vessels and coastal traders, were simply beached and burned (along with their cargoes) or destroyed on the shore where they lay, their crews left to make their escape. In relatively few cases, where larger, valuable vessels were captured, were the ships and their cargoes taken intact and sailed as prizes to England with skeleton crews.[9] The British squadron simply had too few men to scatter them amongst captured prizes and send them back to Britain; on the spot destruction was the simplest plan. In the event, huge quantities of stores were destroyed in raids and bombardments. Any coastal town showing signs of resistance or trying to prevent the destruction of its ships and stores found itself being shelled and immense damage was done. *Miranda* and her sister ships must have been filled to the gunwales with ammunition!

Since the possibility of an attack on Archangel had been abandoned, the squadron turned its attention to the regional centre of Kola, lying 30 miles upriver from the Kola Inlet at the confluence of the Kola and Tuloma Rivers. The thirteenth-century river port – the oldest town in the region and the capital of Russian Lapland – had been fortified since 1565 and initially flourished as a base for fishing in the rich Arctic waters and for naval expeditions into Arctic regions. But although re-fortified under Peter the Great, it went into decline as Russia began to concentrate on developing its Baltic presence. By the nineteenth century, although still an important local trading and political centre, Kola was becoming something of a backwater, signified by its use as a place of exile by the Tsarist government. It was, nevertheless, regarded as an attractive and historic town, famous for its monastery and the beautiful Cathedral of the Annunciation (1800–10).

The Royal Navy had been there before; in 1809, when Russia was briefly an ally of Napoleon, two British gunboats had navigated their way down river and destroyed two Russian ships lying at anchor, but they had not damaged the town itself. In August 1854, things were very different. The squadron's commander, Captain Ommanney of *Eurydice*, deputed Edmund Lyons in *Miranda* to investigate the town. One has to admire the great skill with which George Williams, Master of the *Miranda*, navigated the ship down the tortuous river,[10] especially as the last 5 miles were uncharted and the river was dangerously narrow in places, but what Lyons then did to Kola surely reflects little credit on him, even if it was the capital of an 'enemy' territory, and was roundly criticised by elements of the British press.[11]

On 23 August, having cautiously brought his ship down river and setting it 'within point blank range of the city's batteries', Lyons sent Lieutenant Buckley under flag of truce to demand nothing less than the surrender of the town and all its government property, its fort and armaments. A truce was arranged for the governor to consider the offer but when no answer came by next day – the men on board *Miranda* being kept 'at quarters' all night – *Miranda* hauled down her flag of truce and opened fire with no further warning. Thus began a day-long bombardment of the town on 24 August which literally reduced the whole place to rubble without the warship suffering a single casualty.[12] In less than an hour the small docks, the river defences and the gun emplacements were destroyed by red-hot shot, grapeshot and canister. Landing parties of sailors and marines under 1st Lieutenant J.F.C. Mackenzie and the Mate, Charles Manthorpe, came ashore under cover of *Miranda's* continuing overhead fire and seized the enemy's guns. They and the governor's house might have been deemed to be fair game, but *Miranda* destroyed everything else – the beautiful cathedral and monastery, private houses, warehouses and shops. All were burned. By 7.30pm, according to a chilling contemporary account, 'Kola was expunged off the list of capitals [and] one tower of the fortified cathedral alone now stands to mark the spot where Kola once stood'.[13] It seems very hard on the local people and the effect on the region must have been felt for years. In the event, Kola never recovered from the attack and although slowly rebuilt, was gradually superseded as a regional centre with the modern expansion of the nearby city of Murmansk.

After Kola, *Miranda* and the other ships continued their patrols, capturing and destroying another half a dozen enemy vessels in the Litscha Inlet and Gulf of Motow. But the year ended with no signal achievement for the allied squadron (save the destruction of Kola). The flotilla withdrew with the advancing ice of the winter of 1854 and by late September had returned to home waters.

Early in the spring of 1855, government ministers were asked in the Commons whether they intended to re-establish a strict blockade of the White Sea and replied that such a blockade was indeed intended, as soon as the ice allowed the free movement of shipping. And just as operations in the Baltic in both the seasons of 1854 and 1855 were forced to concentrate largely on harassing local trade rather than bringing about any significant victory, so the White Sea in 1855 was to offer no opportunities for a general naval action. The allies decided to continue the 1854 policy of cruising the White Sea and its environs, trying to capture or destroy shipping and stores belonging to the Russian government but as far as possible leaving unharmed private property and those not engaged in running the blockade. However, as some merchant ships had used the neutral ports of Norway to evade to some extent the blockade of 1854, it was decided to impose a rather more stringent control on the movement of all shipping in the new year.

In April 1855 a British squadron under Captain Thomas Baillie in *Maeander* was readied for service in the far north and with the arrival of better weather set off on 19 May for the Russian Arctic. They rounded the North Cape on the 31st and were in position off the Russian coast by 11 June, when the blockade was officially announced.[14] The squadron comprised the 44-gun *Maeander* under Baillie, the 8-gun steamer *Phoenix* – recently returned from Arctic exploration[15] – under Commander J.M. Hayes and the 9-gun screw vessel *Ariel* under Commander John P. Luce. Arriving off Archangel early in June, it was joined by an augmented French contingent under Captain Guilbert of *La Cléopâtre*, with *Cocyte* and *Pétrel*.

The renewed blockade was to include without exception all the ports, harbours and creeks in the White Sea from Point Orlofka to Cape Kanoushin and especially the larger ports of Archangel and Onega. However, it was found that the White Sea had been freed from ice at an earlier date than usual and that neutral trading vessels had taken the opportunity to carry cargoes of wheat and other goods to and from Archangel. As many of these vessels had reached Archangel before the blockade was formally re-established, it was deemed reasonable to allow them to leave, either in ballast or with any cargo they had loaded by the date of the new blockade. As a result, some Norwegian, Danish, German and American merchants were allowed to leave the area, mainly carrying grain, timber and flour.

Ships of the Anglo-French squadron were employed, as in 1854, blockading ports and scouring the sea in search of enemy merchant ships; unsurprisingly, there was no sign of Russian warships, from Archangel or anywhere else. As in the Baltic, however, it was soon discovered that over the winter the main towns and ports had not been slow to strengthen their defences or build new ones and around Archangel in particular Russian land forces had been brought in to defend the coast. A force of light cavalry, 12,000 infantry[16] and militia was deployed around the city, whilst the forts defending the channel leading to the port were mounted with powerful new batteries of artillery; the town's citadel had been enlarged and two new bastions constructed. Under the command of Admiral Kruschtscheff, Governor General of the province and military commander in the city, Archangel was confidently believed by its citizens to be impregnable.

During the blockade of 1854 the apparently wanton destruction of small craft, most worked by local traders and fishermen and of no great significance in the greater scheme of things, had been badly received by elements of public opinion in Britain and in part of the British press. Although there was plenty of right-wing support for prosecuting the war to the full, regarding any enemy possession as a legitimate target, it was widely thought that Britain's image as a civilised nation was being tarnished by the damage done to helpless local people; ruining the livelihoods of Lapps, Finnish fishermen and small coastal traders was not deemed to be a worthy policy. Added to this was criticism of the effect of the blockade on the maritime trade of neutral countries (like Norway and the USA) which was seriously disrupted[17] and the resulting shortages of some foodstuffs which was causing severe problems and price inflation around Scandinavia; Sweden, for example, normally obtained most of its wheat from Russia.

As a result, the allied blockade orders for 1855 did allow that small coastal craft would not be seized or destroyed so long as it was clear that they were not contributing to the war effort and were simply going about their business. However, this more liberal approach came to grief very quickly when it was discovered that some boats were being used to ferry weapons and ammunition from Archangel along the coast to supply defensive positions or simply to arm local people.[18] In response, the Admiralty altered its orders and the blockade returned to its former policy of preventing the movement of any enemy vessel, boarding, confiscating or destroying those that took the risk of taking to sea or running the blockade. The principle of blockade was again enforced to its utmost, by checking the passage of any vessels or boats, however small, in any direction. By October, sixty vessels had been seized and either burned or returned to Britain as prizes; neutral ships were forced to linger in port – many in Norway – rather than try to run the blockade and by the arrival of autumn, the maritime trade of the White Sea had been completely disrupted, if not wholly destroyed.

Actual operations continued very much as in 1854, with warships patrolling the coast, intercepting ships and burning enemy merchant vessels and stores. On one such voyage, the *Ariel*, cruising in the Gulf of Migen, sent boat parties ashore to explore the area around Migen, a town of 1,500 inhabitants. It was found to hold no government stores or shipping and was left alone, but on the return journey the boats investigated a smaller village whose menfolk approached the sailors with no great show of hostility, their wives and children having fled into the woods. Here the village itself was left but three small ships amounting to 300 tons were burned. *Ariel* then joined the *Maeander* off Cross Island on 9 July and the next day they joined *La Cléopâtre* to sail for Archangel. On 21 July, most of the blockading squadron was assembled off Archangel but they found no change to the port since the last reconnaissance – no new ships had attempted to get into or out of the Dvina – and they withdrew to continue their searches.

During the 'season' of 1855, there were countless minor incidents involving pursuits, captures, burnings and destruction undertaken by the blockading squadron. Sometimes ships' boats would investigate the rivers flowing into the White Sea, row up a few miles, reconnoitre both sides and then return. If anything like a Russian or Finnish boat was seen, it usually became the object of attack and was burned but villages without shipping were usually left in peace. This depended, of course, on the conduct of the inhabitants; if they resisted a search or fired on the invaders, it generally led to the destruction of their village by shell fire or landing parties. A more usual practice was for the villagers to flee and remain hidden until the enemy had gone. Partly as a result of the treatment they had received from allied vessels, and being largely defenceless, some villages initially showed a willingness to co-operate with the allies and sell food and provisions to the warships when requested. However, an order from the Tsar threatened severe penalties – death or exile to Siberia – to anyone helping Russia's enemy and thereafter landing parties frequently met not only with sullen hostility but with active resistance. For example, on 16 July, *Maeander* was off Kouzemen, in the mouth of the Gulf of Kandalak. A powerful landing party of 60 men under Lieutenant H.M. Eliot found itself opposed by an armed group of over 350 local people, but since nothing was to be gained by a pitched battle on the shore, the ship's Captain, Thomas Baillie, ordered the boat party to withdraw.

The Russian press frequently and understandably made much of supposed 'clashes' between allied landing parties and local Finnish or Russian villagers. One was said to have occurred at Liamtsi, in the Onega district, on 9 July where, it was stated, an English steamer – reported in Britain as the *Phoenix* – sent in four fully manned boats. Some of the villagers, under an old retired soldier, fired on the landing parties and compelled them to return to the ship, whereupon the steamer opened a fire of ball, grape and rockets, which it continued for three hours. Then two boat parties were launched towards the shore but the villagers were said to have met them with such courage that they could not land and withdrew, leaving the warship to continue its bombardment through the night. It had achieved nothing but the shelling of a poor coastal village. In the English press, the incident is painted as far less dramatic, with the *Phoenix*, cruising near the coast, sending two boats with a flag of truce and an interpreter to buy provisions; when villagers fired at the boats, they were hastily recalled and the *Phoenix* sent a few balls and rockets into the village to punish the inhabitants for their disregard of the white flag.

On 12 July, HMS *Ariel*, having relieved *Phoenix* in the Gulf of Onega, proceeded to visit Kem, Solovetski, Sosnovia, Umba and the Gulf of Kandalak. Near Kandalak, her landing party was attacked, wounding three sailors, but they drove off the enemy under cover of fire from the ship and the town was burnt as a reprisal. Plans to attack larger villages like Soumet, Kerret and Kema were abandoned when it was discovered that Russian government stores and vessels had already been removed.[19] *Phoenix*, *Maeander* and *La Cléopâtre* were involved in similar incidents at other small coastal villages like Shelua, Megra and Zolititsa and other places whose insignificance might well have shielded them from the fear of attack.

The allied squadron remained on station off the coasts of the White Sea somewhat later than in 1854, leaving only on 9 October 1855, when the onset of the Arctic winter weather and increasing sea ice again forced the ships to withdraw and the blockade was effectively ended. It was not renewed in 1856 and apart from confirming the fact of allied naval domination of the coasts, it cannot be said to have affected the Russian war effort very greatly. Local people and local trade seem to have been the main victims.

Chapter 6

Operations in the Pacific, 1854–5

At a time when Russian imperial expansion eastwards across Siberia was still in its infancy,[1] there were few major Russian settlements on the Pacific coast that might merit the attention of the allied fleets. The only sizeable Russian towns in the region were Okhotsk and Petropavlovsk,[2] along with the fur and fish trading port of Sitka in Alaska.[3] Smaller fishing and trading settlements hardly merited attention, as did the local communities on Sakhalin Island or around the estuary of the River Amur, former Chinese territory which had only recently been brought under Russian control. The port of Petropavlovsk, situated on the Kamchatka Peninsula and sheltered in Avocha Bay, was the largest Russian settlement on the Pacific coast.[4] Founded as recently as 1740 by the Danish explorer Vitus Behring (1681–1741), after whom the Behring Sea and Strait were named, the port recalled his two ships, *St Peter* and *St Paul*. It was developing as an important fishing and whaling port, a base for voyages into the Arctic seas to the north and as a link with Russian trading settlements in Alaska. In 1854, it was also an anchorage of the Russian Pacific squadron, the Okhotsk flotilla.

Had it not been for the fact of a Russian naval presence in the northern Pacific the region might well have been left alone by the allies, since it was so remote and of little economic significance. Added to that, British (and presumably French) knowledge of the region was minimal and sea charts just about non-existent. Nevertheless, a Russian naval squadron did exist, though its exact size and location were unknown, and would have to be dealt with, since there was some concern that if unmolested Russian warships might 'injure' British whalers or traders operating in the Pacific or moving to and from the USA, China and Australia. It was therefore decided in the summer of 1854 that Anglo-French naval forces would indeed operate against Russian interests in the region. The aim, as in the other naval theatres, was to seek out and destroy Russian warships (in this case the small Okhotsk squadron), to attack shore-based military targets and to disrupt trade, which largely meant the fishing and whaling industry and trade with Russian Alaska.

The Russian naval presence in the northwestern Pacific was, not surprisingly, very small. Her fleet in the China and Japan seas in 1854 was commanded by Rear Admiral Yevfimy Putyatin,[5] a highly experienced explorer,

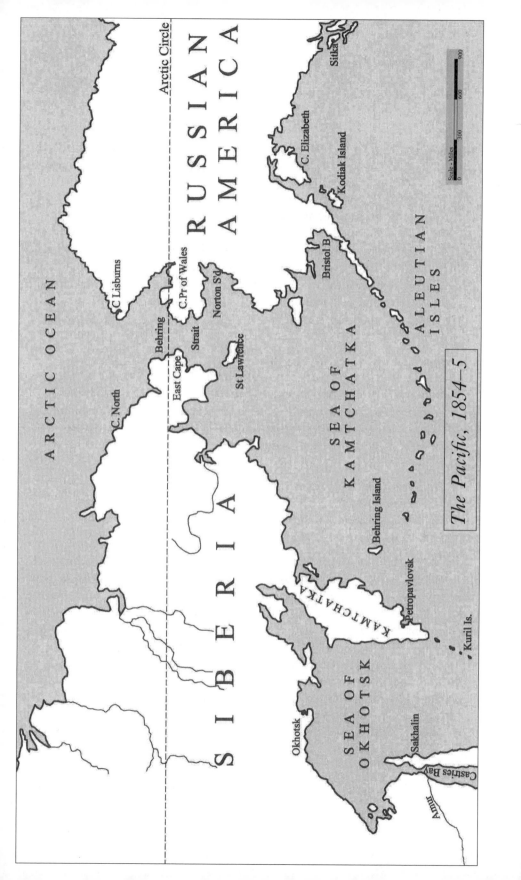

The Pacific, 1854–5

diplomat and naval officer who had under his immediate command only the aged 60-gun frigate *Pallada* (or *Pallas*), the frigate *Aurora* and the armed transport *Dvina*. The last named had only recently refitted in Portsmouth! Putyatin knew very well that his enemy could deploy a far greater force against him and wisely sought to avoid a naval engagement. The frigate *Pallada* he sent for safety far up the River Amur, whilst the *Aurora* and *Dvina* were dispatched to the shelter of Petropavlovsk[6] where they could not only find a refuge but also help in the defence of the port if required.

The allied squadron deployed to operate in the north Pacific was drawn from warships usually on the China Station or patrolling the American Pacific coast, which could be rapidly diverted for active operations against Russian interests. The chosen ships gradually assembled in the Marquesas in May and June and finally concentrated at Honolulu late in July 1854, where in a leisurely manner they completed their repairs and took on water and provisions. The combined force comprised:

British
>   *President* (flagship), a 50-gun frigate under Captain Richard Burridge.
>   *Pique*, a fifth-rate frigate under Captain Sir F.W.E. Nicolson, Bart.
>   *Trincomalee*, a *Leda*-class frigate under Captain Wallace Houstoun.[7]
>   *Amphitrite*, a *Leda*-class frigate, under Captain Charles Fredericks.
>   *Virago*, a paddle-steamer under Commander Edward Marshal.

French
>   *La Forte* (flagship), frigate under Captain de Miniac.
>   *L'Eurydice*, frigate under Captain de la Grandière.
>   *L'Artémise*, corvette under Captain L'Evéque.
>   *L'Obligado*, brig under Captain Rosenavat.

The French contingent was under Rear Admiral Auguste Fébvrier-Despointes (1796–1855) but overall command lay with the British Rear Admiral David Price commanding the British squadron in the Pacific. Having duly received his orders from the Admiralty, on 9 May Price issued instructions from *President*, then at Callao in Peru, to his subordinate commanders requiring that 'we should forthwith commence and execute all such hostile measures as may be in our power ... against Russia and against ships belonging to the Emperor of Russia or to his subjects or others inhabiting within any of his countries, territories or domains'.[8] Having detached the *Amphitrite*, *Trincomalee* and *Artémise* to cruise for commerce protection off the coast of California, the allied squadron still mounted over 200 guns, with 2,000 men and was what one writer called 'a very respectable force of ships to meet the Russians with'.[9] Setting off from Honolulu on 25 July in search of enemy warships, the allies headed first for the Russian fur-trading port of Sitka in Alaska, hoping to locate the Russian squadron there. When nothing was found, the combined fleet turned for the Kamchatka Peninsula and on 28 August 1854 arrived in Avocha Bay.

Such is the distance between St Petersburg and Petropavlovsk that the military governor of Kamchatka in 1854, Rear Admiral Vasili Zavoyko, had only heard that a state of war existed between Russian, Britain and France in mid-July. Although Petropavlovsk already had some established fortifications, the Admiral lost no time in strengthening its defences, realising that the port would be an obvious target for a naval attack. He ordered the construction of new entrenchments, batteries, banks and ditches and enrolled local men into a form of 'town guard'. Merchant ships already in the bay were dispersed and the only Russian warships in the port, the recently arrived *Aurora* and *Dvina*, were withdrawn deeper into the bay, moored in such a way that their guns would serve as additional batteries defending the approaches to the port. The *Aurora* took shelter behind a large sand spit, additionally defended by an 11-gun shore battery and both ships' crews were landed to join the defenders. Nevertheless, Zavoyko had only 67 heavy guns and less than 1,000 armed men (including the naval contingent) to defend the entire town. He could then do no more than wait for an enemy to appear.

Having found no worthy targets in Alaska or at sea over the past five weeks, Admiral Price arrived off Petropavlovsk on 29 August and went aboard the steamer *Virago* to reconnoitre the port. He found it defended by four small batteries and a larger work, Fort Schakoff, mounting five heavy guns and itself defended by flank batteries, each of twelve 36-pounders. Holding a council of war aboard *President*, Price decided to attack the port on 30 August. Early that morning, the ships were cleared for action and the *President, Pique, La Forte, L'Eurydice* and *L'Obligado* entered the harbour. But after only a few rounds had been fired at the Russian defences, a disaster occurred. Just after the firing began, Admiral Price retired to his cabin below decks on the *President* and shot himself in the heart; he died some hours later. Whether it was the accidental discharge of his own pistol, as was tactfully suggested at the time, or the suicide attempt of an officer overwhelmed by his responsibilities and sense of inadequacy will never be known. On 1 September his body was taken by *Virago* to be buried on the nearby island of Tarinski.

The unfortunate Rear Admiral Price (1790–1854) was typical of the gerontocracy which dominated the Royal Navy in the 1850s and whose employment in the Baltic and elsewhere was to cause such comment. Universally regarded with respect as a courteous and tactful man, Price was quite out of his depth as the commander of a combined squadron on active service. He was then 64 years old, had been a post captain for nearly forty years before his recent promotion to rear admiral and had seen no service at sea for over a generation.

In his early career, he had been a brave and resourceful officer, seeing extensive action during the Napoleonic Wars, from Copenhagen in 1801, through numerous naval clashes with the French and during the American War in 1814. But thereafter he had led a quiet life, with six years in retirement (1838–44) as JP for Brecon. Returned to service, from 1846 to 1850 he was superintendent of Sheerness Dockyard, being promoted rear admiral in November 1850, and then for some unaccountable reason, apart from the merit of his long service, given active command of British naval forces in the Pacific in August 1853. The tragedy of his sudden death at Petropavlovsk naturally caused the complete disruption of the planned attack. As next senior British naval officer, overall command of the British ships was quickly transferred to Captain Sir Frederick Nicolson of the *Pique*, who postponed the attack and ordered the immediate withdrawal of the squadron. Thereafter, the French Admiral Auguste Fébvrier-Despointes directed operations; he too was to die aboard his flagship *La Forte* in 1855.

At 8.00am on 31 August, the allied squadron once again sailed into the harbour and began the bombardment of Petropavlovsk in earnest. But indecision ruined any chance of success. Fearful of serious damage to the ships, the French Admiral kept them at long range – in fact too far to do any serious damage to well-defended batteries. The main target was the large 11-gun battery, which was actually silenced by fire from *La Forte* and *President*. The Russian ship *Aurora* returned a damaging fire from behind her defended position, though she suffered quite severely from the allied response. Finally, a landing party from *Virago* under Captain Charles A. Parker, RM actually captured one 3-gun shore battery and spiked its guns before withdrawing. But by nightfall little had been achieved and the squadron again withdrew; overnight, the Russians repaired the damage to their batteries ready for the next onslaught.

In council with his officers, Fébvrier-Despointes decided to launch a combined land and sea assault on 4 September. Whilst the warships bombarded the Russian defences, a Naval Brigade of 700 sailors and 100 marines drawn from the *Pique* and the *Eurydice*, nearly half of the entire manpower of the allied squadron, would be landed to seize gun positions north of the port prior to an attack on the town itself. This force was placed under the command of Captain de la Grandière of *L'Eurydice*, with Captain Burridge of the *President* and the marine contingent again under Captain Parker. The three warships *President*, *Virago* and *La Forte* would occupy the attention of the shore batteries (which incidentally did a great deal of damage to the ships' masts and rigging), whilst the shore parties carried aboard *Virago* dealt with the guns at close quarters and would then attack the town. The main landing beyond the town initially went well, though the site was badly chosen, overlooked as it was by a hill which turned out to be well defended. Gunfire from *President* and *Virago* silenced two shore batteries and the immediate land objective, the Russian Battery No. 4, was quickly taken. However, it was found simply to have been abandoned by its small crew under Lieutenant Popoff, who withdrew to No. 2 battery, having spiked its three guns. The warships maintained their previous long-range barrage, especially at the *Aurora* and at the large No. 2 battery under Lieutenant Prince Maksutoff but the shore party soon got into difficulties and the entire attack collapsed. In face of the strong enemy landing, Russian defenders had been positioned on a wooded hill overlooking the route of the advance and in concealed positions in thick brushland. As the Naval Brigade and marines pushed inland towards No. 2 battery, impeded by dense brambles and undergrowth, they were met with heavy and accurate fire from concealed positions, followed by a counter-attack by Russian sailors. Captain Parker and two French officers, including Captain Lefebvre of *L'Eurydice*, were amongst the first killed and nine other British and French officers were quickly wounded. With these losses amongst their leaders and under heavy and concentrated fire, the rest fell back and a retreat to the shore was ordered. By the time the fighting stopped, 107 British and 101 French sailors and marines had been killed or wounded in what was an ignominious repulse. The survivors regained the ships by 10.45am and although a desultory firing continued until nightfall, nothing significant was achieved.[10] The ships withdrew beyond range in the evening to repair and to treat the wounded and overnight the Russians again re-occupied or repaired their damaged gun positions.

Needless to say, this setback in the Far East was greeted with a mixture of amazement and derision in Britain, where the failure to achieve anything concrete against so remote an enemy was scarcely credited. The reputation of the Russians as defenders and as opponents capable of supplying and holding on to even the most remote Imperial outpost was greatly enhanced and greatly admired. There is no doubting the bravery of the officers and men on both sides – the casualties amongst the allied officers perhaps indicating a rather reckless disregard for their own safety – but it is equally clear that the landing was badly thought-out, with little accurate information on the nature and strength of the enemy positions they were attacking. The Russians proved to be determined and effective defenders – apparently much to the surprise of the officers of the allied fleet, who seem to have expected a complete collapse and withdrawal by the Russians.

The fleet withdrew to repair and after the allied dead were buried on Tarinski Island on the 5, 6 and 7 September the squadron simply left the area, its commanders considering it too weakened to renew the attack. The Russians reported 115 casualties – 40 killed and 75 wounded, amongst whom was Lieutenant Prince Maksutoff, mortally wounded – and damage to the town's fish warehouse and 13 other buildings from the naval bombardment. Although *Virago* and *President* managed to capture the Russian trading schooner *Anadis* and the 10-gun transport *Sitka* on 7 September,[11] these were slender rewards achieved at great cost. The British element sailed for winter stations in Vancouver and the French to San Francisco.

There were no further naval operations in the Pacific that year. The debacle in August and September forced a complete restructuring of the allied squadron made available for operations in the Russian Pacific and the deployment of new warships to the theatre. Rear Admiral Henry William Bruce, commanding Britain's Pacific Squadron, was appointed to the command in November 1854 but nothing was done until the better weather of the spring of 1855. There were two British squadrons available to provide ships to tackle the Russian presence in the Pacific. The Pacific Squadron generally patrolled the western coasts of the Americas whilst the other was the established China Squadron under Admiral Sir James Stirling. Between them, they would provide a larger force for operations against the Russians and initially put under Admiral Bruce the *President*, flagship, the *Pique*, *Trincomalee*, *Dido*, *Amphitrite*, *Brisk*, screw, *Encounter* and *Barracouta*. The French element, commanded by Rear Admiral Martin Fourichon after the death of Fébvrier-Despointes, comprised, as in 1854, *La Forte*, *L'Eurydice* and *L'Obligado* with *L'Alceste*.

In April 1855, Admiral Bruce ordered the *Encounter* and the *Barracouta* simply to watch Petropavlovsk and report the movement of Russian ships, if any. The city had in fact been heavily re-fortified in the early months of 1855 but the allied plans for a renewed and successful attack were suddenly rendered obsolete. The defenders of the city, under Admiral Vasili Zavoyko, were well aware of the danger they faced from a renewed onslaught by a much more powerful force. In a remarkably audacious and resourceful move, they cut passages through the ice to release their trapped ships and under cover of snow and dense fog on 17 April 1855, the entire Russian garrison of about 800 was withdrawn from the town and carried southwards to safety in the estuary of the Amur River in the *Aurora* and *Dvina* and any other available merchant ship. The remaining civil population to the number of about 1,300 people fled overland to take refuge in the inland village of Avatcha, far from the danger of naval gunnery. The town's guns were spiked, removed or buried. It was all swiftly, efficiently and effectively carried out, without the allied observers even being aware of the movement.

When in May 1855, the new allied squadron under Bruce sailed into the harbour of Petropavlovsk, it was immediately clear that the town was deserted – apart from two American traders who hoisted the 'Stars and Stripes' as a friendly signal. Landing parties destroyed the remaining batteries and gun platforms and burned the arsenal and magazines, but did no damage to private property – unlike the fate of the unfortunate town of Kola in the White Sea. A stranded Russian whaler found in the inner harbour was burned but no attempt was made at any stage to follow the Russian ships into the Amur, since they were reported to be very well protected. Having nothing else to achieve at Petropavlovsk, Bruce and Fourichon directed their ships to Sitka but since it was found to be undefended and with no Russian shipping in port, it was left unharmed. The British press later leveled special criticism against the commanders of the *Encounter* and the *Barracouta* for allowing the entire garrison of Petropavlovsk to escape by ship along channels that were not even marked on the Admiralty charts. They did not, however, face any investigation by the authorities.

Despite the change of commanders and an increase in strength, the allied Pacific campaign of 1855 was to be another depressing failure, characterised by a round of seemingly pointless (and certainly ineffective) patrols in largely unknown waters. They simply could not find the Russian Pacific Squadron – or at least, could not close with it – and unlike allied ships in the Baltic and Azoff seas made little attempt to damage the largely insignificant local trade or local communities. Sporadic naval operations by various ships drawn off the China station continued throughout the year. In April, HMS *Spartan* was detached to patrol the Kuril Islands, with no result, and ships cruised in Japanese and Korean waters[12] searching for Russian vessels. Allied warships visited the Japanese port of Hakodate[13] and from there sailed north, examining largely insignificant settlements on scattered islands; at Urup in the Kuril Islands, they seized the possessions of the Russian-American Company. More alarmingly, Commodore Elliott, with the 40-gun *Sybille*, the screw *Hornet* and the *Bittern*, reported sighting a Russian squadron in Castries Bay on 20 May. They were identified as the ships *Aurora*, *Dvina* (both recently escaped from the Amur), *Oltenitza*, the 6-gun *Vostok*, and two other unidentified armed vessels. With his three small ships – and no charts or knowledge of the those waters[14] – Elliott did not feel strong enough to enter the bay to try to 'cut out' the enemy vessels and apart from *Hornet* lobbing a few long-range shells at the *Dvina*, nothing could be done. Having failed to frighten or induce the Russian ships out of the bay to fight in the open sea, Elliott dispatched the *Bittern* to bring up reinforcements and spent a fruitless week cruising with *Hornet* and *Sybille* trying to watch the Russians in Castries Bay. By the time *Bittern* returned with part of the China Squadron under its Admiral, Sir James Stirling,[15] the Russian vessels had escaped back into the Amur, simply by-passing Commodore Elliott's slight blockade – a fact that caused some caustic comment in London. The *Pique*, *Barracouta* and *Amphitrite*, joined by the French vessels *Sibylle* and *Constantine*, were then detached under Elliott to patrol the Sea of Okhotsk, unsuccessfully searching for the vanished Russian ships.

Admiral Bruce's squadron, having cruised to no great effect in the estuary of the Amur and then amongst the Kuril Islands in August and September, simply dispersed as winter set in; most of the British vessels headed once more for the dockyards on Vancouver Island, Britain's nearest Pacific port, whilst the French again sailed for San Francisco. The last act of the Pacific campaign, if it can be called such, was the seizure by *Barracouta* of the brig *Greta*, out of Bremen but under US colours, which was found to have on board most of the crew of the Russian frigate *Diana*. The 50-gun *Diana* had had an exciting time. Laden with ammunition and other supplies intended to re-supply Petropavlovsk, she had come all the way from Cronstadt in 1854, eluding the allied blockade of the Baltic in its early days. After an epic journey around the world, she was eventually wrecked off the coast of Japan in November 1854 and her non-arrival at Petropavlovsk was another other reason for the town's abandonment in May 1855. *Greta* was sent under Lieutenant R. Gibson to Hong Kong and claimed as a prize.

The operations in 1855 were as limited and as unsuccessful – though less costly in lives – as those in 1854 and again caused an outburst of indignation in England. That such large, expensive and powerful fleets could do so little was beyond conception in Britain. The naval authorities on the spot were accused of 'knight-errantry' in pointlessly cruising distant, largely uncharted seas with no apparent goal, in dividing their forces up into squadrons too small to tackle any sizeable Russian force that remained and especially in allowing the flight of the Russian squadron in Castries Bay. A correspondent of *The Times* summed up the whole operation in October 1855:

> The result of the expedition was most unsatisfactory and indeed, its commencement was of the same character. Petropavlovski, which was found 14 or 15 months back defended in such a manner as justified a hostile attack, actually repelled the allied forces; and this year when visited, it was disarmed and of course spared. The Russian settlements in the Amoor River turn out to be a mere myth. Finally, the Russian Pacific Squadron appears before our officers just to disappoint their hopes and, when the British Admiral is ready, eludes all pursuit. The Russian ships are, no doubt, at this moment snugly ensconced behind some choice sandbanks in the Sea of Okhotsk.[16]

Unsurprisingly, there were no significant allied naval operations in the Pacific in 1856.

Chapter 7

The Campaign in the Baltic, 1855

The perceived failure of the allied expedition to the Baltic in 1854 – if indeed it was actually a failure – led to acrimony in Britain and the removal of its commander, Admiral Sir Charles Napier.[1] But it did at least force their Lordships at the Admiralty to reconsider the aims and needs of the naval force for the campaign season of 1855. It was becoming clear that the old sailing 'wooden walls' and even the larger screw warships, powerful as they were, were not the right sort of vessel for the coasts and waters of the Baltic or for the operations being planned there. Attacks on harbours and strongly defended installations required a more manoeuvrable but powerfully armed fleet which could deliver overwhelming firepower against static land targets, not just enemy warships. Consideration would also have to be given to the carrying of sizeable land forces for possible operations ashore.

The Admiralty announced in February 1855 that no sailing warships of any kind would be sent to the Baltic in the new season, experience having shown that 'the mixture of screw and sailing ships was not conducive to the interests of the service'; the new Baltic Fleet would consist only of steamers, twenty of which would be ready for service within two months.[2] In particular, it was expected that in 1855 there would be a greater degree of planning and concerted action than seemed to be the case in 1854. A correspondent in the *United Service Gazette* wrote: 'The general subject of complaint last year in the Baltic was that no plan of operation appeared to have been determined upon. From Kiel the fleet went to Kioge. They went up the Gulf of Finland and came down again – they buzzed about everywhere without fixing anywhere and they did not take Bomarsund until it was nearly time to conclude the campaign.'[3] The writer went on to urge attacks on the fortresses of the Baltic since 'the most complete plans and drawings of the chief Russian fortresses are in the possession of our government'. It seems that the Emperor Napoleon III was equally anxious that some degree of proper planning should go into the new campaign – he understood that the French navy would play second fiddle to the British, but nevertheless thought that Britain's reputation had suffered ('terribly shaken by the nullity of our campaign in the Baltic last year') and urged that thorough planning must be in place.[4] Interestingly, the French reduced their Baltic contingent in 1855, perhaps in view of the strength of the

British fleet and considering that their greatest efforts were needed in the Crimea.

The result in Britain at least was the creation of a new Baltic Fleet for 1855.[5] There were to be over 100 vessels comprising *only* steam-powered ships, both screw and paddle, many of them smaller, faster vessels of shallower draught capable of operating in the waters of estuaries and rivers. But, in stark contrast to that which had set off so hopefully a year before, the impressive new fleet that sailed from Spithead on 4 April 1855 did so without any great show or pageantry; it left simply as a fighting force with a job to do and with no ceremony or public celebration.[6] It was a powerful fleet:

> The Baltic Fleet this year is in all respects much stronger than the last; it has more steam power, more guns, a new class of gun-boats and floating batteries, adapted for creeks and shoals and – what more than anything else marks a resolution to do something – a new commander ... We certainly had wished that after last year's experience we should have less of such floating castles as the *Duke of Wellington* and the *Royal George* and rather more of the gun-boats and other small craft on which we must mainly rely in our offensive operations[7]

The 'new commander' was Rear Admiral Richard Saunders Dundas.[8]

Since the total blockade maintained in 1854 was to be resumed, the 1855 campaign season began with the dispatch of an 'advanced squadron' under Captain Rundle Watson (in *Impérieuse*) on 20 March, which reached the Baltic in mid-April and formally declared a renewed blockade on the 17th.[9] At much the same time, most of the larger warships of Dundas' fleet were passing through the Kattegat, heading for anchorage at Kiel, where they concentrated on 13 April.[10] Most of the fleet remained there for nearly a month, waiting for the last of the solid winter ice to recede, but Dundas finally left Kiel on 2–3 May with twenty ships, joining the advanced squadron at Gothland on the 7th. Whilst the main fleet then proceeded to Nargen Island, opposite Reval, which became Dundas' advanced base, smaller squadrons were deployed as in 1854 to range around the Baltic – to reconnoitre Sveaborg, Riga, Cronstadt, the Åland Islands and Hängo Head, to blockade the Gulfs of Riga and Finland and the coast of Courland[11] and to intercept enemy trading vessels.[12] Although the fleet at Nargen was in easy reach of Reval, any thought of an attack on the town was quickly abandoned, given that its defences had been massively strengthened over the winter. The truth is that the Russians had used the winter very well, not only to strengthen or fortify many of their previously un-defended smaller ports but to deploy large forces of infantry, guns and cavalry at strategic points along the Baltic shores to fend off possible allied landings.[13]

Allied landing parties were to find a much warmer reception in 1855 than they had in 1854.

The French squadron under Rear Admiral André Pénaud joined on 1 June when Dundas was reconnoitring Russia's great Baltic base at Cronstadt, which was clearly the most important potential target of allied efforts in 1855. Dundas had over thirty vessels off Cronstadt in June and repeated reconnaissance picked out at least twenty-eight Russian warships at anchor in the harbour. But they showed no signs of coming out to give battle and the allies, despite long discussions on the possibility and method of an attack, really saw no hope of success with a naval assault. Similarly, Dundas himself, having personally reconnoitred Cronstadt in *Merlin*, reached the conclusion that 'no serious attack appears to me to be practicable with the means at my disposal'.[14] As at Reval, Sveaborg and other Baltic ports, the tranquility of winter had allowed a significant strengthening of the port's defences and outer approaches, which included submarine piles and the novel deployment of two sorts of underwater mines (or 'infernal machines') which were a largely unknown and much-feared weapon.[15] If Cronstadt had been considered unassailable in 1854, it was equally so in 1855. A completely different sort of naval force was required even to consider the attempt – one with a mass of small gun and mortar vessels and with a significant landing force. As a result of the experiences in the Baltic in 1855 (see below), 'The Great Armament' of 1855–6 set out to rectify this need and eventually produced the necessary type of vessels in large numbers, but in the campaign season of 1855 they were simply not available.[16] The case was quickly closed: however closely Cronstadt might be 'watched' over the rest of the season, it could not be attacked by sea in 1855.

The only major incident of this early period was the so-called 'Hängo Massacre' on 5 June, an event that greatly occupied the British and even European press for some time. The *Cossack* under Captain E.G. Fanshawe landed a boat party under Lieutenant Louis Geneste and Midshipman Sullivan near Hängo Head to formally notify the inhabitants of the renewed blockade, to release several captured Finnish sailors and, perhaps as an afterthought, to negotiate with the locals to buy food. What actually happened was the subject of conflicting reports depending on the loyalties of the writer, but it seems that the landing party, which was effectively unarmed since its weapons were left in the boat, was unexpectedly fired on by concealed Russian soldiers when it came ashore under flag of truce. All of those who landed were killed or wounded, apart from Lieutenant Geneste, who was taken prisoner, and when the Russians attacked the boat itself they managed to kill or capture the rest of the crew. Of the 22 crew and their Finnish captives, 6 were killed, 7 wounded and 15 captured. Remarkably, one wounded seaman, John Brown, managed to row back to *Cossack* that night and relate what had happened. Captain Fanshawe had already sent a second boat under Lieutenant John Field to locate the first, but Field, seeing their object aground and riddled with holes, feared an ambush and did not land. Fanshawe felt able to do nothing more than fire off a few angry rounds at a deserted shoreline and then steam away to report the matter to Admiral Dundas.

The incident became something of a cause célèbre, especially since it seemed to involve a breach of international law with an attack on an unarmed party bearing a white flag. All the details were, of course, greatly disputed and in the Finnish and Russian press the incident was blown up into the signal defeat of a major enemy attack. Furious diplomatic correspondence between Dundas and the Russian authorities at Helsingfors only served to muddy the issue, the Russians asserting that no flag of truce had been seen and (possibly with some justification) that British naval forces had previously approached villages under flag of truce and then proceeded to destroy Russian property. The prisoners were apparently roughly handled at first, the officers eventually being sent to Helsingfors but held separately. After a few months in confinement, all were exchanged for Russian prisoners and sent home.[17]

The summer of 1855 continued with desultory operations – the odd shelling of a Finnish coastal village and the seizure of Russian shipping attempting to break the blockade; Captain H.A. Story, in the *Harrier*, as an example, managed to stop and destroy no fewer than forty-seven Russian trading vessels off Nystad in two days, 23–4 June. Whilst Dundas remained with the bulk of the allied fleet off Cronstadt, with no sign of a Russian response, warships cruised the Baltic coast and attacked wherever they felt they could do some damage. Much more than had been the case in 1854, there was a greater response in 1855 to allied action along the coast. Sometimes there were exchanges of shots with shore batteries – many of them newly constructed – or forces of Russian infantry along the coastline and there were many small-scale actions. One of the most impressive was the destruction on 21 July[18] of new land batteries at Fredrikshamn near Helsingfors by *Magicienne*, *Cossack*, *Arrogant* and *Ruby* under Captain Hastings Yelverton and the attack by the same ships, augmented by four mortar vessels,[19] on the fortified island of Kotka on the 26th. Here, all the marines of the force were landed (the garrison already having fled) and 3 barracks, 4 storehouses, 4 magazines and a number of other detached buildings, along with workshops and supplies, were all destroyed. Captain Yelverton in *Arrogant* had a particularly active time; not only did he go on to shell Cossack forces in Kounda Bay and installations at the mouth of the Portsoiki, but he even attacked the town of Loviso on 5 July, burning government property and then destroyed Fort Svartholm.[20] The larger town of Viborg, which Yelverton boldy considered attacking, proved to be too well protected for even him to risk.

Such fairly minor incidents – and there were many of them in the summer of 1855[21] – were no doubt briefly exciting and meaningful to the officers and crews engaged, but did nothing more than confirm allied domination of the Baltic; in terms of the greater war with Imperial Russia, they were of little significance. As a fairly monotonous and largely unexciting round of naval patrols resumed in the summer of 1855, the commanders in the Baltic may have reflected that the efforts of Sir Charles Napier and the fleet of 1854 had indeed been unfairly criticised; their crews, perhaps hoping for greater successes and rewards, were equally forced to accept that they too were unlikely to come home covered with glory. It is possible that Dundas himself developed some sympathy for his predecessor Napier and the criticism he had faced in view of his much publicised 'lack of activity' with the great fleet of 1854. Dundas certainly felt the need for some concrete achievement to offer to his superiors and to the British public. At any rate, in August 1855, he and his senior officers decided that one significant target might yet be attempted, especially in view of the continued strengthening of its fortifications. If Cronstadt was unassailable, it was just possible that the defended islands of Sveaborg, protecting the approaches to Helsingfors and the base of a Russian division, might be vulnerable to the powerful force Dundas had under command. Repeated reconnaissance had shown that work was continuing to strengthen the forts and batteries – nearly twenty new ones since 1854 – and that any viable attempt on 'the Gibraltar of the North' would have to come sooner rather than later.[22]

The Sveaborg defences constituted a complex and formidable position. They covered six islands, Langorn (the central and principal island), West Svarto (West Fort), East Svarto, Lilla East Svarto, Vargon and Gustafsvard, besides other rocky outcrops. The forts on all the islands were built of granite on granite foundations; five of the islands were linked by bridges, sandbars and causeways and the channels between them were impassable, two of them being further defended by warships (*Russia* and *Hezekiel*) moored broadside on. The original defences were built after 1748 by the Swedish military engineer Augustin Ehrensvärd (1710–72) when Finland was under Swedish rule and were intended to defend the capital in response to Peter the Great's construction of the Russian naval base at Cronstadt. They came under Russian control when Finland was ceded to Russia in 1809 and, apart from defending Helsingfors, were regarded as part of the defences to the approaches to Cronstadt and the capital city. In addition to the actual fortifications, at the centre of the island complex a naval dockyard had been constructed to house part of the Swedish Baltic Fleet and the Russians extended and added to the defences after 1809.[23]

In the campaign season of 1854, Admiral Napier had on several occasions considered an attack on Sveaborg (and perhaps on Helsingfors) and had the islands reconnoitred and 'watched'. But, to the consternation of many of his younger subordinates, he refused to be drawn into what he regarded as a futile attack; he did not believe his firepower great enough to reduce the forts, he did not have mortar or gun vessels that could do serious damage and he had no land forces to operate ashore if the forts fell. His brief from Sir James Graham at the Admiralty was, after all, very clear – he was not to endanger his fleet on desperate enterprises against fixed defences. In the campaign season of 1855, the situation was somewhat different. Since the Admiralty had at least learned something from the omissions of 1854, the new Baltic Fleet under Admiral Dundas was better equipped to take on some of the fortifications that had been beyond Napier's capacity in 1854. In particular, he had powerful gunboats and a number of mortar vessels capable of heavy bombardment with some hope of doing damage.[24] The allied attack on Sveaborg in 1855 was to be the largest purely naval operation in the Baltic but the allied fleet did not, however, carry anything in the form of significant land forces to serve ashore, so any attack could never be more than a demonstration of allied naval might. It could do whatever damage it liked at long range, but it could not seize or permanently hold the forts or operate on shore from them. The Russians, for their part, clearly believed that although no attack on Sveaborg had been made in 1854, there was every likelihood that a new, more powerful fleet would make an attempt in 1855.

Leaving Admiral Sir Robert Baynes with a squadron to blockade Cronstadt,[25] Admiral Dundas assembled at Nargen a fleet of 22 steamers, 16 gunboats and 16 mortar vessels,[26] carrying an armament of the largest ordnance used in naval warfare up to that time. They were joined by a French contingent under Rear Admiral Pénaud in *Tourville*. Once extra supplies of ammunition had been received from England, the admirals agreed their plans and steamed from Nargen for Sveaborg, where they brought their vessels into battle array on 8 August. In his dispatches Dundas stated that by erecting batteries on every advantageous position (including the shore around Helsingfors, which was heavily defended) the Russians had so commanded all the approaches to the harbour that he abandoned any intention of making a general attack, limiting his operations to a naval bombardment of the islands and the destruction of any fortresses and arsenals that could be reached by mortar shells and gunfire. The plan for the bombardment was largely adopted from that written in 1854 by Captain B.J. Sulivan of *Lightning*; he now commanded the larger *Merlin* but in the event was not allowed to exercise overall command of the attack and was in fact angered by suggested changes to his plan.[27] It was difficult to find suitable positions for the long line of 16 British and 5 French mortar vessels amid the rocks and islets, but ultimately these boats, towed to into position by steamers, were ranged in a curved line facing the island defences at a range of 3,300 yards and 4 lighter mortars were placed on the islet of Otterhall. The larger warships – *Magicienne, Vulture, Euryalus* and *Dragon* – were 400 yards behind them ranged in line. Operating in front of all of these, closer to the actual defences at a range of about 2,500 yards, were the French and British gunboats. The rest of the allied fleet lay at anchor further to the rear of the battle lines between the islets of Skogsholm and Skogskar.

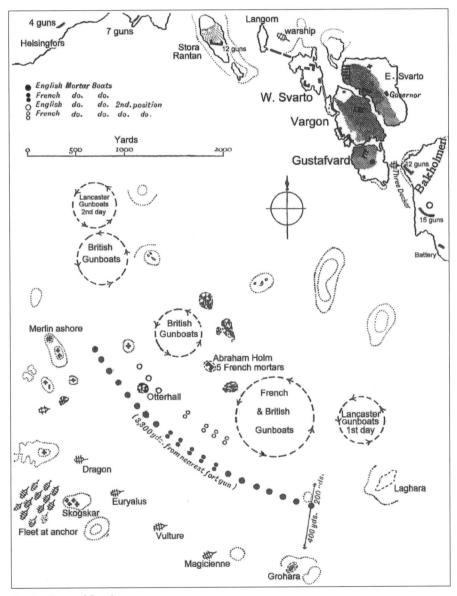

Bombardment of Sveaborg.

At 7.00am on the 9th the bombardment began, employing the moored mortar boats, a French sandbag battery on a rocky outcrop and the gunboats. The gunboat flotilla, wheeling round in large circles to bring their few heavy guns to bear,[28] was under the command of Commodore Hon. F.T. Pelham. The gunboats and sandbag battery fired nearly horizontally against the forts, whilst the 12-inch and 13-inch mortars fired at a high elevation, over the other ships, so that their shells, about thirty an hour, dropped into the interior of the defences or between them and Helsingfors, to destroy magazines, ships,[29] stores and buildings. The largest island and seat of the governor, East Svarto, was somewhat sheltered by Vargon but could nevertheless be hit by high-angled dropping fire. Some of the larger warships cruised to the east and west, to distract the attention of troops and batteries visible on shore.

This heavy bombardment was returned with great resolution by the defenders but before long the whole line of defences was being pounded by thickly falling shells and shot and hit by falling fragments of buildings, roofs and burning timbers. Dundas recorded that

> about 10.00 o'clock in the forenoon, fires began to be observed in the different buildings and a heavy explosion took place on the Island of Sargon [Vargon], which was followed by a second an hour later. A third and far more important explosion occurred about noon on the Island of Gustavsvard, inflicting much damage upon the defences of the enemy and tending to greatly slacken the fire from that direction ... [there were] continued fresh conflagrations which spread extensively on the Island of Sargon.[30]

As night arrived, the gunboats withdrew and the fleet's smaller boats, armed with rockets, took over, firing into the forts throughout the night so that the interior of Sveaborg's defences was engulfed in a spectacular sheet of flame, filling the air with masses of smoke. Early in the morning of 10 August, some adjustments having been made in the line of mortar boats, the full-scale bombardment recommenced. Once again, columns of smoke and flashes of flame lit up the sky and the depots on East Svarto were soon seen to be in flames. Again, the firing continued all day so that, as Admiral Pénaud recorded in his dispatch to the French government, Sveaborg looked like 'a vast fiery furnace' so numerous were the fires and explosions of magazines, storehouses, barracks and other buildings. As before, the attack was continued through the night by rocket boats. It was clear by dawn the next day that just about everything – short of a landing and occupation – that could be achieved by naval firepower had been done.[31]

In Helsingfors, the local population, many of whom had crowded onto high points to watch the action, now prepared to flee the city, certain that an allied landing would follow. But as the ships could not penetrate further into the intricate channels between the islands, the allies brought operations to a close and no further action ensued. The attack had used, it was estimated, over 100 tons of gunpowder and 5,000 tons of iron shot and shell in 48 hours. Nevertheless, the actual seaward defences of the forts and batteries seemed comparatively undamaged and the admirals could only point to the destruction of property within the interior as proof of the success of their operations. Considering that the mortars and guns fired at an average distance of more than 2 miles from their targets, it was no great surprise that the stone forts were so little damaged.

One unusual feature of this action was that the larger ships were virtually spectators, since the admirals did not want to risk them in close action; their crews, agog with excitement at the sight of the burning forts, could only envy those in the mortar boats and gunboats and could do nothing but run up the rigging to get a view and shout and cheer whenever a good shot from the gunboats struck the forts or a shell from the mortar boats burst within the defences. Some of the larger ships – the *Cornwallis, Hastings, Amphion, Arrogant, Cossack* and *Cruiser* – did manage to put some shots into the forts, especially one at Sandhamn, 6 miles from the main action[32] but the smaller boats did most of the work. The bombardment of Sveaborg was yet another example of the value of heavily armed, lighter-draught, manoeuvrable ships rather than the old line-of-battle heavyweights.

When the great effect of the gun and mortar boats was made public in England, Sir Charles Napier wrote to the newspapers, demanding as an act of justice that his operations in 1854 should be judged in the light of the action of 1855: this seemed no more than fair, seeing that he had neither gunboats nor mortar boats and could not have done what Dundas was able to do.[33] The letter he had written to the Admiralty on the 12 June 1854 – over a year before Dundas' attack – is worthy of notice:

> The only successful manner of attacking Sveaborg that I can see . . .
> is by fitting out a great number of gun-boats carrying one gun with
> a long range, and placing them west of Sveaborg and south of
> Helsingfors; every shell from them would tell somewhere, and per-
> haps not five per cent. from the enemy would take effect; back them
> by the fleet to relieve the men, and in the course of the summer
> Sveaborg would be reduced to ashes, and Helsingfors also, if it was
> thought proper.[34]

A French report, printed in the *Moniteur*, stated that during the 2 days' bombardment of Sveaborg, the allied fleet destroyed 2 powder magazines, 2 shell magazines, a flax and rope storehouse, 2 granaries filled with corn and flour, a pitch manufactory, a medicine store, the house and office of the governor general and 17 private houses. Besides this, a 3-decker and 18 other Russian vessels were more or less damaged by shot and shell, whilst 2,000 Russians were killed or wounded. Not surprisingly, the Russian papers produced rather different statistics and their accounts of the damage, related in various European newspapers and in official Russian reports, naturally varied enormously; some reported immense damage and loss of life, whilst others belittled the 'insignificant' damage and long-term effects of the allied action and claimed serious loss in the enemy fleet. One dispatch, published in the *Invalide Russe*, claimed that the allied fleet numbered no less than 80 vessels of various kinds and that their marines had been prevented from landing on the island of Drumso; that the excellent fire of the defenders' artillery caused great damage and loss to the gunboats that came within range; that 1 battery sent such a volley against 2 screw steamers, as to compel them to retreat, 1 towing the other; that although the fire of the allies was tremendous, resulting from 21,000 projectiles thrown during 2 days, and although many conflagrations and explosions occurred, the damage done to the main fortresses and to the batteries in general was insignificant and, finally, that the loss of men was by no means severe, comprising 65 killed and 201 wounded. In the end, it has to be assumed that no accurate picture of the damage done or casualties sustained by the defenders could really be established.[35]

Remarkably – and again largely because of the range – there was little damage to the allied vessels and few casualties. The gunboats had steamed round slowly in a wide circle, firing first their bow gun, then their midship gun and reloading both whilst completing the rest of their circuit; the Russian gunners simply could not take accurate aim at such continually moving targets and hardly a ship was hit. The mortar vessels, which were moored and thus more or less stationary, suffered rather more damage but much of this was simply from the sheer rate of their own fire which severely damaged the new mortars; several burst[36] after firing literally dozens of rounds and many others were temporarily put out of use by overheating or the risk of fracture. But remarkably not a single sailor was killed throughout the allied fleet during two days of continuous firing, though several suffered minor wounds and burns or injury from the premature bursting of rockets.[37]

The flotilla of steam gunboats, nicknamed the 'Mosquito Squadron', really did demonstrate its power and worth here for the first time in a significant action. The result was spectacular. The Admiralty became so convinced that these small, light boats represented the future of naval operations against fixed land targets that they immediately embarked on the mass construction of gun and mortar vessels. In a radical building programme over the winter of 1855 – really nothing less a than the rapid construction of a massive new fleet in what became known as 'The Great Armament'[38] – over 200 new gunboats, 11 armoured floating batteries and 100 mortar vessels and rafts were laid down to be ready for use in 1856. A huge strain was placed on Thames-side construction yards (for example, at Blackwall where many of the *Dapper* class were laid down), so that on the whole private tenders were taken for the basic building of the ships whilst the official or royal dockyards were employed for finishing – equipping them with engines and armament. New steam battleships were also prepared (for example, *Conqueror*). The ultimate target of all this activity would no doubt have been the mighty defences of Cronstadt itself, but as the war ended before the new fleets could be deployed in 1856, they were never tested. Only a 'flying squadron' of steam frigates and two new battleships, *Caesar* and *Majestic*, reached the Baltic for what would have been the campaign season of 1856. In fact, the end of the Russian war saw a rapid return to pre-war Anglo-French tensions and naval rivalry which required, from Britain's point of view, the construction of larger steam battleships and frigates, rather than a host of small gunboats.[39]

The rest of 1855 – with the mortar vessels quickly sent home[40] – saw no significant action; the usual blockade and ship searches continued, with the bulk of the allied fleet based at Nargen. A familiar round of shore bombardments, landings to destroy shipping and supplies ashore and the arrest of coastal vessels went on as it had before. On 2 August at Brandon, 'the harbour of the town of Wasa' and 'a great ship building place', *Firefly*, *Harrier* and the French *d'Assas* anchored 400 yards off the town, 'sprung the broadside' to cover the place and sent boat parties in to destroy magazines and warehouses; many were already empty but large stocks of naval stores were found and destroyed in some. Four ships were also sunk there.[41] The inland town of Räfsö was attacked by *Harrier* and *Tartar*, again with the French corvette *d'Assas* on 9 August, after a difficult journey upriver, and eleven boats captured, including a useful steamer.[42] In the Gulf of Riga, Captain Heathcote in *Archer*, accompanied by *Desperate* and *Conflict*, attacked shore positions at Windau. Having first negotiated with its Russian commander that his men should evacuate the town, Heathcoate landed marines to burn government buildings; he then set fire to boats and barracks near Capel Wik.[43] Similar operations continued in the Gulf of Riga throughout August, the most significant being an 'engagement with the enemy's batteries and gun-boats' at the mouth of the River Dvina.[44] With *Desperate* and *Hawke*, Captain Erasmus Ommanney – who was exceptionally busy with such actions throughout August – was suddenly faced by a flotilla of twelve gunboats which 'swept out boldly from the river' to defend local coasters. All the Russian gunboats opened fire ('which was well directed') on the British warships and 'a very sharp and spirited cannonade' was kept up. From 5.30am until 7.00pm the ships engaged the gunboats and nearby shore batteries (whose shot pierced both the ships' hulls) until the Russian gunboats withdrew into shallow water and could not be pursued. An attempt to reach them slightly later was equally fruitless but the shore batteries were successfully shelled before the British ships withdrew; Ommanney was able to give a good account of the size and strength of the defences at the mouth of the Dvina, the approaches to the city of Riga.[45] Ommanney carried out similar operations at Dromeness with *Hawke* and *Conflict* in the middle of the month, shelling land positions, scattering enemy forces and landing parties in six boats to burn the town.[46] There were also thirty-seven small boats destroyed at the same time. On one occasion, on 2 September, it finally looked as if the Russian fleet from Cronstadt was actually going to emerge to fight. A Russian squadron of one screw 90-gun ship, a screw frigate, a paddle-wheel steamer and 'several' gunboats left Cronstadt and headed towards *Colossus* and *Impérieuse*, which had been watching the port. However, as soon as the two British warships got under weigh and headed for the Russians, the latter decided that discretion was the better part of valour and turned tail, retreating into the harbour whilst the two British ships resumed their station. It was all rather disappointing.[47]

And so it continued, until winter set in from the middle of September. The ships once again began to disperse as ice formed and the weather worsened, initially directed towards Kiel and then to their home ports. By then, no fewer than 106 larger vessels, 50 sloops and over 50 storehouses, magazines and buildings had been destroyed around the shores of the Baltic; *Harrier* claimed the largest haul, she alone having destroyed 55 ships, only one being sent intact to Britain.[48] Admiral Baynes remained on station to maintain the blockade till the last possible moment, but the bulk of the allied fleet had left the Baltic by the end of November and all were back home by Christmas. There were those who deemed the campaign something of a success – after all, Sveaborg had been attacked and once again, large Russian forces (and their stores and supplies) had been kept more or less inactive on the Baltic coasts. Russian merchant trade had been paralysed and the losses to Russian and Finnish shipping had been immense. Other observers were less charitable and felt that once again a powerful (and expensive) fleet had not shown to great advantage; as one observer remarked: 'When the war broke out, it was supposed that because we had steam as a propelling power instead of sails, we were about to see great results obtained by means of our Navy. But the ships were built to meet and vanquish ships and we were beginning to see that this was not a naval war.'[49]

It was hoped that as a result of 'The Great Armament' of the winter of 1855, 'a formidable fleet reinforced by a great number of gun boats and floating batteries will re-enter the Baltic in 1856 ... and blockade all the coasts, whilst the army,[50] commanded by General Canrobert, will simultaneously operate in Finland and the three Russian provinces of Courland, Estonia and Livonia'.[51] But it was not to happen. Into the early months of 1856, as the war petered to a close elsewhere, a few steamers kept up the blockade and an attempt at warlike operations, cruising off the Kattegat to block possible Russian shipping movements into the North Sea. During these patrols, the 5-gun steam-sloop *Polyphemus* was wrecked off Jutland, thus having the doubtful honour – at the very last minute – of being the only allied ship to be lost in the Baltic blockade.[52]

Chapter 8

Scouring the Sea of Azoff, Summer 1855

Anglo-French naval operations in the Sea of Azoff[1] were a natural adjunct to their land campaign in the Crimea and their general policy of action against Russia's trade and economy. In addition, they gave a much more effective role to the powerful Anglo-French fleet, anxious to contribute to the campaign but more or less reduced, apart from the odd bombardment, to the inglorious role of ferrying troops and supplies. The Sea of Azoff extends about 90 miles northwards from the Strait of Kertch (now usually Kerch) to Berdiansk and from the Spit of Arabat in the west to the mouth of the Don it stretches for about 190 miles. The northern shore is broken by bays and long projecting sand spits, whilst its eastern coast is low, sandy and broken by *limans*, or lagoons. The southern coast is pierced by the only access into the Sea of Azoff, the narrow Straits of Kertch or Yenikale, whilst the western coast is dominated by the long Spit of Arabat. The sea is an unusually shallow stretch of water with considerable variations in depth and tidal flow and was unsuited to the deployment of larger deep-draught warships – a fact known to the Russians and on which they placed some hope of safety. Its greatest depth is under 50 feet but most is much shallower – as little as 4 feet in places – and as most of the coastline is bordered by shoals, mudflats and shallow water, inshore navigation could be difficult and dangerous. An unusual feature was the Sivash or 'Putrid Sea',[2] an area of shallow stagnant water lying to the west of the Spit of Arabat, which was frozen in winter and pestilential in summer;[3] it joins the Sea of Azoff at Genitchi Strait. Along the coast, the most important trading centres and ports were Azoff, Rostov and Taganrog around the estuary of the Don, Mariaupol, Berdiansk and Genitchi on the north coast and Arabat in the south-west. In and around the straits are the ports of Kertch, Yenikale and Taman, with Anapa and Kaffa lying nearby on the Black Sea coast. The sea and its hinterland provided highly important arteries of trade into and around the Black Sea and (during the war) with the Crimea. To the Russian armies in the Crimea and in the Caucasus, the Sea of Azoff offered major sources of supply for foodstuffs (principally fish and grain) as well as of timber, hay, tar, coal and other goods and also facilitated the movement of troops and war materiel from other parts of the Empire.[4] Disrupting – if not destroying – its maritime trade and coastal economy was an obvious goal of allied ambitions and throughout the campaigning season of 1855, before the sea began to ice up in the winter, British and French warships wrought havoc in the Sea of Azoff and along its coastal hinterland.[5]

Rear Admiral Sir Edmund Lyons was the moving force behind the adoption of active operations in the area. Although the allied fleets were not in a position to attempt the Strait of Kertch and the Sea of Azoff until the summer of 1855, as early as 21 December 1854 he had prepared a 'Memorandum on the Sea of Azoff':

> The importance of the Sea of Azoff, considered merely as a channel of communication between Central Russia and the armies of the Crimea and Caucasus, can hardly be over-rated. It is of value in other respects from the fisheries at the mouth of the Kouban and the Don, and to the training which these supply to a hardy race of marsh men. But the great value of the sea to Russia consists in the facility which it affords in moving troops and *materiel* of war cheaply and without fatigue to points which otherwise could not be reached without great expense and loss of life, from the necessary privations attending the land journey ... The heaviest articles, such as iron, and even large fir trees of a size to serve as masts for small frigates, [as well as] tallow,

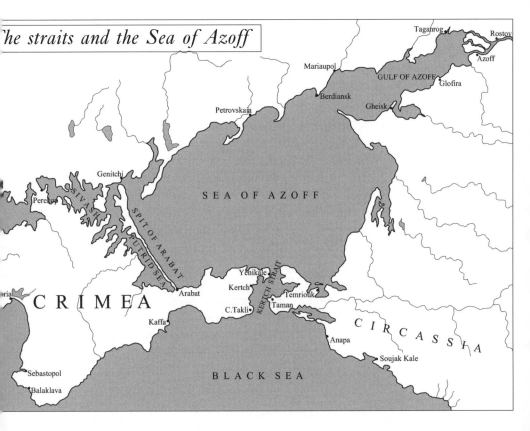

cordage, timber for shipbuilding and all other articles requisite for constructing and arming gun-boats, are conveyed across by land carriage and embarked on the Don, by which they descend as far as Rostov. From Rostov all merchandise is usually conveyed as far as Taganrog in barges and at Taganrog transferred to sea-going vessels. This arrangement arises from the circumstance of the mouths of the Don being nearly closed by the alluvium, so that nothing can pass which draws more than four feet water; and in some seasons there is not even this.

. . . an enormous traffic continually goes on in summer by means of barges, in winter on the Volga by sledges. The chief interruptions will of course be at the seasons which stop the one kind of convey-ance and compel a resort to the other. But the times of the ice becoming strong enough to bear traffic and the rivers being open for navigation are uncertain, especially in the southern part of the route.

. . . [it] seems not impossible that the reinforcements which are said to have lately arrived in the Crimea are drawn from the can-tonments of the army of the Caucasus[6] . . . [and] have been conveyed in small boats from the northern embouchure of the Kouban (near the site of Temriouk, which is within the Sea of Azoff) to the [Crimean] Peninsula.

Lyons pointed out the great 'obstacles to the entrance of a British flotilla into the Sea of Azoff and to its operations therein': the shallowness of the channel in the Strait of Yenikale 'where it would be unsafe to reckon on more than 11 feet of water', a shallowness that continues throughout the sea itself, caused by the silting up of the waters, and the frequent bouts of severe weather, which would 'render the employment of small vessels somewhat hazardous'.[7]

Reconnaissance of the strait had shown that entry to the sea was difficult – through narrow channels that hardly featured on British charts and which had been further blocked by scuttled ships and past the defended ports of Kertch and Yenikale. Clearly, operations in the Sea of Azoff would rely on the allied control of the 'Kertchine Peninsula' and strait and would therefore require the occupation of the ports, so that a land campaign would be needed.

Even before the operations of 1855 began, reconnoitring squadrons had been sent towards the region, largely to look at its Black Sea coast, but avoiding the strait and the shallow Azoff Sea. Early in March, Captain Gifford, cruising nearby, detached the steamer *Viper* to examine Kuban *liman*, or bay, between Anapa and the Strait of Kertch; Lieutenant Armytage, commanding the steamer, dispersed a few Cossacks on the shore and destroyed a fort, battery, barrack and granaries. But only towards the end of April 1855 were plans

Crews leaving
Portsmouth to join the
Baltic Fleet, March 1854.

(*Left*) A contemporary print showing Vice Admiral Sir Charles Napier. (*Right*) A contemporary print
the Baltic Fleet under sail, 1854.

HMS *Lynx*, *Beagle* and
ow in the Baltic, 1854.

ed ships off Cronstadt, July 1854.

HMS *Hecla* and
Valorous during the
raid on Bomarsund,
21 June 1854.

A reconnaissance of
Cronstadt in summe
1854.

The attack on the
Bomarsund forts.
(*Tyrell*)

HMS *Hecla* and
Arrogant attack Ekn
19 May 1854. (*Tyrell*)

Fort Notvik after its capture; Fort Prästö is seen in the background, across Bomar Sound, August 1855.

HMS *Archer* in the ice at Wingo Bay, 1854.

The bombardment of Odessa. (*Tyrell*)

HMS *Spitfire* at the destruction of Sulina, 17 July 1854.

The allied anchorage at Baljik.

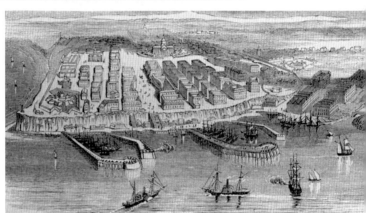

A view of Odessa in 1854. (*Chambers*)

The allied fleet leaving Varna for the Crimea 7 September 1855.

Rear Admiral R.S. Dundas. (*Clowes*)

A contemporary print showing Rear Admiral Sir Edmund Lyons.

(left) French naval commanders, left to right: Admirals Hamelin, Bruat and Deschênes.
(right) A contemporary print showing a view of Sebastopol.

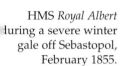

HMS *Royal Albert*
during a severe winter
gale off Sebastopol,
February 1855.

View of Balaklava harbour. (*W. Simpson*)

HMS *Trafalgar* with *Retribution* (foreground) at the bombardment of Sebastopol, October 1854.

Allied ships off Anapa, 1855.

Leopard, Highflyer, Swallow, Viper and *Fulton* attack Soujak Kaleh on the Black Sea coast, 13 March 1

(*ft*) The docks at Sebastopol. (*W. Simpson*) (*Right*) The reverse of the Crimea Medal, to a naval
∘ipient, with clasps for Sebastopol and Azoff.

∘ied ships off the seafront at Eupatoria.

∘ied warships
∘porting the defence of
∘atoria, March 1855.

Part of the Naval
Brigade camp before
Sebastopol, 1855.

Sailors dragging siege guns from Balaklava, March 1855.

The naval battery and mortar on Greenhill, May 1855.

(*Left*) No. 2 Sailors' Battery on Greenhill. One gun is s on its naval carriage.

(*Below left*) Captain Willia Peel of HMS *Diamond*. (*Clo*

(*Below right*) A contempor print of the allied landings near Kertch, 24 May 1855.

MS *Snake* in action against Russian ships off Kertch, 24 May 1855.

lied warships off Kertch, 25 May 1855.

rkish troops landing at Yenikale, June 1855.

Captain Peel (standing centre) with a Lancaster gun in the *Diamond* battery. (*W. Simpson*)

The attack on Fort Arabat, 28 May 1855.

Cowper Coles' gun raft *The Lady Nancy* in action off Taganrog. A rocket boat can be seen in the foreground.

HMS *Miranda* off the town of Kola, 24 August 1854.

The attack on Novitska in the White Sea, 23 July 1854.

HMS *Miranda* with prizes in Litscha Bay, August 1854.

Captain Edmund Lyons HMS *Miranda*. (*Clowes*)

HMS *St George* refitting for the Baltic in March 1855.

The second Baltic Fleet at anchor, April 1855.

The Royal Yacht *Fairy* (centre) reviews the new Baltic Fleet, March 1855.

HMS *Duke of Wellington*, April 1855.

A small gunboat in the Baltic, 1855.

The gunboat HMS *Recruit*.

(*Left*) The screw gunboat *Wrangler* in the Baltic.

(*Below left*) Vice Admiral J.W.D. Dundas. (*Clowes*)

(*Below right*) HMS *Cossack* off Hängo Head at the time of the 'Hängo Massacre', 5 June 1855.

A contemporary print showing British ships off Cronstadt, 1855.

A view of the island of Cronstadt with its outlying sea defences.

The island of Cronstadt and its outer forts.

A view of Sveaborg. (*Tyrell*)

A contemporary print of the bombardment of Sveaborg viewed from a small gun vessel, 1855.

Allied ships, including HMS *Geyser* and *Archer* patrolling off Riga, May 1855.

(*Left*) HMS *Magicienne* iced up in the Baltic, February 1855. The effects of the often severe weather on operations in the Baltic should not be ignored. (*Right*) Reverse of the Baltic Medal, showing Britannia seated; in the background is the fort of Bomarsund (left) and Sveaborg (right).

HMS *Magicienne* with burning and captured prizes off Cronstadt, June 1855.

Landing guns on the spit at Kinburn, 15 October 1855.

The bombardment of Kinburn seen from the allied landing place.

The forts at Kinburn under attack, 17 October 1855.

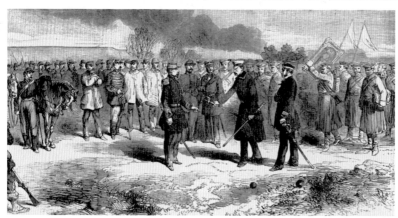

The surrender of Kinburn, 17 October 1855.

The allied bombardment of Petropavlovsk on Russia's Pacific coast, 31 August 1854.

agreed for a full-scale naval expedition. Early in May preparations were made for dispatching a fleet of heavily armed steamers, with several gunboats, under Sir Edmund Lyons and his French counterpart Admiral Bruat,[8] to test the strength of the Russian fortifications at Kertch and Yenikale.

On 3 May a fleet of over 50 ships set off from Kamiesch and Balaklava, carrying 12,000 troops, the British contingent of infantry and two batteries of artillery under Sir George Brown. However, just after the British and French ships rendezvoused close to the Strait of Kertch on the 5th, a French steamer arrived with the shocking news that the French element was to be withdrawn in the light of orders received directly from Napoleon III in Paris. This was, incidentally, one of the fruits of the new Black Sea electric telegraph completed only on 3 May[9] – close contact with the allied capitals and (as in this case) the interference of the French Emperor. The French military commander in the Crimea, General Francois Canrobert,[10] though he had never been very keen on this large-scale 'combined operation' which he considered something of a diversion from the main task of taking Sebastopol, was angered and frustrated by the order, but felt bound to obey his Emperor and instructed Admiral Bruat to return at once. Without the French contingent (not least their land forces) the expedition was deemed too weak to proceed against what was, by and large, an unknown target. Shorn of his ally's support, Admiral Lyons could do nothing more than bring the British fleet back to Balaklava. It was a humiliating and dispiriting end to a much-anticipated project.[11] It transpired that Napoleon was reluctant to see the weakening of French forces in the Crimea; neither did he want his fleet diverted from the task of carrying reinforcements and supplies from Constantinople to the immediate seat of war.[12] However, he is said not to have known that the expedition to Kertch had actually sailed and to have been furious that it was then recalled; he apparently expected Canrobert and Bruat to use their own judgment 'on the spot'. At any rate, it was all too much for Canrobert; the French withdrawal left relations with the British command at a low ebb and facing the increased prospect of being controlled 'by wire' from Paris, he resigned his command on 17 May.[13] He was succeeded by the 61-year-old Aimable Jean-Jacques Pélissier, a hard, experienced and aggressive commander, known forbiddingly as '*l'homme brutal*'.[14]

The only result of this wasted enterprise, apart from the palpable sense of disappointment and failure that spread through the allied fleets, was that the Russians were warned of the possibility of an allied attack and began to strengthen the defences and garrisons of the principal towns guarding the straits – Kertch, Yenikale, Taman and Anapa, where considerable numbers of troops and guns were known to be based.

No sooner was Pélissier placed at the head of the French army than a new spirit entered the French high command and a second Kertch expedition was

The Crimea and the Strait of Kertch.

agreed on 20 May 1855. A fleet of over 60 ships would carry a larger landing force of 18,000 men; the French would provide about 7,500, the Turks 5,000 and the British about 4,000,[15] supplied with equipment for constructing earthworks and other defences at any occupied position. There was also some hope that allied landings in the Strait of Kertch would encourage, with active Turkish assistance, a Circassian revolt which might also divert or hamper Russian forces; Commander Sherard Osborn reported that the Turkish General Mustapha Pasha had already reconnoitred the Circassian coast in *Vesuvius* to look at potential landing sites.[16]

For this major operation, Sir Edmund Lyons, Admiral Stewart and the French Admiral Bruat had under their command an impressive fleet. The British element was *Royal Albert, Hannibal, Algiers, Agamemnon, St Jean d'Acre, Princess Royal, Sidon, Valorous, Leopard, Tribune, Simoom, Furious, Highflyer, Terrible, Caradoc, Sphinx, Spitfire, Gladiator* and *Banshee*. This was a combination of larger line-of-battle ships which might be needed at Kertch or Yenikale and smaller steam vessels. Other small steamships would be deployed in the Sea of Azoff itself once the straits had been secured. The French fleet under Admiral Bruat was equally powerful and comprised the battleships *Montebello, Le Napoléon* and *Charlemagne*, the steam frigates *Pomone, Caffarelli, Mogador, Cacique, Descartes, Asmodée* and *Ulloa*, the steam corvettes *Véloce, Primauguet*,

Phlégethon, *Berthollet*, *Roland* and *Caton*, the small steam sloops *Lucifer*, *Mégère*, *Milan*, *Brandon*, *Fulton* and *Dauphin* and the mortar boat *Vautour* with other support vessels. The troops were carried on the lager warships.

If the seizure of the straits and their principal ports went according to plan, Captain Edmund Lyons[17] was to be given command of a 'flying squadron' consisting of gunboats and light steamers, less ponderous and more man-oeuvrable than the larger line-of-battle ships. It was to become, in the terms of its own operational orders, the most successful allied fleet to be deployed in the Russian war and comprised the *Miranda*, *Vesuvius*, *Stromboli*, *Medina*, *Ardent*, *Arrow*, *Beagle*, *Lynx*, *Snake*, *Swallow*, *Viper*, *Wrangler* and *Curlew*. Captain Lyons retained his flag on the *Miranda*, the ship he had already commanded with such success in the White Sea. In addition, five French steamers were to operate alongside Lyons' squadron in the shallow waters of the Sea of Azoff.

The allied armada with its military contingents left Kamiesch and Balaklava on 22–3 May 1855, reached the entrance to the Strait of Kertch on the 24th ('on her Majesty's birthday') and anchored opposite the village of Ambelaki, close to where the Strait of Kertch joins the Strait of Yenikale. The British and French military contingents under the command of Sir George Brown[18] and General d'Autemarre respectively had been carried in the lighter steamers so that they could be brought as close to the shore as possible and were then transferred into the ships' boats for the actual landing. Although the steamers' guns offered covering protection to the landing force, none was needed, since there was no opposition and Ambelaki was immediately occupied. Soon after-wards, the sound of loud explosions in the distance proved to be the destruc-tion by the Russians of their own batteries and barracks at Fort Paul and throughout the day other Russian defences in the direction of Kertch were heard being blown up by their own men.[19] The Russians clearly considered that the small works defending the strait were untenable in the face of such a large-scale enemy attack and operated something like a minor 'scorched earth' policy; several large granaries were burned near Kertch, along with two steamers in the harbour, and Russian cavalry destroyed nearby farmhouses, timber and forage supplies. It was later found that as much as 4,000,000lb of corn and 500,000lb of flour had been destroyed since they could not be carried away. Throughout the day and all through the night, the allies landed the men, stores and equipment they would need for the advance to Kertch, which began next morning. The French contingent took the lead, followed by the Turks and then the British.

Kertch and nearby Taman were major Russian military command centres, with large, well-equipped and sizeable forces available to them. Rather more resistance was expected of them by the allies, but they had received little support from the Russian high command, despite repeated requests for assistance and further reinforcement. The arrival of a major enemy naval and land force was enough to convince the Russian military in Kertch that opposition was pointless and rather than face a siege or mass captivity, Russian forces abandoned Kertch and fell back towards the coastal towns of Arabat and Kaffa. Captured documents later revealed that up to 6,000 Russian soldiers had been in garrison at or near Kertch and that their commander, General Wrangel, had appealed to St Petersburg for reinforcements, but to no avail. It was widely believed that if the allied cavalry force had been larger, the retreating Russians could have been brought to battle and decisively defeated 'in the field' but in the event, no such encounter took place and the allied army quietly entered Kertch and took possession of the city with its government buildings, harbour and defences. They later found 17,000 tons of coal which the Russians had failed to destroy or remove, and appropriated all of it for the use of the steamers. Leaving a garrison at Kertch, the allies immediately continued along the coast northeastwards towards Yenikale. Once again, their entry into the port was entirely unopposed and once again they found that the Russian defenders had fled and that, rather more than at Kertch, it had been abandoned by its terrified civilian population. This was the cue for a mass looting of the town by the allies and though in their respective accounts all laid the blame on the other, there is no doubt that French, British and Turkish soldiers and sailors pillaged what they could before some degree of control was restored.

Kertch, occupied by the allies on 25 May, was a prosperous commercial centre and an ancient and fine-looking town – once described as 'a Naples on a small scale'. Like many other cities around the Black Sea, Kertch was a very ancient foundation, established by Greek colonists in the seventh century BCE; it had only been taken from the Turks as recently as 1774. Lying on a semicircular bay, it possessed a fine stone quay and harbour, tall churches, grand merchants' houses of white stone or painted wood, good shops and numerous public buildings of some stature. As a regional administrative and military centre, Kertch housed extensive magazines, stores, factories, saw mills, shell and ball foundries, a dockyard, batteries and other military and naval buildings. Few of these had been destroyed by the Russians, so rapid was their flight and the change of owners.

But the allied soldiery fell into an appalling orgy of looting and pillaging during the first few days of the occupation of Kertch,[20] ably assisted by the heterogeneous mix of people who had remained behind and, apparently, by people from the surrounding countryside who were not slow to take advantage. Hardly any house – rich or poor – was left untouched; everything portable was taken and what could not be carried was burned or destroyed. Wealthier inhabitants who could manage it had fled, leaving their houses and furniture unprotected, whilst the poorer population was left behind. But all property became a target for the looter. The town's museum, famous for its classical collection, was destroyed and its contents scattered and broken; the governor's house was similarly wrecked and drunken men of all nationalities, soldiers and sailors alike, laden with spoil, were seen staggering about the streets in wild disorder. The other of the twin towns controlling the strait, Yenikale, was similarly occupied by allied troops and became the headquarters of the British land commander, Sir George Brown. Yenikale was important because of its closeness to the Sea of Azoff and although smaller than Kertch, had many public buildings and fine houses owned by the wealthier inhabitants. Sir George at first had problems maintaining order amongst his soldiers and as at Kertch, there was much looting and theft, with 'trophies' being taken away by all and sundry. However, Brown soon imposed strict discipline on his men and by setting a stern example in a few instances quickly brought the rest to reason and re-established order within the town.

Once established at Kertch and Yenikale, the allies proceeded to destroy all Russian government property that they could not carry away or use, the Turks being delighted to find some of the guns that the Russians had seized at Sinope eighteen months earlier. The allies found huge quantities of useable naval stores of all kinds in the dockyard and divided them up between themselves; what they did not want was simply thrown into the sea. W.H. Russell recorded:

> The dockyard magazines at Kertch contained quantities of military and naval stores – boiler plates, lathes, engineers' tools, paint, canvas, hemp and chain cables, bales of greatcoats, uniform jackets, trousers and caps, knapsacks, belts, bayonets, swords, scabbards, anchors, copper nails and bolts, implements of foundry, brass, rudder pintles, lead etc. The French were busy for a few days taking the clothing etc. out of the storehouse and destroying it. The valuable stores were divided between the allies, according to their good fortune and energy in appropriation. Numbers of old boats, of large rudders, covered with copper and hung on brass, of small guns, of shot, shell, grape and canister, were lying in the dockyard ... Outside the wall of the dockyard which was filled with oxen and horses, was another long range of public buildings and storehouses which had nearly all been gutted and destroyed. Soldiers' belts, caps, trousers, cartouche boxes, knapsacks and canteens were strewn all over the quay in front of them. In a word, Kertch has ceased to be a military or naval station and the possession which Russia so eagerly coveted a few years before was of no more use to her than the snows of the Tchatir Dagh.[21]

Arrangements were immediately made for securing the defences of the town, in case a Russian force attempted to return; but no enemy appeared and the military had to leave it to the steam squadron to achieve any further glory. Some of the smaller allied steamers had already begun to hunt down Russian vessels trying to flee from Kertch, some laden with government property and stores. The first actual engagement – if it can be so called – was fought by HMS *Snake*. Once Fort Paul had been destroyed by its own defenders, leaving part of the strait undefended, Lieutenant Henry M'Killop[22] of *Snake* was given permission to press on northwards in pursuit of a Russian vessel seen trying to leave Kertch Bay. This proved to be the war steamer *Argonaut*, part of a fourteen-ship squadron based at Kertch under Rear Admiral Wulff. Exchanging shots with a battery at Kertch as he passed, M'Killop succeeded in preventing the ship's escape into the Sea of Azoff but not before she had run under the protection of the guns of Yenikale, still at this time manned by their Russian defenders. *Snake* opened on the Russian vessel, setting it on fire; run ashore by her crew, she shortly afterwards blew up. In what was one of the few examples in the entire war of a Russian naval response, at least two other gun boats of the Kertch squadron, believed to be the *Goets* and the *Berdiansk*, emerged into the strait to challenge *Snake* and a brief firefight followed. But *Snake* skillfully outmanoeuvred them all, preventing their escape into the Sea of Azoff. With the British steamer *Recruit* and the French *Fulton* and *Mégère* joining in the chase, the Russians grounded and then burnt their own steamers, under the gaze of a delighted allied fleet. At much the same time, several other sailing vessels were intercepted, burned or captured as they tried to flee the ports and shortly afterwards the magazines and batteries at Yenikale were destroyed by their own defenders. The Russian naval commander, Admiral Wulff, having burned most of his squadron at Kertch, managed to flee into the Sea of Azoff with his last four remaining steamers.

This action by *Snake*[23] and her companions was one of several small incidents in the strait, though much of the damage to Russian shipping seems to have been self-inflicted. On the night of 24 May Captain Lyons anchored his steam squadron just off Yenikale, beyond the range of its guns and was there when the Russians fired their magazines. Early next day, Lyons ordered his ships to close with the shore defences but the sight was enough for the defenders who blew up the remaining fortifications and fled. As the Master of Lyons' ship *Miranda*[24] had by now buoyed a safe passage through the narrow and shallow waters, he found himself able to pass through on the afternoon of the 25th and, as the land forces occupied Kertch and Yenikale, an allied steam squadron duly entered the Sea of Azoff. Sir Edmund Lyons reported back to their Lordships in the Admiralty: 'The Allied forces are now masters of the Straits of Kertch and . . . they have in the Sea of Azov a powerful steam flotilla of light draught capable of cutting off the enemy's supplies and harassing him at all ports'.[25] This in itself was some achievement: the sea had been regarded by the Russians as a vital source of foodstuffs and other materials and something of a 'safe haven', deemed to be so inaccessible that its coasts were not strongly defended.[26] The mere fact of the allied entry into the Sea of Azoff was proof enough of their naval domination and what was to follow – destruction on a huge scale – was a vital blow against the Russian war effort.[27] The real value of smaller steam vessels was well demonstrated during this particular campaign; *Miranda*, with fifteen guns, was the largest vessel and the only British warship mounting more than eight guns. Lyons with thirteen British steamers and his French counterpart Captain Sedaiges with five French vessels left the main fleet behind them and began what was to be a remarkable and destructive campaign of economic warfare. As one writer noted:

> It was like bursting into a vast treasure house crammed with wealth of inestimable value. For miles along its shore stretched the countless storehouses packed with the accumulated harvests of the great corn provinces of Russia. From them the Russian armies in the field were fed; from them the beleaguered population of Sebastopol looked for preservation from the famine which already pressed hard upon them.[28]

The town of Berdiansk was to be the first to feel the effect of the allied intervention.[29] On 26 May, Lyons took his steam flotilla straight across the Sea of Azoff to its northern coastline and found the remaining four war steamers of Admiral Wulff's Kertch squadron burned out at the water's edge;[30] since Russian gunboats (supposedly guarding the estuary of the Don) were said to have fled to Rostov, it appeared that there were no Russian warships in the entire Sea of Azoff and therefore no chance of a Russian naval response.[31] On 27 May, Lyons sent a boat to demand the surrender of all Russian government property in the port of Berdiansk. The governor, not surprisingly given the unexpected presence of an enemy fleet right on his doorstep, was eager to comply and a party of sailors and marines under Commander Rowley Lambert was sent in to carry out the destruction. Stores of corn and shipping on the shore near the town were burned, whilst other allied ships chased merchant vessels plying to and from the harbour and towards the Don. Russian forces known to be nearby made no effort to intervene. Here, as everywhere else during the naval campaigns, it was the intention that private property and innocent civilians would remain unharmed, though inevitably over shooting and uncontrolled fires often caused damage beyond what was intended or required. Once again, much was made of this sort of thing in the Russian press which constantly emphasised not only the uncivilised destruction of private property but the general irrelevance of the damage the allied warships inflicted on stores destined for Russia's armies.

Having dealt with government property at Berdiansk, Lyons headed westwards for the small port of Arabat, at the southern end of the Spit of Arabat, 70 miles in length, detaching *Curlew* to investigate the mouth of the Don and *Swallow* and *Wrangler* to visit Genitchi[32] at the entrance to the Sivash. Here, boat parties under Lieutenant Campbell Mackenzie destroyed three Russian vessels and seized three others as prizes but were unable to block completely movement in and out of the 'Putrid Sea'.[33] On 28 May, Lyons arrived off Arabat and immediately engaged its fort, which was perhaps the best constructed and best armed fort on the Azoff coast. Surrounded by a broad dry ditch, with recently repaired stonework and 'bombproof' internal buildings, it mounted 17 guns facing the seaward approach and was believed to be garrisoned by up to 4,000 men. For over an hour there was a fierce artillery duel, with some damage done to the fortress, including the explosion of its magazine, but in the end Lyons decided to end the engagement and withdraw. He did not have enough men to attack the fort from the land and there was nothing ashore at Arabat that was deemed safe to attack under fire from the fort.[34]

In just three days of patrolling – the first days of the allied invasion of the Sea of Azoff – Lyons' ships destroyed over 200 enemy vessels, 90 on 29 May alone. Many of these were refugees from the Black Sea which had crowded for supposed safety in the creeks and harbours of the Sea of Azoff. There was some

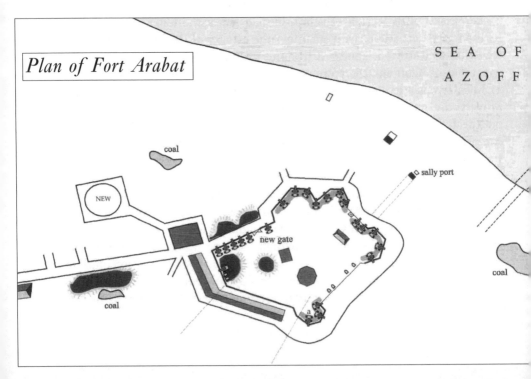

Plan of Fort Arabat

criticism – as there had been in the Baltic – that valuable stores that could have been used by the allies in the Crimea were wantonly destroyed[35] but Lyons made it clear that he simply did not have the crews to sail captured prizes or the ships to escort them if active operations were to continue at the same level. Lyons then crossed to Genitchi on 29 May. As before, under flag of truce a boat, this time under Commander F.A.B. Craufurd, was sent in to demand the surrender of government shipping and property. Here the reception was rather different; Genitchi had its own defence force of infantry, Cossacks and artillery and its officers bluntly refused to comply. Lyons followed what was going to be a very familiar process in the Sea of Azoff.[36]

> At 6 o'clock this morning I sent Commander Craufurd with a flag of truce, to demand the immediate surrender of all these vessels and of the immense corn stores for the supply of the army in the Crimea, and of all Government property of every description; stating that if these terms were complied with I would spare the town and respect private property, but that if not, the inhabitants were immediately to leave the town ... Commander Craufurd was met by an officer, of apparently high rank, who refused to accede to these terms, saying that any attempt to land or destroy the vessels would be resisted. The enemy at this time had six field pieces in position and with about 200 men with them and, visible from the mast-head, drawn up behind the town a battalion of infantry, besides Cossacks.
>
> Having allowed until 9.00am for reconsideration of the refusal to deliver up the vessels and stores and receiving no answer, I at that time hauled down the flag of truce and placed the steamers as near to the town and the passage into the 'Putrid Sea' as the depth of the water would allow, but they were only able to approach within long range. Seeing that if the enemy, who had removed his guns from their former position, could place them in the town, so as to command the passage, and that if he could place his infantry in a similar manner, it would be impossible for the boats to pass the channel and destroy the vessels and stores, I directed the ships to shell the town, which they did effectually, so that the [ten] boats ... under the command of Lieut. J.F.C. MacKenzie, got safely through the passage, and set fire to the shipping (73 in number), and the corn stores. This service was ably performed by Lieut. MacKenzie, and the boats returned without accident.
>
> The wind having shifted about two hours after the boats came off, some of the corn stores did not catch fire; conceiving the destruction of this corn, as well as some of the more distant vessels in so

favourable a position for supplying the Russian armies in the Crimea, to be of the utmost importance, I sent the boats again, commanded and officered as before, although I was aware that from the enemy having had time to make preparations, it would have been a hazardous enterprise. The ships accordingly resumed their fire upon the town, and the boats proceeded. Lieut. Cecil W. Buckley of this ship; Lieut. Hugh T. Burgoyne, of the *Swallow* and Mr. John Roberts, Gunner of the *Ardent*, volunteered to land alone and fire the stores; this offer I accepted, knowing that the imminent risk there would be in landing a party in presence of such a superior force, and out of the gunshot of the ships. This very dangerous service they most gallantly performed, narrowly escaping the Cossacks, who all but cut them off from their boats; at the same time, Lieut. MacKenzie pushed on and burned the remaining vessels, the enemy opening a fire from four field guns and musketry, placed almost within point blank range of the boats.[37]

The landing parties on both occasions returned without suffering a single casualty.

Taganrog, one of Russia's most important ports and a major depot for goods, especially grain, moving down the Don into the Sea of Azoff, was next to suffer. Taganrog remained the base of the small Azoff flotilla,[38] though this, in the event, never ventured beyond the defended estuary of the Don. HMS *Curlew*, which had been detached to watch the estuary, steamed towards the port on 30 May and found its approaches shallow and dangerously convoluted. Since its early days as a commercial centre under Peter the Great its coast, as at many other towns around the Sea of Azoff, was gradually silting up, so that Kertch had overtaken Taganrog as a port. Nevertheless, Taganrog was a sizeable town, with attractive white houses stretching down to the shore and extensive warehouses and government buildings. Captain Lyons with the rest of the steam squadron joined *Curlew* on 1 June but found that because of the unmarked shallows it was dangerous and impracticable to bring the warships nearer in than several miles; only the light *Recruit* could steam closer to shore. Since heavier guns than could be carried by the usual ships' boats were thought to be needed for the reduction of Taganrog, the novel idea was proposed of using two 32-pounders, mounting one on a specially constructed raft and another in a cutter. The raft, devised by Commander Cowper Coles of *Stromboli*[39] was called *The Lady Nancy* and proved to be very effective. In addition, Lyons requested the dispatch of some of the ships' boats and their crews from the larger allied warships anchored near Kertch; the boats of *Agamemnon, Princess Royal, Algiers, Hannibal, St Jean d'Acre* and *Royal Albert*, carrying mortars and rockets, thus had their only opportunity for actual service within the Sea of Azoff.

With these reinforcements and adaptations, Lyons and Sedaiges were ready to strike against Taganrog and on 3 June followed what was becoming the standard procedure: under flag of truce, a boat was sent in to demand the surrender of government property. On this occasion, the town's military governor Count Tolstoi, with 3,000 local troops under General Krasnov,[40] felt confident that he could defend the place and once his refusal was known, Lyons prepared for what was to be a major assault. No less than forty small craft under Commander Cowper Coles – gun rafts, rocket boats, launches, cutters and paddle-box boats –were fitted out to attack the town. Their job was quickly and effectively carried out; rockets and shell fire from the boats destroyed shipping and granaries, whilst boat parties landed and carried the destruction further ashore, burning the customs' house and all other government stores and buildings. 'An immense loss of supplies' was again inflicted on the enemy[41] whose troops tried vainly to repel the attackers and halt the destruction, but were fought off at every attempt. But the assault on Taganrog was an occasion when not all went according to plan; such was the extent of the burning that the flames carried into the town and great damage was done to private houses. Nevertheless, by 4.00pm the landing parties and boats had done all that they could easily accomplish, whilst under continuing rifle fire from Russian soldiers who remained under cover of the buildings. Remarkably, there were no serious casualties to the allied landing forces by the time a withdrawal was ordered.[42]

There was simply no let up or respite in this relentless attack on Russian interests right around the Sea of Azoff.[43] With the ceaseless energy and dedication to duty which characterised the naval commanders of the 'flying squadron', Lyons immediately turned to the important corn-exporting centre of Mariaupol,[44] a main link on the trade route between Taganrog and Berdiansk. On 4 June, only a day after the destruction wrought at Taganrog, the squadron anchored before the town. As at Taganrog, a request for surrender was refused and boat parties again burned everything that could be considerer government property. Next day, nearby Gheisk[45] – whose governor, Colonel Borskoff, had the sense to accept the offer of surrender and let the boat parties under Lieutenant Nugent Macnamara go about their work without resistance – was subjected to five hours of unopposed action which destroyed immense quantities of hay and corn.[46] Shortly afterwards, the Queen telegraphed 'Her Majesty's extreme satisfaction at the successful operations in the sea of Azoff'.[47]

In the meantime, whilst Captain Lyons ranged around the coast of Azoff, smaller expeditions were sent southwards from Kertch to seize nearby Russian towns. Both Anapa and Soujak Kaleh,[48] on the Black Sea coast southeast of the Strait of Kertch, retained Russian garrisons and would clearly have to be reduced. The mere threat of action by a joint Anglo-French military force[49] rapidly led to the abandonment of Soujak Kaleh, whose defenders retired having destroyed their guns and magazines on 28 May. But at Anapa the French once again threatened to be hamstrung by direct instructions by telegraph from Napoleon III, ordering that no attack should be made. Fortunately, the French high command, Pélissier and Bruat, who anyway felt inclined to ignore their Emperor, had the matter taken from their hands by the sudden abandonment of the town by the Russians on 5 June, leaving 114 guns to fall into allied possession; most had been disabled and were simply thrown over the cliffs. This was the last town on the Circassian coast to retain a Russian garrison and to fall to the allies.

By 13 June 1855, the allied command at Kertch and Yenikale had decided that the retention of large forces in the area was no longer necessary and decided on a return to Balaklava and Kamiesch. Much had been achieved at hardly any cost: the Russians had been forced to evacuate Kertch, Yenikale, Fort Paul, Anapa and Soujak Kaleh and the light squadron had destroyed shipping and stores at Arabat, Genitchi, Berdiansk, Mariaupol and Taganrog. Leaving largely Turkish garrisons[50] at Kertch, Anapa and Yenikale, and the 'flying squadron' to continue to scour the Sea of Azoff, the bulk of the allied expeditionary force returned to Sebastopol to rejoin the continuing siege. This included Captain Lyons in *Miranda*, withdrawn from the Azoff flotilla by his father's orders to take part in the forthcoming attack on Sebastopol. Here, he was wounded during a small-scale naval attack on Sebastopol on 17 June, part of a series of night-time naval bombardments in preparation for the major land assault on 18 June. He died of gangrene at Therapia hospital in the Bosphorus a few days later, to the universal regret of the fleet.

Captain 'Jack' Lyons was succeeded as commander of the Azoff gunboat squadron by the equally dynamic and tireless Commander Sherard Osborn[51] of *Vesuvius*. In what may be regarded as a second tranche of operations, Osborn directed his first attention to Genitchi. His target here was the wooden cable-ferry or floating bridge (Tchongar Bridge) which connected the town to the Spit of Arabat and, more importantly, allowed the free movement of troops and supplies to and from the Crimea. On 3 July, he sent Lieutenant W.N.W. Hewett of *Beagle* to destroy the bridge. The work was done by two boat parties, including Osborn himself with Lieutenants John Commerell and William Horton, who cut the hawsers linking the rafts, but not without serious risk and under close rifle fire.[52] Osborn remained in the area for some days, regularly sending out boat parties to investigate shore installations and to destroy anything and everything that might conceivably be of use to the Russians – guard posts, barracks, boats and stores of fish, grain, hay and timber on and near the Spit. Leaving ships to watch Arabat, Osborn then made for Berdiansk[53] and destroyed its huge (and newly acquired) stocks of corn and hay. All around the coast, from Fort Petrovskaia between Berdiansk and Mariaupol to the eastern shores and from Genitchi[54] to Taganrog, Osborn destroyed everything in the way of stores and shipping within reach of landing parties, including fisheries which had been supplying Sebastopol.[55] Off Fort Petrovskaia on 24 June *Vesuvius* was fired on, hitting the ship several times, but the batteries (which, Osborn believed, were manned by the crews from the four Russian warships scuttled at Berdiansk) were silenced by the ships' guns. At that time, Osborn thought that he did not have enough power to destroy all the fortifications, so on 17 July he returned with a larger force of ten British and two French warships.[56] The fort, which had been reinforced and repaired since the recent bombardment, was shelled and this time completely destroyed by the warships, which were positioned 1,000 yards offshore. A party under Lieutenant Hubert Campion of *Vesuvius* was landed to complete the destruction of the fort defences and nearby stores. On the same day, 17 July, at Glofira Spit near Gheisk, Osborn sent *Fancy*, *Grinder*, *Boxer*, *Curlew*, *Cracker*, *Wrangler* and *Jasper* under Commander Rowley Lambert with additional boat parties from *Swallow* and *Vesuvius* to burn corn and fish stores, though the presence of large parties of Cossacks prevented a landing at the town of Glofira itself.

Osborn reconnoitred Taganrog in *Jasper* on 19 July and a few days later the only significant loss to the Azoff squadron occurred, and not through enemy action.[57] HMS *Jasper*, under Lieutenant J.S. Hudson had been detached to cruise off the mouth of the Don and near Taganrog and when relieved by *Grinder* proceeded on 23 July to join *Swallow* to examine the Krivaia, or 'Crooked Spit'. However, whilst waiting to meet *Swallow* the ship ran aground at night. When day broke, the Russian defenders on the Crooked Spit had the considerable surprise of seeing a British warship lying stranded before them and were not slow to open fire. Commander F.A.B. Crauford, coming up in *Swallow*, advised Hudson to lighten the ship, including throwing overboard his guns and ammunition and anything else that could be moved. But nothing worked and Hudson had the dubious pleasure of ordering the crew to abandon *Jasper* and then firing his own ship, having stripped her of whatever could be carried away.[58] Later, British vessels returned to the wreck and over the course of four days some of her gear and one 68-pounder gun were salvaged. She was then blown up with powder casks.

Only at the end of July did the pace slacken and for much of August the sea and its coasts were left in a degree of peace. The town of Azoff itself was deemed to be too well defended to approach and the other important potential target which had so far escaped attention was the major port and city of Rostov on the Don. Developed after 1749, Rostov was one of the most important regional trading centres, especially for grain and timber. On 10 August Osborn detached *Vesuvius* to reconnoitre the mouth of the Don to look at the feasibility of moving upriver for an attack on the city, its dockyards and its shipping. But as with so many places around the Azoff coast, the channels leading into the estuary and river were found to be tortuous, silted and narrow and the single navigable approach was partially blocked by a wooden stockade, defended by earthworks mounting guns and surrounded by miles of mudflats. Without proper charts or a detailed survey (which was not feasible given the presence of an estimated 2,000 Russian troops in the area), Osborn wisely declined to consider an attack and Rostov was left isolated but unmolested.[59]

Of the Azoff operations up to that time, one commentator noted:

> Not a boat of so much as one ton burden was left afloat; not a store-house was erected but a landing party discovered and burned it. Often it happened that the work had to be done again for as fast as we destroyed their storehouses the Russians rebuilt and refilled them; yet no sooner was this done than they were again attacked and reduced to ashes.[60]

Since most of Osborn's steam squadron was then dispatched southwards into the strait for the final series of operations in that region (see below, p. 127ff.) it was not until late August and September that renewed patrolling revealed the existence of rebuilt or new installations around the Azoff coast and the round of landings and destruction began again. No one can claim that the Azoff squadron was not active! At the end of August, the *Ardent*, *Weser* and *Cracker* under Commander William Horton destroyed stocks of forage near Arabat[61] and *Recruit* under Lieutenant George F. Day, with *Fancy* and *Curlew*, rounded the Berutch Spit and on 1 September destroyed what he called 'immense quantities of forage' at Kiril on the south side of the Ouliouk *liman*.[62] Meanwhile, Captain Osborn, with *Vesuvius*, *Grinder* and *Wrangler* patrolled off Mariaupol and towards the estuary of the Don; he found Taganrog strongly fortified and *Grinder* was fired on as she approached. It was during operations on 31 August at Lyapina near Mariaupol that one un-fortunate incident occurred. Lieutenant Hugh Burgoyne of *Wrangler* landed men to destroy large quantities of corn and forage, which was successfully achieved, but during the action three of his men were captured by the Russians – Mate Charles Odevaine, Bosun Joseph Kellaway[63] and Able Seaman Robert Thirston.[64]

Despite the fact that the siege of Sebastopol was clearly coming to an end – concluded with the fall of the city after the assault on 8 September and the Russian evacuation, operations elsewhere would continue. September and

October saw a continuing round of attacks in the Sea of Azoff to destroy stores ashore; Rear Admiral Lyons was able to report that 'the squadron in the Sea of Azoff maintains its wonted activity in harassing the enemy, notwithstanding the remarkably bad weather which they have encountered during nearly the whole of the summer'.[65] In mid-September Lieutenant Day of *Recruit*, accompanied by *Curlew* and *Fancy*, sailed from Genitichi to reconnoitre the northern mouths of the Don, where he found large numbers of Russians working on the shoreline defences and a number of small 'row gun boats' and schooners. Determined to attack them, he had to wait off Taganrog for a sudden squall of rough weather to abate and when on 13 September he set off to round Otchakov Spit, he had only a disappointing time; he found that the boats had gone (scattered into the shallow waters of the Don) and the second target, hay stores near Stanits, were unassailable because of the shallow water.

Meanwhile, only a few incidents enlivened the life of the garrison left at Kertch. The largest took place on 17 September, when a cavalry skirmish occurred about 15 miles from the town, in which the French *Chasseurs d'Afrique* and part of the British 10th Hussars routed a body of Cossacks who were trying to remove all the wagons in the neighbourhood. On the 24th, part of Osborn's steam squadron was temporarily removed from the Sea of Azoff – *Lynx*, *Snake*, *Arrow* and *Harpy*, with nine French gunboats. They embarked at Kertch three companies of the 71st Highland Light Infantry and six companies of French infantry, bound for the Russian military centre of Taman, on the opposite shore of Kertch Strait. The troops landed just east of Fanagoria[66] on the south coast of the Bay of Taman, covered by the fire of the gunboats directed against a body of cavalry. They found that Fanagoria had been evacuated and after dispersing about 600 Cossacks, occupied the fort and its buildings. The capture proved to be of little value, as the buildings – a hospital, two magazines and some storehouses – were nearly empty, and sixty-six pieces of artillery had been rendered unserviceable before the Russians left them. Taman was found to be equally deserted, with anything of value removed or destroyed. Although the possession of Fanagoria gave the Allies control of the Taman Peninsula, it was not thought necessary to retain the place; the troops destroyed the few buildings and returned to Kertch on 3 October, taking with them the wood of the destroyed buildings for use as fuel.[67]

It was arranged that whilst operations were in progress at Taman and Fanagoria, the recently promoted Captain Osborn would make an attack on Temriouk – these three fortified posts being the only places of any importance on the Taman Peninsula. Captain Robert Hall of the *Miranda* and Captain Bonet of the *Pomone* led the naval element whilst Major Hunter of the 71st HLI commanded the British troops, 300 in number, the French force comprising about 600 marines under Captain Dill. On 23 September, Osborn proceeded towards Temriouk with *Vesuvius*, *Curlew*, *Ardent*, *Wrangler*, *Beagle*, *Fancy*, *Grinder* and *Cracker* and was joined at daybreak on the 24th by the French steamers *Milan*, *Caton* and *Fulton* under Captain de Cintré. The water was so shallow that not even the armed boats could reach the town and as there was a large body of Russian cavalry and infantry nearby, with some guns, the attack was called off. Osborn then tried to cut off communication between Temriouk and Taman and succeeded by destroying a bridge which crossed the channel connecting the Sea of Azoff with Temriouk Lake and prevented the 2,000-strong garrison of the town from coming to the relief of Taman and Fanagoria.

Returning into the Sea of Azoff after these operations in the strait, Osborn took *Vesuvius*, *Curlew*, *Recruit* and *Ardent* northwards to Bieloserai Spit, where the Russians had placed a considerable force in the ruins of the old fishing establishments, digging rifle pits and constructing breastworks. On 15 October, *Recruit* destroyed seven boats and five fishery stations there, but could not dislodge the riflemen who kept up a heavy fire. On the 20th, the *Ardent* went further east to Krivaia, or 'Crooked Spit', and destroyed another three boats, despite the opposition of a large body of cavalry. *Vesuvius*, struggling against bad weather and in very shallow water, approached the Bieloserai Spit on the 24th, and Osborn shelled the riflemen from their pits, effected a landing, and destroyed the barracks, a fishery and eleven small boats. That same day, *Recruit*, in the neighbourhood of Mariaupol, destroyed two large fisheries and several launches mounted on land carriages. And so it continued.

There were those who criticised the destruction of fisheries and fishing tackle as being unworthy acts of war really directed against poor local fishermen, but since huge quantities of dried fish were known to be sent to or intended for the Sebastopol army, their destruction inevitably followed. Captain Osborn, in one dispatch to Sir Edmund Lyons, said:

> The extraordinary efforts made by the enemy to prosecute their fisheries upon this coast are the best proof of their importance. They sometimes move down 200 or 300 soldiers, who escort large launches placed upon carriages and arabas [wagons] drawn by oxen laden with nets and gear, as well as fishermen to work them. The fish, directly they are caught, are carted off into the interior; and when it is remembered that we have destroyed over 100 launches upon one spit alone, some idea can be formed of the immense quantity of fish caught and consumed on this coast; and in proof of its being a large item in the sustenance of Russian soldiers, hundreds of tons of salted and dried fish were found and destroyed by us in the first destruction of the military depots at Genitchi in May last.[68]

Whilst Captain Osborn was engaged on the northern coast of the Sea of Azoff, Lieutenant Commerell of the gunboat *Weser*, succeeded in crossing the Spit of Arabat, entering the 'Putrid Sea' and executing an extraordinary and dangerous feat that was to win him the Victoria Cross.[69] He found out that large quantities of corn and forage were stored on the banks of the rivers Karasu and Salghir, which entered the western (Crimean) side of the 'Putrid Sea' and whose mouths lay opposite the centre of the spit. Although a Russian guard house and signal station were close by, he decided to attempt the destruction of the stores. At 4.00am on 11 October, Commerell, accompanied by only four others, Mate N.D. Lillingstone, Quartermaster William Rickard and Seamen Milestone and Hoskins, manhandled a cutter across the sandy spit and launched it on the exceptionally shallow waters of the 'Putrid Sea' to get to the rivers. Leaving Lillingstone and Hoskins to guard the boat, the three others forded both rivers, walked over 2 miles in the dark to reach the corn and hay and at daybreak set fire to it all, destroying about 400 tons. Not surprisingly, the twenty or thirty Cossacks camped as guards in a nearby village soon reacted and gave chase. The retreating party was so hard pressed that, but for the fact that the last 200 yards were over deep mud where the cavalry could not go, and the cover of rifle fire from Mate Lillingstone and Seaman Hoskins, guarding the boat, they would never have escaped. Having re-crossed the spit, they returned to the *Weser* that morning. The conduct of William Rickard, Quartermaster of *Weser*, was highly commended; he went back under heavy fire to assist the exhausted Milestone who had collapsed in the mud and was unable to free himself.

Early in November, Captain Osborn again disturbed the collection of stores and provisions for the Russian army. Sir Edmund Lyons had learned that the enemy were accumulating large quantities at and around Gheisk, intended to be transported over the ice and frozen snow during the winter to the neighbourhood of Sebastopol. He therefore sent back to the Sea of Azoff several of Osborn's gunboats which had been detached from his squadron for the attack on Kinburn and Osborn, duly reinforced, at once steamed for Gheisk, near the eastern end of the sea. On 3 November, leaving the *Vesuvius, Weser, Curlew* and *Ardent* standing offshore, Osborn entered the bay with his ships' boats and the gunboats *Recruit, Boxer, Cracker* and *Clinker*. In quick time, the landing parties burned stacks of newly harvested corn, hay and fuel; in this, as on other occasions, the ships fired 'carcasses' – incendiary shells – into the corn ricks lying near the shore and stretching for a distance of 4 miles around Vodina and Glofira. The quantities were immense and as they were guarded by Cossacks and infantry the burning did not take place without a fight, in which lives were lost on both sides. A new entrenchment, designed to defend the town, was also shelled during the operations. On 6 November, the same squadron 'visited' Gheisk itself, where enormous haystacks were seen. For once, a considerable fight ensued when the 200 men, mainly marines, landed at different points and were opposed by 3,000 Cossacks and other Russian troops defending the place. Nevertheless, Osborn did not retire until the destruction had been accomplished. The quantity of stores destroyed was so great that none of the British naval officers could even estimate the amount. Osborn wrote to Sir Edmund Lyons:

> I despair of being able to convey to you any idea of the extraordinary quantity of corn, rye, hay, wood and other supplies, so necessary for the existence of the Russian armies both in the Caucasus and in the Crimea, which it has been our good fortune to destroy. That these vast stores should have been collected here so close to the sea while we were in the neighbourhood is only to be accounted for by their supposing that they could not be reached by us.[70]

Later in the month, Captain Osborn, whose ships had now been very actively engaged in the Sea of Azoff for six months, found that severe winds, frequent fogs and the appearance of ice warned of the onset of winter. The time was clearly approaching when active operations would not be possible. Various ships, nevertheless, kept up their harrying work over the course of November, *Recruit* in particular being very active in attacking and destroying shipping off the 'Crooked Spit', off White House Spit and at Mariaupol. As a final act of the campaigning 'season', Osborn carried out one last grand 'sweep' and reconnoitred once again the ports of Mariaupol, Taganrog, Berdiansk, Gheisk, Genitchi and others, to confirm that Russian trade had indeed ceased for the winter;[71] he then took his squadron back to Kertch having brought to a conclusion the most completely successful series of naval operations in the whole war.[72] Admiral Lyons reported to the Admiralty on 24 November:

> As the ice is now forming on the shores of the Sea of Azoff and the squadron is withdrawn, I feel it is to be due to Captain Osborn to record that under circumstances of great difficulty, occasioned by unusually tempestuous weather, he had most ably continued through the summer and brought to a successful close in the autumn operations novel in their nature and extremely detrimental to the enemy, which commenced auspiciously in the spring under the direction of the late Captain Lyons of the *Miranda*, nor is it too much to say that both commanding officers were supported throughout by as dashing and intelligent a band of young officers, seamen and marines, as ever shone in the British navy.[73]

The whole Azoff expedition had been a resounding success in terms of the destruction of enemy shipping, foodstuffs and stores. Important Russian supply lines to their armies in the Crimea and the Caucasus had been severely disrupted and although no great naval engagement had taken place and no ports or forts occupied, the economic damage had been truly stupendous. The hinterland of the Sea of Azoff must have suffered long after the allied fleet withdrew.

Chapter 9

Black Sea, 1855 and the Attack on Fort Kinburn

The formal blockade of the Black Sea was announced on 1 February 1855.[1] Although the Russians had sensibly abandoned a number of remote military bases along or near the eastern coast which were incapable of being supported by land (their navy, of course, being scuttled or trapped in Sebastopol), they still defended the more significant towns of Anapa and Soujak Kaleh on the Circassian coast. Since their capture would not really achieve anything – and they continued to bottle up Russian forces – it was initially decided simply to 'watch' these ports rather than to attack them. Nevertheless, on several occasions between 20 and 24 February 1855, the paddle-steamer *Leopard* under Captain George Giffard attacked Russian troops moving along the coast near Anapa, landing parties that captured some of their guns, and destroyed nearby buildings. Similarly, on 8 March the 4-gun steamer *Viper* under Lieutenant William Armytage landed men to destroy a fort[2] and barracks at Djemetil near Anapa. A more serious effort was made on 13 March when *Leopard*, *Viper*, *Highflyer*, *Swallow* and the French *Fulton* joined in a direct attack on the defences of Soujak Kaleh, though without adequate landing parties their bombardment was little more than a gesture. It was hoped that local Circassian chiefs would be encouraged to rise up against their Russian overlords and there was indeed talk of the Circassians joining in with attacks on Russian coastal bases like Soujak Kaleh, but in the end, little materialised.[3]

Throughout the spring and summer of 1855, the siege of Sebastopol continued, with the Naval Brigade of nearly 1,000 men and the Royal Marine battalions continuing their support of the land operations (see Chapter 4); the naval guns, for example, shelled the Mamelon on 18 March. But apart from the continuing work of ferrying troops, dispatches and supplies across the Black Sea from the Bosphorus, and the campaign waged in the Sea of Azoff, purely naval operations around the fringes of the Black Sea during the summer of 1855 were necessarily few. The allies were determined to range around its coasts as in every other region, but found little to give them any serious trouble or occupation. On 28 May the Russians finally evacuated the isolated coastal town of Soujak Kaleh after destroying all the main buildings, sixty guns and six mortars so that 'the place is now a mere mass of ruins'.[4] More important still, the Russians evacuated Anapa itself on 5 June. The allies had been anxious that such an important location on the main trade routes should not remain in the hands of the Russians, so Rear Admirals Stewart and Charnier directed their attention to the town and its fortifications, intending to launch a land attack under Generals Brown and d'Autemarre, if necessary. But the Russians saved them the effort by completely abandoning the port after exploding the powder magazines, disabling most of the guns and burning the barracks, granaries and coal stores. The defences had been remarkably strong, with fifteen mortars, twenty-one howitzers and eighty 'long guns', which could have maintained a formidable fire against any attacking force. The garrison of no less than 8,000 men retired across the River Kuban, a withdrawal forced by the inability of the Russian military to support or supply their garrison in the face of the allied actions in the Sea of Azoff.

Further to the north and west, the town of Eupatoria, on the coast 40 miles north of Sebastopol, was strongly fortified by the allies. It had been reconnoitred as a possible landing place as early as 28 April 1854 and when the allies landed in Kalamita Bay a force was detached to hold Eupatoria at the same time, in case a base for operations further north was needed. The port surrendered without opposition, since it had no Russian garrison and no fortifications and on 15 September, *Retribution* and *Valorous* were sent to take possession, followed by a detachment of 400 marines under Captain S.W. Brock of *Britannia*. Brock's first task was to construct a basic defence line around the perimeter of the straggling town, linking strong buildings and houses with lines of sandbags and breastworks and defended by ditches. From the start, Eupatoria was blockaded by the Russians, who maintained a sizeable force around the port and as early as 19 September 1854 and again on 12 October it was indeed attacked by Cossacks, who were driven off by Captain Brock. Shortly afterwards, HMS *Leander* arrived, landing 100 of her crew, soon joined by 500 French and Turkish marines to reinforce the garrison. Later, 2,000 Turks, supported by British and French infantry were placed in occupation under a French governor and Turkish forces continued to be built up until over 25,000 were in garrison there.[5]

The prime function of an allied army based at Eupatoria would be to block Russian supply and reinforcement routes to or from Sebastopol via Simferopol or across the Isthmus of Perekop into southern Russia. The problem was the relative isolation of Eupatoria and the Russians, well aware of the threat posed by a large allied force along their main routes to the north and south, were not slow to probe the defences. Several clashes took place, so that at various times British and French warships were stationed offshore to offer additional firepower if the town was seriously threatened.[6] The Russian retreat in the Balkans had enabled the redeployment of much of the Turkish army to Sebastopol and Eupatoria[7] so that Eupatoria became a major Turkish base when a large force arrived there under their commander-in-chief, Omar Pasha[8] and the number of allied warships there was gradually reduced as the Turks took the burden of the defence. A Balkan Croat turned Turkish Muslim, Omar Pasha was a highly regarded commander, who became internationally famous as the defender of Silistria in the recent fighting in the Balkans. The Turks had already driven off a Russian attack in October 1854 and did so again following the great hurricane of 14 November (see above, pp. 67–8). During the storm, serious damage was done to transports and warships moored nearby, including the grounding of two French warships *Henri IV* and *Pluton* and the Russians, quick to take advantage of the disarray caused by the storm, launched an attack on the town. For over an hour 10,000 troops attacked the outer defences but were driven off by the Turkish garrison aided by naval rockets and by the gunfire of the grounded warships that managed to bring their guns into action.[9]

During the spring of 1855, there were repeated rumours of a pending Russian attack on the place since it was so isolated from the allied force besieging Sebastopol and equally from supplies of food and ammunition. The greatest attack – a considerable but now forgotten Crimean action – came on 17 February 1855 when a Russian force of up to 20,000 men with heavy artillery under General Khrouleff was launched against the Turkish defences after a heavy artillery bombardment. The gunfire of British ships under Captain Hon. G.F. Hastings – *Curacao, Furious, Valorous* and *Viper*, aided by the French steamer *Véloce* and the Turkish *Schefer*, helped the Turkish garrison once again to repel the Russian attack. The ships were able to move from point to point to support any threatened area and coming in close to the shore could bring their powerful broadsides to bear on the attackers. The battle lasted from dawn until 10.30am, by which time the Russians had been forced to withdraw having suffered 800 casualties in several attempts to storm the perimeter defences.[10]

That was the last attack launched against Eupatoria and little else happened to disturb the peace there (where the large Turkish army stagnated through the summer).[11] Once Sebastopol had been evacuated in September 1855 – which of course did not bring an end to the war itself – there was some talk amongst the allies of continuing operations inland using Eupatoria as a base but the peace treaty in 1856 ended hostilities before anything had been planned.

Following the fall of Sebastopol in September 1855, with the final destruction of its magnificent docks[12] and the remains of the Russian Black Sea Fleet, the Naval Brigade was rapidly re-embarked, the Royal Marines leaving only a few weeks later. The Admiralty had on several occasions expressed its disquiet with the fact that so many men and guns had been removed from its ships (rendering them 'inefficient' as a naval force)[13] so that now the Naval Brigade's immediate role ashore was over, they were very quickly restored to the fleet. Within a matter of days, the naval contingents were marched down to Balaklava harbour, and to the accompaniment of regimental bands and the resounding cheers of soldiers drawn up in their honour, boarded their ships and sailed away.[14]

But although allied naval domination of the Black Sea was long ago secured, the high command considered one further naval objective in the Black Sea as a possible preliminary to further land operations against Russia. This was planning for an 1856 campaign season beyond the Crimea and as part of that planning what turned out to be the last significant naval operation of the Russian War was launched – the allied fleet's attack on the fortress of Kinburn.[15]

Kinburn lay about 40 miles east of Odessa and 150 miles northwest of Sebastopol, where the Dnieper enters the Black Sea. It guarded the entry to Kherson Bay, the bay or *liman* of the Dnieper and the southern approaches to the important towns of Kherson and Nikolaev. Technically, the allies' ultimate goal was Nikolaev.[16] Standing 25 miles upriver on the Bug as it made its way into the Dnieper, Nikolaev was important for its arsenal and large naval dock-yards, where most of Russia's Black Sea warships were built. The area had already come under attention in the early days of the war in October 1854 when Russian reinforcements heading for the Crimea from the Nikolaev area had been seen by *Sidon* (watching Odessa) and had been shelled near Otchakov by the French steamers *Cacique* and *Caton* as they tried to cross the bay. After Odessa, which had remained undisturbed since the bombardment on 22 April 1854 at the beginning of the war,[17] Nikolaev was an obvious point of attack for an allied force anxious to further damage Russian interests in the hinterland of the Black Sea and impede the movement of troops and supplies. It was also conceivable that in 1856 the town and area would form the base for further land operations.

The fortress of Kinburn, and its nearby village, was built on the western end of a long, low-lying and desolate sandy spit, stretching westwards from the coast. It dominated the southern access to the bay of the Dnieper, whose shallow waters were known for their dangerous sandbanks and shoals. Opposite on the mainland stood the small town of Otchakov whose batteries (especially the nearby Fort Nikolaev) guarded the northern approaches to of the bay. Kinburn's defences comprised a large stone-built citadel dominating the spit, supported by 2 smaller earthwork batteries to the west, which themselves mounted 12 and 20 guns. The main fort was a solid stone structure with case-mated embrasures mounting 55 guns and mortars, additionally protected by an earth parapet 15 feet thick and a wet moat. The entire defence force under

Major General Kokonovitch was about 1,500 men and the total armament on the spit was reported to comprise 80 guns and 20 mortars, though not all of these seem to have been in place at the time of the allied attack in October 1855.

On this occasion, nothing was left to chance; this was going to be an expeditionary force that would be capable not only of destroying the forts from the sea, but also of landing and occupying the site and possibly even operating further inland. A British and French infantry force of over 9,000 men, the British element of about 4,000 troops under Brigadier General Hon. A. Spencer[18] and the French under General Achille Bazaine, was taken aboard the chosen ships and sizeable contingents of engineers and artillery accompanied the force. The major British warships selected for the expedition were *Royal Albert*, *Algiers*, *Hannibal*, *Sidon*, *Princess Royal*, *St Jean d'Acre* and *Arabia*, with a large flotilla of smaller frigates, gunboats and mortar vessels amounting in total to no fewer than fifty-two warships, transports and tenders, the majority of them steam powered. The French squadron was equally powerful and included the *Montebello*, *Ulm*, *Jean Bart* and *Wagram*, with smaller gunboats. The French contingent aroused great interest because of the presence of three brand-new types of warship which had just arrived from France – the iron-armoured 'floating batteries' *Dévastation*, *Lave* and *Tonnante*. Napoleon III was apparently concerned at the losses suffered by French warships during the bombardment of the Sebastopol harbour forts and pressed for the development of a new type of ship that would be heavily armoured and could withstand a close-range pounding. The result was the rapid construction of these 3 flat-bottomed vessels each of 1,400 tons, armoured with 4½-inch iron plates, with a crew of 320 and mounting 30 guns in 2 broadsides.[19] Intended for use against Sebastopol, they had arrived just too late to be of any value and so were directed to join the Kinburn expedition, where these revolutionary vessels would be used in action for the first time.[20]

After several days anchored in Kamiesch and Kazatch bays waiting for the weather to clear, the attack force set sail on 6 and 7 October 1855. The rendezvous point for the fleet was just off Odessa – which caused wild alarm there as the warships passed close to her shores and anchored within sight of the city on 8 October. The combined fleet of over eighty ships anchored off the coast, remaining there for six days; it has been suggested that this was to draw Russian forces away from the Kinburn, Nicolaev and the coastal area (in preparation for the possible defence of Odessa) but it seems to have been more to do with severe weather and the need to send survey vessels to sound the channels around Kinburn.[21] This surveying and the delay in setting off to attack the forts naturally gave the Russians time to strengthen the defences of what was clearly the intended target.

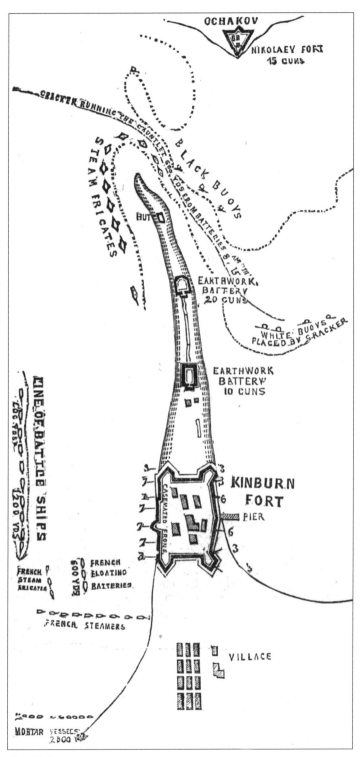

Fort Kinburn.

Command of the naval operation lay with Vice Admiral Bruat (leading the French squadron),[22] with Sir Edmund Lyons himself and his second-in-command Rear Admiral Sir Houston Stewart.[23] Their plan was to deploy the major line-of-battle ships at a range of 1,000–1,400 yards to bombard the main citadel on Kinburn spit and engage the two low sand-bar forts. The mortar vessels and gunboats, anchored further off, would join the bombardment and other elements of the fleet like the smaller frigates would actually enter the bay and engage the forts from the north. Once the defences had been destroyed or silenced, the Anglo-French landing force would occupy what was left.

The first moves were made on 14 October when the gunboats *Fancy*, *Boxer*, *Cracker* and *Clinker*, with the French *Tirailleuse*, *Stridente*, *Mutine* and *Meurtrière* entered the estuary. They were fired on from both Kinburn and the shore batteries near Otchakov as they passed but without any serious damage being done and, once in place, effectively blockaded the northern shore of the spit, preventing Russian naval forces along the Dnieper and Bug (if there were any) from coming to the aid of Kinburn. On the 15th, French troops under General Bazaine and British infantry under Brigadier General Spencer were landed under the protection of the gunboats on the spit 3 miles east of the fort and, having marched within closer range, began to dig-in 400 yards away from it, so that the defenders of Kinburn were effectively isolated by land and sea.

The mortar boats began with a brief bombardment on the 15th, recorded by Edmund Cree aboard *Odin*:

> About 2.00pm our mortar vessels opened fire, in which we joined with our long 64s, throwing shot and shell into the fort, which they returned in a plucky manner, although their range was indifferent, their shot dropping short or going over, except for one shot which destroyed the boat of the mortar-vessel *Camel*. Most of our 13-inch shells fell – burst – inside the large fort and must have done immense damage, but the enemy would not give in, although they must have seen how useless was their resistance to such an overwhelming force as we brought against them. One of their storehouses in the fort was ablaze and as they saw our troops advancing against them on the land side they set fire to the village outside the fort.[24]

However, apart from ranging shots and minor exchanges of fire on the 16th, bad weather and heavy seas interrupted the planned assault until 17 October – fortuitously the anniversary of the first major bombardment of Sebastopol a year earlier. It was to be the first naval operation fought entirely by steam vessels and the first use of iron-armoured warships in action in the form of the three French 'floating batteries'. Not surprisingly, it was completely successful, as it should have been given the size of the forces involved. The chosen warships were in bombarding positions south of the main fort by 9.00am and under Rear Admiral Stewart and his French counterpart Rear Admiral Odet Pellion a heavy fire was directed against the defenders from a formidable naval force: *Valorous, Gladiator, Odin, Arrow, Viper, Lynx, Beagle, Snake* and *Wrangler* and the mortar boats[25] *Raven, Magnet, Camel, Hardy, Flamer* and *Firm*. They were supported by French vessels, including the new armoured floating batteries *Dévastation, Lave* and *Tonnante*, noted by Cree as 'great square looking iron boxes ... crawling up slowly against the large fort'.[26]

At noon, as the Russian fire slackened, Sir Houston Stewart moved his own squadron, augmented by *Firebrand, Furious, Sidon, Leopard, Stromboli, Spiteful* and *Gladiator* and supported by the French ships *Asmodée, Cacique* and *Sané*, through the channel between Otchakov and Kinburn to join the ships already there and engaged the north side of the fort from the shallow waters of Dnieper Bay. This mighty armament continued to batter the main fort and the sandbank batteries from the north, receiving heavy fire in return from the determined and gallant Russian defenders.

When Stewart's powerful force went into action to the north of the spit, the larger line-of-battle ships under the direct command of Sir Edmund Lyons, including *Royal Albert, Algiers, Agamemnon* and *Princess Royal*, with four French ships, continued the shelling of the main fort from the south. In addition, *Curacao, St Jean d'Acre, Tribune* and *Sphinx* bombarded the larger earthwork battery and *Hannibal, Dauntless* and *Terrible* the smaller one on the western end of the spit. Many of the larger warships, operating in shallow water from closer in, suffered numerous hits and sustained minor damage, but casualties were remarkably light with only two men wounded in the entire British fleet.[27] Nevertheless, it was the mortar vessels anchored to the south of the forts, operating at greater range but lobbing high-angle shots, supported by the gunboats and the new French floating batteries,[28] which were especially effective in reducing the stone fort. It was another example of the fact that large wooden warships could indeed take on coastal defences but, having to come in much closer, were put at greater risk than the mortar vessels and gunboats, which could effectively pound an enemy at longer ranges, doing the job without the casualties.[29]

Firing was continuous from 9.30am. After midday, the combined bombardment from two sides had set the buildings within the fort complex ablaze and large sections of its defensive works had been reduced to rubble, the fire from the heavy guns bringing 'down the outer wall of the fort in cartloads [and] crumbling away the wall by tons'.[30] On land, the military forces had little to do – other than keep away from the bombardment. There was some shelling of the forts by the artillery and long-range rifle fire against the Russian battery crews, but to little useful effect compared with the damage being wrought by the ferocious naval attack.[31]

Kinburn was no Sebastopol or Cronstadt or Sveaborg and the surrender of the fort and outlying batteries was inevitable. The Russians had put up a gallant resistance under terrible fire, much admired by their enemy but 'their resistance to such an overwhelming force' could not be long maintained. Rear Admiral Lyons, anxious that no more casualties should occur once the main works were clearly beyond defence, was anxious to offer terms to the defenders. Under flag of truce, he sent a request for the surrender of the governor and garrison. There seems initially to have been real opposition on the part of some of the Russians to the idea of a humiliating surrender after such a staunch defence. The governor, Major General Kokonovitch, personally went out to meet Generals Spencer and Bazaine and, albeit with a sense of deep humiliation, agreed to surrender his forts and the garrisons. Somewhat to their disgust, and without being able to further disarm their own guns, over 1,400 Russians were marched out to lay down their arms;[32] most were handed to the British authorities and put aboard HMS *Vulcan*, whilst others were removed by French warships and all were sent as prisoners to Constantinople. Estimates of the Russian casualties vary widely, depending on source, from 45 to 200 killed during the bombardment and 130 to 400 wounded,[33] many of whom were later tended by naval or army surgeons with the allied forces. George Tryon, by then Lieutenant of *Royal Albert*, 'was sent ashore directly the place surrendered, in charge of the fire-parties of the fleet. We isolated the buildings on fire and let them burn out quietly',[34] whilst Edmund Cree, eager as ever to get ashore to look around, recorded: 'We landed at the second spit battery and then walked to the main fort to examine the destruction there. All in ruin, as bad as Sebastopol on a smaller scale; scarcely a gun remained serviceable, some capsized and broken, their carriages smashed, scarcely a square yard untouched by shot and shell.'[35] No fewer than 174 pieces of artillery – many of them unmounted but being prepared for use – and large stores of ammunition were captured with the forts. One side-effect of the successful destruction of the Kinburn defences was that the headland Fort Nikolaev and batteries across the estuary at Otchakov, which had kept up a long-range but largely ineffective fire against the warships on that side, were destroyed by their own defenders and abandoned on 18 October.

What to do next? Lieutenant Tryon wrote home from Kinburn that:

> I cannot learn we are likely to follow up our success. We are certainly carrying on the war in a sleepy manner. I suppose this success at Kinburn has opened to us one hundred miles of water as yet

unexplored, over which supplies for the Crimea have been transported, and here we are with the door open and have already given
them four days to remove their vessels to a place of safety.[36]

The obvious reason for the attack on Kinburn (and a probable attack on
Otchakov if necessary) was indeed to free the Dnieper estuary for operations
further upriver towards or against Nikolaev. It was already known that sizeable
Russian forces had been assembled in the area, initially intended for the
defence of Kinburn and to protect the large regional centre of Kherson, and
that they were relatively safe from anything other than a major military
landing. On 20 October, Sir Houston Stewart took a flotilla of the lighter
vessels, British and French, into the Dnieper to reconnoitre as far as its
confluence with the River Bug. *Stromboli*, *Spiteful*, *Grinder* and *Cracker* were
sent further north towards Nikolaev, the river passing through fairly empty
and desolate steppe land, until they were eventually halted by fire from Russian
batteries, with which they exchanged shots. The British ships then returned to
the estuary and on the next day, 21 October, French gunboats made the same
journey and exchanged fire with the same battery. These two reconnaissances
showed that the Russians had taken the possibility of allied action into the
Bug very seriously and had begun to reinforce and strengthen their defences
across the region; they were not only defending the river approaches but were
also building other defences and Cossack units were burning farms and even
villages in the vicinity, presumably in expectation of an allied land assault.[37]

Although the destruction of Kinburn offered a late 'victory' in the Russian
War, gladly welcomed by public opinion in Britain, it was clearly meant to
herald greater things.[38] In Kinburn itself, as it had been decided to garrison the
spit and leave a strong military force there over the winter of 1855, the land
forces were put to repairing the defences. On 18 and 19 October General
Bazaine took over 4,000 French troops, with some British artillery, northwards
towards Paksoffka in a sort of 'reconnaissance in force', but, like the ships that
patrolled upriver, he met with nothing but poor villages, which, if they had not
already been burned by the Cossacks, were destroyed by the French. Russian
cavalry skirted and watched Bazaine's force but no engagement took place and
he returned to Kinburn.

Nothing much more than the river reconnaissance was done by the formidable naval force that had been deployed; it was found that the shallow waters
and the huge sandbanks and shoals really made a military landing from the
ships unsafe, since they would not be able to offer effective close support and
Russian military force in the area was clearly being increased day by day.
Desultory operations in the Dnieper estuary devolved into a miniature version
of the exploits already seen in the Baltic and Sea of Azoff – light warships

ranged around the estuary and coastline looking for targets. The most significant achievement – if it can be called that – came when *Stromboli*, *Triton*, *Wrangler* and *Snake* intercepted and seized huge rafts of timber intended for the dockyards at Nikolaev.

All in all, the capture and destruction of Kinburn was a small victory for so much effort – and after arousing such large expectations, since it clearly hinted at a major land offensive beyond the Crimean Peninsula. Public and press opinion in Britain, as so often before during this war, seriously questioned the whole project and criticised the plan and its execution. On 27 October preparations for a large-scale withdrawal began; as many men as could be housed in the repaired and re-armed fort complex would be left to winter over – a fairly depressing prospect for them – whilst a small squadron of warships would remain on station to protect the garrison from attack across the estuary. By the first days of November, as ice began to form in the shallow waters, the bulk of the allied fleet had sailed for Kazatch Bay and the French garrison of 1,800 men settled down to face a cold and dismal winter – awaiting a renewed campaign in the spring of 1856?

By this time, all hope of further operations from the Crimea, military or naval, seem to have ended and the break up of the allied fleets soon began. Many ships had been on station off the Crimea or in the Black Sea since the earliest days of the war in 1854. In November, *Agamemnon* and *Algiers* were ordered to Malta and shortly afterwards Sir Houston Stewart led *Hannibal*, *Princess Royal*, *St Jean d'Acre* and *Sphinx* out of the Black Sea, through the Bosphorus and towards the Ionian Islands. Most of the other ships, excepting some retained on station in the Black Sea,[39] gradually made their way back to Constantinople, heading ultimately for the Mediterranean Fleet anchorage in Malta or for home ports.

Where would the allies strike next? An allied council of war met in Paris in the spring of 1856 to consider further military action – north from Sebastopol (possibly from Eupatoria)? In the Odessa or Dnieper region? From Kaffa Bay? Along the Circassian coast or further east? Or was the Baltic to be the key point for a campaign in 1856, with the possibility of an actual attack on Cronstadt and even St Petersburg?[40] In the end, whatever allied strategic planning considered, no further military or naval action was necessary; the Russians came to the negotiating table and in March 1856 a peace treaty was finally concluded in Paris.

Conclusion

The fall of Sebastopol in September 1855 was by no means as conclusive an action as it may appear when judged through the eyes of many modern histories of the war. The allies had, in fact, captured only the southern half of the bay and the port, although this did render the rest of Sebastopol untenable and forced its evacuation. One great Anglo-French goal, the destruction of Russia's Black Sea naval base and fleet, had at least been accomplished. But this was simply one limited victory and much more would be required to bring the huge Russian Empire to its knees. The land campaign in the Crimea, difficult and damaging as it was, did not win or end the Russian War and the loss of Sebastopol did not lead to a Russian collapse; it was after all only one city, no matter how significant the port or embarrassing the loss. And where could the allied army go next to continue the land campaign? From the viewpoint of manpower, supply and resources, a march from the Crimea into southern Russia seemed to be out of the question,[1] whilst the operations against Kinburn seemed to presage a further land campaign northwards from the Dnieper estuary. Was either logistically possible?

Given the amount of time and effort that had gone into taking Sebastopol, the port was perhaps the logical base for continued land operations in 1856 but plans for a new campaign moving inland towards Perekop and perhaps into southern Russia were never formalised. Similarly, although a possible inland advance from the Turkish base at Eupatoria was considered by an allied council of war in Paris in January 1856, nothing was agreed and the same is true for potential operations inland from the Dnieper estuary following the fall of Kinburn. The fact of the matter is that any major land operations in 1856 would have presented enormous problems for the allies in terms of manpower, supply, security and movement. In fact, given the logistical problems these operations presented, a renewed and more determined naval campaign in the Baltic was a much more obvious option. This could employ the expanded and remodelled British fleet[2] to tackle Cronstadt (and the attack on Sveaborg in 1855 had shown that such fortresses could be challenged by the right combination of naval power) and would threaten St Petersburg itself. It would, of course, require a powerful army, presumably provided largely by France, but offered at least one way to threaten Russia more directly; an attack on

St Petersburg would damage Russia much more than distant operations in the southern Crimea, Azoff, the White Sea or the Pacific. There is, however, little evidence that plans for a renewed Baltic campaign were ever fully formulated for 1856.

As the new year dawned, there were some hopes that Sweden and Austria would openly side with the allies and that Poland (and even perhaps Finland) would rise in revolt against Russia – an alarming thought for the Russian government and one that they had had to keep in mind throughout the war.[3] Tsar Alexander II was not anxious to begin his reign with the threat of internal revolt or in the midst of a possibly escalating European war, which, as it seemed, Russia could not win. By the spring of 1856 he was more receptive to the idea of a peace settlement and more responsive to the intense diplomatic pressure that the European powers were exerting. In the end it was really the international pressure put on Russia, not least by Austria and Prussia, that forced the Tsar's government to the negotiating table in Paris in February 1856.

Although discussions on the finer points of a settlement continued into April, the war was formally ended by the Treaty of Paris on 30 March 1856. Amongst its terms were freedom of navigation on the Danube (whose lower reaches were formally ceded to Turkey) and Russian abandonment of claims over the Danubian Provinces and for a protectorate over the Turkish Christians. More importantly from the point of view of Franco-British strategic concerns, the treaty imposed the demilitarisation of the Åland Islands[4] and, most significantly, of the Black Sea itself, allowing Russia no major warships or fortifications in its waters or on its shores. These 'Black Sea Clauses' were famously repudiated by Tsar Alexander in 1870 when Europe was otherwise engaged with the Franco-Prussian War and the French in no position to respond. In fact, the effects of the war on Russia itself seem to have been quickly reversed. Although Bomarsund was never refortified, the defences of Sveaborg were quickly rebuilt,[5] as was Sebastopol and its harbour; one assumes that the coastal and commercial trade of the White Sea, the Baltic and the Sea of Azoff were equally restored in time.

But there were of course other outcomes. For the navies of Britain and France, many lessons had been learned by the experience of the Russian War. It is of course well known that the British army that served through the Crimean War had experienced a wealth of embarrassing and well-publicised failings in just about all aspect of its command, equipment, supply and organisation and was forced to undertake a systematic process of reform which, speeded by the growth of Prussian power, continued into the 1880s. In general, the Royal Navy had shown to much better light in most respects during the war, but it too had serious lessons to learn – not least the provision of an adequate system of manning, training and reserves, the need for accurate charts via surveying and mapping and perhaps the need for a much more professional approach to the management and training of the 'people' and even the officers of the fleet. The warships themselves – and many of their commanders – had performed impressively well. The dominance of steam power over sail, already a demonstrated fact by 1854, was absolutely confirmed by 1856, as was the superiority of screw over paddle. After 1856, major warships were steamers driven by propeller; the day of the centuries-old sailing warship and the more recent paddle-steamer was effectively over. Similarly, although demonstrated only briefly late in the war at Kinburn, the value of armour plating warships was apparent. The three French armoured floating batteries, whatever their defects,[6] had shown that steam warships could be effectively armour plated; the fact was brought home perhaps more forcibly during the American Civil War of 1861–5 by the much-publicised deployment of armoured ships like the *Monitor* and the *Merrimac*. From the 1860s, major new warships were 'iron-clads', propelled by steam-driven screws.

The navies of Britain and France had worked very well in concert during all their joint operations around the globe. The French squadrons generally acted as subordinates to British naval commanders but no animosity seems to have been aroused by this agreed relationship and it is quite evident from surviving personal accounts that both officers and men worked in harmony as allies and indeed in a spirit of friendship. This is perhaps all the more remarkable given the history of Anglo-French naval relationships and the fact that prior to 1854 both nations looked to each other as potential enemies against whom their respective naval armament and strategic policies were directed. Sadly, the end of the Russian War also ended this spirit of cooperation and both countries quickly reverted to their pre-war policy of naval rivalry. Britain's construction of the magnificent and revolutionary HMS *Warrior* in 1860 was proof of how seriously this renewed rivalry was taken – and of Britain's ability to contain the threat posed by French naval developments.

As far as the Royal Navy was concerned, the war of 1854–6 was framed by two great naval assemblies in 1853 and 1856. In August 1853, as the crisis with Russia developed, the Spithead Review had put on display what appeared to be a mighty armament of warships, ranging from the most powerful 'wooden wall' sailing ships ever built to a range of screw and paddle-steamers of the latest design. At a time of international crisis and the threat of war, they were clearly designed to impress on a possible enemy the potential naval strength of Great Britain; most had gone on to serve in the Baltic and some in the Black Sea. Nearly three years later, on St George's Day, 23 April 1856, as part of the nation's victory celebrations, a radically enlarged and very different British fleet was inspected by Queen Victoria. The review was primarily intended to celebrate the victory over Russia and to show the British public what their fleet had become and to celebrate what it had achieved. But it was, of course, no less intended to impress the host of foreign diplomats, guests and reporters who joined the crowds as official and unofficial observers.

Arrayed for the Queen's inspection and public display at Spithead in April 1856 were no less than 240 British warships, including 24 major line-of-battle ships and 19 screw frigates, along with a host of the new, small gun and mortar vessels, many of them veterans of the Baltic, Black Sea and Azoff campaigns. The lines of warships stretched for 6 miles and to add to the spectacle of the occasion, the ships were, for the first time, lit up at night as an element of the display. Their mock attack on Southsea Castle was meant to give some indication of what the ships had actually done at Bomarsund or Sveaborg or even Sebastopol, but in reality the 1856 Review put on display for friend and foe alike the massive naval might that Britain could now assemble against any enemy. She demonstrated to the world that her power at sea was quite simply not to be challenged.

Chronology

1853

31 May	Russian ultimatum to Sultan demanding agreement to claims over the Balkan Christians.
16 June	Turkey rejected Russian demands.
2 July	Russian forces entered the 'Danubian Principalities' of Wallachia and Moldavia.
4 Oct.	Turkey declared war on Russia.
14 Oct.	British and French warships sent into the Dardanelles.
20 Oct.	First fighting in Central Asia – defeat of Russians at Orelle.
1 Nov.	Turkish forces crossed the Danube to engage the Russians.
4 Nov.	Russians defeated at Oltenitza. Turks attacked Giurgevo.
26 Nov.	Turks defeated at Akhaltzik.
27 Nov.	Turks renewed attacks on Giurgevo.
30 Nov.	Ships of the Russian Black Sea Fleet under Admiral Nakhimov destroyed the Turkish squadron at Sinope.
2 Dec.	Russian ships returned to Sebastopol.
24 Dec.	Allied warships ordered into the Black Sea.

1854

Jan.	Turkish actions along the Danube.
3 Jan.	Allied warships entered the Black Sea; returned to the Bosphorus on the 24th.
12 Jan.	Russia officially notified that France and Britain would protect Turkish interests.
2 Feb.	Britain, France, Austria and Prussia agreed to maintain the integrity of the Ottoman Empire.
7 Feb.	Allied ships escorted Turkish forces to Batum and Trebizonde. Allied warships reconnoitred eastern Black Sea coast.
22 Feb.	First contingent of British troops left for Malta.
27 Feb.	France and Britain demanded Russian withdrawal from the Danubian Provinces.

3 March	Russians began to evacuate their smaller garrisons on the Circassian coast of the Black Sea.
4 March	British and French missions to the Tsar demanded withdrawal from the Danubian Provinces.
10 March	Queen Victoria reviewed the Baltic Fleet at Spithead.
11 March	First division of the British fleet sailed for the Baltic under Admiral Napier.
16 March	Second division of British fleet under Admiral Corry sailed for the Baltic.
19 March	Russia rejected Anglo-French demands. British Baltic Fleet united at Wingo Sound.
21 March	British, French and Turkish ships entered Piraeus (Athens) to demand neutrality of Greece. Anglo-French forces at Malta.
23 March	Major Russian army crossed Danube. Successes in the Dobrudscha region.
24 March	The Anglo-French fleet entered Black Sea.
26 March	The Baltic Fleet passed through the Great Belt into the Baltic.
27 March	Britain declared war on Russia; France followed next day.
29 March	The Admiralty ordered ships 'on all stations' to begin 'hostile measures' against Russian shipping and other targets.
31 March	French troops landed at Gallipoli.
1–3 April	Russian defeats in Wallachia.
4 April	British declaration of war read out on ships in the Baltic. Admiral Hanway Plumridge with a 'flying squadron' sent to Gulf of Bothnia.
5 April	First British troops landed in Gallipoli.
8 April	HMS *Furious* fired on whilst under flag of truce at Odessa.
9 April	Declaration of War received by Anglo-French fleets anchored in Baljik Bay.
10 April	Formal treaty of alliance between Britain and France, joined by Turkey on the 15th.
12–14 April	The Baltic Fleet sailed for the Gulf of Finland.
22 April	The bombardment of Odessa by allied warships.
23 April	Russians begin withdrawal from Wallachia.
28 April	Russian attacks on Silistria.
28–9 April	Allied Black Sea Fleet sailed for Sebastopol to reconnoitre the port and engage the Russian fleet; no Russian response.
4 May	The Turkish fleet sailed to join Anglo-French naval forces in Baljik Bay.

5 May	Allied fleet returned to Varna from Sebastopol.
	Allied squadron detached to patrol eastern coast of Black Sea as far as Batum.
9 May	Allied senior commanders began to arrive in Gallipoli.
	Allied commander in the Pacific ordered 'hostile measures' against Russian shipping and other interests.
10–12 May	Russians defeated in Wallachia.
11 May	Siege of Silistria began.
12 May	HMS *Tiger* ran aground near Odessa and destroyed.
17 May	HMS *Amphion* and *Conflict* attacked Libau in the Baltic.
19 May	An allied conference agreed to adopt Varna as the main Black Sea base.
	Attack on Redut Kaleh by allied warships and Turkish troops.
20 May	HMS *Arrogant* and *Hecla* engaged at Eckness in the Baltic.
21 May	*Eurydice*, *Brisk* and *Miranda* under Commander Ommanney sailed for White Sea.
22 May	Attack on forts at Hängo in the Baltic.
25 May	The first French troops left Gallipoli for Varna.
26 May	British and French forces sent to Athens in view of Greek revolt against Turkey.
29 May	Russian attack defeated at Silistria.
30 May	Admiral Plumridge's squadron attacked Brahestad in the Baltic.
1 June	Allied warships began the blockade of the Danube estuary.
1–2 June	Attack on Uleaborg, Finland, by Admiral Plumridge.
5 June	Allied forces established at Varna.
7 June	*Odin* and *Vulture* attacked Gamla Karleby on the Finnish coast.
9 June	Russian attack on Silistria defeated.
13 June	The French naval contingent joined the British fleet off Hängo in the Baltic.
15 June	Exchange of fire between Russian warships from Sebastopol and *Furious* and *Terrible*.
18 June	Serious Russian defeats in the Caucasus.
21 June	*Hecla*, *Odin* and *Valorous* under Captain Hall attacked Bomarsund fort.
22 June	Allied fleet reconnoitred Cronstadt.
	Blockade of the White Sea inaugurated.
	Russians raise the siege of Silistria and withdraw.
24–9 June	*Firebrand*, *Vesuvius* and *Fury* attacked Russian positions in the mouth of Danube.
29 June	The British government agreed to the invasion of the Crimea.

5–7 July	Major Turkish offensive across the Danube drove back the Russians.
6 July	British sailors sent to aid the Turks at Routschouk.
7 July	Captain Hyde Parker killed near Sulina.
12 July	Napoleon III reviewed French troops destined for the Baltic at Boulogne.
15–16 July	French forces sail from Calais for the Baltic in British ships.
16 July	Orders for the invasion of the Crimea reached Lord Raglan and Admiral Dundas.
17–18 July	Attack on the monastery of Solovetski by the White Sea squadron.
	Allied fleet sailed from Baro Sound for the Åland Islands in the Baltic.
20 July	Allied warships reconnoitred Sebastopol.
	Attacks by White Sea squadron on coastal locations.
23 July	The Anglo-French fleet in position off Bomarsund.
	Attack on Novitska in the White Sea.
26 July	Brief exchange of fire between allied warships and Russian ships off Sebastopol.
30 July	French land forces arrived at Ledo Sound in Baltic.
6 Aug.	Turkish troops entered Bucharest as Russians withdrew.
8 Aug.	First Anglo-French forces landed near Bomarsund, Åland Islands.
9–12 Aug.	Allied landings near Bomarsund continued.
10 Aug.	The Allied base at Varna swept by a huge fire.
12 Aug.	Allied blockade of the White Sea formally announced.
13 Aug.	The attack on the Bomarsund forts began.
14 Aug.	The French captured Fort Bränklint, Bomarsund.
15 Aug.	British forces captured Fort Notvik, Bomarsund.
16 Aug.	Fall of the main fortress at Bomarsund following land and sea bombardment.
24 Aug.	HMS *Miranda* destroyed Kola in the White Sea.
26 Aug.	The occupation of Wallachia by Austrian forces, in agreement with the Turks.
25 Aug.	The French announced the decision to land an army in the Crimea.
29 Aug.	Allied troops began to embark at Varna for the Crimea.
	Final destruction of the captured forts in the Åland Islands began.
30–1 Aug.	The allied squadron in the Pacific attacked Petropavlovsk.

5 Sept.	Allied senior commanders sail on *Caradoc* and *Ville de Paris* for the Crimea.
6 Sept.	Allied warships and transports assembled off Baljik Bay.
7 Sept.	The allied expeditionary force sailed for the Crimea.
8 Sept.	The various elements of the allied Black Sea armada united off Cape Tarkan.
	Senior commanders reconnoitred possible landing sites in *Agamemnon*, *Caradoc*, *Sampson* and *Primaguet*.
11 Sept.	The allied command agreed to land forces near the Old Fort in Kalamita Bay and at Eupatoria.
13 Sept.	The occupation of Eupatoria without opposition.
14–18 Sept.	Allied landings near the Old Fort in Kalamita Bay. British warships shelled Russian forces nearby.
16 Sept.	Final evacuation of the Danubian Principalities by Russian forces.
19 Sept.	The allied advance into the Crimea began.
	Cossacks attacked Eupatoria.
	The French Baltic Fleet sailed for France.
20 Sept.	The Battle of the Alma.
21 Sept.	Elements of the British Baltic Fleet arrived off Nargen to begin the return voyage to Britain.
	Seven Russian warships scuttled to block the mouth of Sebastopol harbour.
25 Sept.	Allied decision to make a flank march to approach Sebastopol from the south.
26 Sept.	Balaklava harbour occupied by British warships led by *Agamemnon*.
28 Sept.	The allies set up their camps to the south of Sebastopol.
2 Oct.	A Naval Brigade landed from British warships to assist siege operations ashore.
	First proposals for operations in the Sea of Azoff.
12 Oct.	Cossacks attacked Eupatoria.
17 Oct.	'First Bombardment of Sebastopol'; the allied fleet attacked the harbour forts.
	Regular bombardment of Sebastopol began.
25 Oct.	The Battle of Balaklava: a major Russian attack on the naval base defeated.
25–7 Oct.	Most ships in Balaklava harbour withdrawn in fear of Russian attack.
26 Oct.	A large-scale Russian sortie near Inkermann defeated.

5 Nov.	The Battle of Inkermann – the defeat of a major Russian attack on allied positions.
14 Nov.	The 'Great Storm' devastated the Crimean coast and the army camps.
	Russian attack on Eupatoria.
29 Nov.	Russian night sortie from Sebastopol defeated by the French.
20 Dec.	Admiral Dundas retired; replaced by Admiral Lyons as commander in the Black Sea. French Admiral Bruat succeeded Admiral Hamelin.

1855

2 Jan.	Seven steamers and two sailing vessels set off from the Thames bringing railway material and 'navvies' to build a light railway from Balaklava to the siege lines.
	Sardinia announced intention to send forces to join the allies in the Crimea.
	Reconnaissance of Kertch by HMS *Leopard*.
5 Jan.	A Turkish army under Omar Pasha left the Balkans for Crimea; 10,000 Turks landed at Eupatoria.
1 Feb.	The resignation of Lord Aberdeen's government following severe criticism of their conduct of the war and the condition of British army.
	The allies declared a renewal of the blockade of the Black Sea.
2 Feb.	Lord Palmertson appointed Prime Minister.
6 Feb.	Reconnaissance of Sebastopol harbour's defences by Admiral Lyons.
17 Feb.	A major Russian attack on Eupatoria defeated.
24 Feb.	More Russian ships scuttled at the mouth of Sebastopol harbour.
2 March	Death of Russian Emperor Nicholas I; accession of Alexander II.
8 March	Attack on fort at Djemtil near Anapa by *Viper*.
13 March	A naval squadron attacked Soujak Kaleh on the Circassian coast.
20 March	The 'Advanced Squadron' of the new Baltic Fleet sailed from England.
22 March	Major Russian attack on the allies ('the Great Sortie'), repulsed by the French.
4 April	The main Baltic Fleet under Admiral R. Dundas sailed from Spithead to renew operations in that sea.
9 April	Unsuccessful 'Second Bombardment of Sebastopol' followed by twelve days of shelling. Decision not to launch a land assault.

17 April	Successful evacuation of Petropavlovsk in Pacific by the Russians.
19 April	'The Rifle Pits' at Sebastopol taken by the British.
26 April	Reconnaissance of Kertch by *Highflyer*.
3 May	First allied expedition to Kertch – recalled.
18 May	Distribution of Crimea medals by Queen Victoria at Hyde Park to returned soldiers, sailors and marines.
22 May	Second expedition to Kertch.
24 May	Allied landings in Strait of Kertch. The occupation of Kertch and the destruction of the Kertch flotilla followed.
	HMS *Snake* in action against Russian vessels off Kertch.
25 May	Allied warships entered the Sea of Azoff. Squadron to Berdiansk and Arabat.
	Occupation of Yenikale.
28 May	Allied warships in action against Fort Arabat.
	Mass destruction of Russian vessels in Sea of Azoff.
	Captain E. Lyons took British warships to attack shipping and stores at Genitchi.
	Baltic Fleet maintained blockade of Baltic and its coasts.
	Soujak Kaleh evacuated by the Russians.
30 May	Allied warships entered the Gulf of Azoff and reconnoitred the mouth of the Don and approaches to Rostov and then moved to Taganrog.
1 June	The French Baltic Squadron joined the British fleet off Cronstadt.
3 June	Allied Admirals reconnoitred Cronstadt.
	Allied warships in action at Taganrog in the Sea of Azoff, aided by flotilla of ships' boats from the larger warships.
4 June	Allied warships in action at Mariaupol in the Sea of Azoff.
5 June	Anapa, the last major Russian garrison on the Circassian coast of the Black Sea, evacuated by the Russians. Allied warships examined the port.
	A General Order to all allied forces announced the triumphs of the squadrons in the Sea of Azoff.
	HMS *Cossack* involved in the 'Hängo Massacre' in the Baltic. Anapa evacuated by the Russians.
6 June	Large-scale destruction of stores at Gheisk in the Sea of Azoff. 'Third Bombardment' of Sebastopol.
7 June	French forces took the Mamelon but were repulsed from the Malakoff; British forces took 'the Quarries'.

9 June	Mass destruction of stores etc. in Kiten Bay in the Sea of Azoff. Allied warships in the Sea of Azoff return to Kertch. Russians began the siege of Kars in Asiatic Turkey.
11 June	Captain Thomas Baillie announced the renewed blockade of the White Sea; maintained until 9 October when ice forced its abandonment.
13–15 June	Most allied forces leave Kertch and return to Kamiesch and Balaklava.
17 June	'Fourth Bombardment' of Sebastopol. Captain E. Lyons wounded in night attack on Sebastopol; died at Therapia.
18 June	Major attack on the defences of Sebastopol; repulsed with great loss.
21 June	The Baltic Fleet began 'minesweeping' operations before Cronstadt; thirty-three found.
23–4 June	Destruction of small Russian trading vessels in the Baltic; at Nystad, 20,000 tons of shipping destroyed.
28 June	Death of Lord Raglan; body sent to Britain on *Caradoc* on 2 July, arriving in Bristol on 24 July.
3 July	Lieutenant Hewett in *Beagle* destroyed the bridge at Tchongar in the Sea of Azoff.
4–5 July	HMS *Arrogant* attacked and destroyed the fort etc. at Loviso in the Baltic and fired on Cossacks at Kounda Bay.
9 July	HMS *Phoenix* attacked Liamtsi in the White Sea.
14 July	*Arrogant* engaged a battery near Viborg in the Baltic.
15 July	Allied ships destroyed huge quantities of stores at Berdiansk in the Sea of Azoff.
16 July	Allied warships attacked Fort Petrovskoi in the Sea of Azoff.
17 July	Reconnaissance of Sveaborg by naval commanders.
18 July	Reconnaissance of Reval by naval commanders.
21 July	*Arrogant*, *Magicienne*, *Cossack* and *Ruby* attacked batteries near Frederickshamn in the Baltic. White Sea Squadron assembled off Archangel.
24 July	HMS *Jasper* grounded and lost near Taganrog.
26 July	Warships under Captain Yelverton attacked the fortifications on Kotka in the Baltic.
Aug.	Various operations in the Gulf of Riga.
2 Aug.	Naval attack on Brandon on the Finnish coast.
8 Aug.	The main allied fleet anchored off Sveaborg in the Baltic.
9–10 Aug.	Naval bombardment of Sveaborg.

13 Aug.	The allied fleet left Sveaborg for anchorage at Nargen.
16 Aug.	The Battle of the Tchernaya (or Traktir) – the last Russian land offensive in the Crimea, defeated by French and Sardinian forces.
17 Aug.	'Fifth Bombardment' of Sebastopol.
19 Aug.	Destruction of eighteen Russian merchant ships near Biorneborg in the Baltic.
	All mortar vessels ordered to return from the Baltic to Britain.
23–4 Aug.	Azoff squadron off Berutch Spit; destroyed stores at Kiril.
25 Aug.	Russians began building a bridge from Sebastopol to the northern side of the bay.
	The destruction of Russian merchant shipping continued in the Gulf of Bothnia.
29 Aug.	Allied warships destroyed stores near Arabat and Genitchi in the Sea of Azoff.
2 Sept.	Russian ships emerge from Cronstadt to challenge British vessels; no engagement.
5 Sept.	The allied squadron reconnoitred the mouths of the Don in the Sea of Azoff.
5–7 Sept.	'The Final Bombardment of Sebastopol'.
8 Sept.	Last allied attack on Sebastopol; the French capture of Malakoff sealed the fate of the city; British forces again repulsed at the Redan with great loss.
	Evacuation of Sebastopol began; all remaining Russians vessels sunk or burned.
10 Sept.	Allied forces finally occupy Sebastopol.
11 Sept.	The Naval Brigade ordered to embark to leave the Crimea.
12 Sept.	A large Turkish force landed at Batum.
17 Sept.	Naval Brigade left Balaklava.
21 Sept.	Minor cavalry skirmish near Yenikale.
23–4 Sept.	Captain Osborn and British ships involved in operations in the Strait of Kertch near Temriouk, Taman and Fanagoria.
29 Sept.	Unsuccessful Russian attacks on Kars.
7 Oct.	Allied warships approach Odessa en route for Kinburn.
9 Oct.	Captain Osborn with *Vesuvius*, *Curlew*, *Recruit*, *Weser* and *Ardent* renewed operations along the coasts of the Sea of Azoff.
	White Sea squadron sailed for home waters.
10 Oct.	Lieuntenant Commerell crossed the Spit of Arabat to destroy stores on the Salgir and Karsu rivers in the 'Putrid Sea'.
14 Oct.	Allied fleet arrived off Kinburn.
15 Oct.	Landing of allied troops (mainly French) on Kinburn Spit.

17 Oct.	Bombardment of Kinburn and surrender of the fort and batteries.
18 Oct.	Fort Nikolaev and batteries near Otchakov destroyed by Russians.
20–1 Oct.	Allied warships reconnoitred the mouths of the Bug and Dnieper.
27 Oct.	Beginning of withdrawal from Kinburn; garrison in occupation.
2 Nov.	Azoff squadron concentrated off Mariaupol.
4–6 Nov.	Osborn with the Azoff squadron destroyed huge quantities of stores etc. around Gheisk and Glofira.
12 Nov.	Gradual dispersal of Baltic fleets; Admiral Dundas remained at Kiel with some ships until mid-November.
13 Nov.	Ice forming in the Sea of Azoff heralded the end of the campaign.
19 Nov.	Death at Toulon of Admiral Bruat, French naval commander in the Black Sea.
19–20 Nov.	Last patrols off Taganrog and Mariaupol in the Sea of Azoff.
20 Nov.	Withdrawal of the Azoff squadron began as the sea began to freeze over.
25 Nov.	Kars surrendered to the Russians.
16 Dec.	Cavalry skirmish near Kertch.
22–31 Dec.	The destruction of the docks and harbour works at Sebastopol began.

1856

Jan.	Various rounds of peace negotiations, proposals and discussions amongst the Great Powers.
1 Feb.	Final destruction of the docks etc. at Sebastopol.
4 Feb.	Fort Nicholas north of Sebastopol destroyed by the Russians.
24 Feb.	Grand Review of 25,000 British troops in the Crimea.
25 Feb.	First meeting of the peace conference at Paris. An armistice was agreed.
28 Feb.	Hostilities in the Crimea suspended under armistice agreement.
13 March	Admiral Charles Napier requests (in the Commons) an inquiry into the operations of the Baltic Fleet in 1854 and 1855. Later withdrawn.
30 March	Treaty of Peace signed at Paris.
2 April	News of the Peace reached the Crimea and celebrated by all the allied armies.

23 April	Grand Review of the British fleet at Spithead – 240 vessels.
29 April	Peace formally announced in London.
4 May	Proclaimed as a day of 'general thanksgiving' for the peace.
24 May	Queen Victoria's birthday celebrated by the British army in the Crimea.
12 July	The last British troops left the Crimea.

The British Fleet Reviewed at Spithead, August 1853

On 11 August 1853, shortly after the Russian invasion of the Danubian Principalities, Queen Victoria conducted a review of a Royal Navy at Portsmouth, which caused great local and national interest. This was the largest Naval Review held in Britain since 1814, when the Napoleonic Wars were apparently at their end and a great national celebration of the conclusion of the war took place:

> But, even in those days of effort and of glory [1814], the navy never presented a force comprising, in a comparatively small number of ships, such a union of strength and skill as may be seen in the squadron now assembled at Spithead. The structure of our vessels is largely expanded and improved; and, although many successive naval administrations have borne the not undeserved reproach of wasted expenditure and abortive experiments, we have now reached a point of excellence from which we look down on all that had been done before. The *Duke of Wellington* and the *Agamemnon* ... are by general consent the finest ships of their class which have been launched from our yards; and, as a sailing three-decker, the *Queen* will support comparison, without disadvantage, against any rivals. The main deck of these colossal vessels is the most striking picture which the eye can behold of the stern preparations and order of war. Armed with guns far exceeding in weight of metal the greatest power of our ships of the line in the early part of this century – with guns directed with a nicety and precision which enable a three-decker to point her broadside as easily as a sportsman aims his fowling-piece – such ships would bring into battle a force which no enemy has ever yet encountered, and which probably no vessel afloat could sustain for half an hour without entire destruction. But, in addition to these improvements and augmentations of marine artillery, a new power has been harnessed to these huge batteries of the ocean, and the fan-like motion of a brazen fin, revolving by the force of an engine placed below the water-line, enables the helmsman to guide and place his

ship, against all the accidents of wind and tide, with as much ease and accuracy as a battery of field guns.[1]

Interestingly, Tsar Nicholas I's two eldest daughters, Maria and Olga, who happened to be visiting England at the time, watched as honoured guests. The major ships on view were:

	No. of Guns	Complement
Duke of Wellington, screw, Captain H.B. Martin, CB, flagship of the Commander-in-Chief Vice Admiral Sir T.J. Cochrane, KCB	131	1,100
Agamemnon, screw, Captain Sir Thomas Maitland, CB, flagship of Rear Admiral Corry	91	820
Queen, Captain Michell	116	970
Prince Regent, Captain Hutton	90	820
London, Captain Eden	90	820
Blenheim, screw, Captain Henderson, CB	60	500
Hogue, screw, Captain W. Ramsay	60	500
Ajax, screw, Captain Quin	58	250
Edinburgh, screw, gunnery ship, tender to:		
Excellent, Captain R.S. Hewlett	58	200
Impérieuse, screw, Captain Watson	51	586
Arrogant, screw, Captain Fremantle	46	450
Amphion, screw, Captain A.C. Key	34	300
Tribune, screw, Captain Hon. S.T. Carnegie	31	300
Sidon, paddle, Captain Goldsmith	22	300
Terrible, paddle, Captain McCleverty	21	300
Highflyer, screw, Captain Moore	21	230
Magicienne, paddle, Captain T. Fisher	16	200
Valorous, paddle, Captain C.H.M. Buckle	16	300
Odin, paddle, Captain Francis Scott	16	270
Encounter, screw, Captain O'Callaghan	14	175
Leopard, paddle, Captain George Giffard	12	240
Desperate, screw, Captain Chambers	8	172
Vulture, paddle, Captain F.H. Glasse	6	200
Vesuvius, paddle, Commander Wilson	6	160
Barracouta, paddle, Commander Parker	6	160

This displayed over 40,200 tons of shipping, mounting over 1,000 guns and with ships' companies that should have amounted to 10,423 hands, but because of shortage in manpower were actually nearer 9,400.

The Times reported on 12 August:

There were no less than 1,076 guns, the smallest 32-pounders, and as large as the largest used in the great sea-fights by which our ancestors won the sovereignty of the seas. The largest throw 84-pound shells, which would be 104-pounders if solid shot were used, and the frightful destructiveness of these missiles may be imagined, exploding on concussion ... The great feature, however, of the armament of the present fleet is its 68-pounders, which produced, when fired, a prodigious effect both upon the imagination and the tympanum of all who witnessed the review. Thus, by its floating batteries of the heaviest description, and by the power of steam to move them rapidly into any position that may be required, the British navy has now become the grandest concentration of force for destructive purposes that can well be conceived. A tonnage of 40,207 tons in one fleet dedicated to such an object reminds one not only of the resources of a country providing such tremendous means of defence, but suggests also how vast must be the interests that require to be so guarded.

The Opposing Fleets at Sinope, 30 November 1853

Imperial Russian fleet

Line-of-battle ships

Veliky Knyaz Konstantin	120 guns
Tri Sviatitelia	120 guns
Parizh	120 guns
Empress Maria	84 guns (flagship)
Chesma	84 guns
Rostislav	84 guns

Frigates

Kulevtcha	54 guns
Kagul	44 guns

Paddle-steamers

Odessa	4 guns
Krym	4 guns
Khersones	4 guns

Ottoman fleet

Sailing frigates

Avni Illah	44 guns – run ashore
Fazl Illah	44 guns (formerly the Russian *Rafail*, captured 1829) – run ashore on fire
Nizamieh	62 guns – run ashore
Nessin Zafer	60 guns – run ashore
Navek Bahri	58 guns – magazine exploded
Damiat (Egyptian)	56 guns – run ashore
Kaid Zafer	54 guns – run ashore

Sailing corvettes

Nejm Fishan	24 guns – run ashore

| *Feyz Mabud* | 24 guns – run ashore |
| *Kel Safid* | 22 guns – exploded |

Steam frigates or corvettes

| *Taif* | 12 guns – escaped to Constantinople |
| *Erkelye* | 10 guns – destroyed |

Appendix 3

Russian Ships of the Black Sea Fleet at Sebastopol, 1854–5

Those marked * were present in the action at Sinope, 30 November 1853.

*Grand Duke Constantine**	120 guns
City of Paris	120 guns
*Tri Sviatitelia**	120 guns
*Empress Maria**	84 guns (flagship)
*Chesma**	84 guns
Brave	84 guns
Flora	
Iagudil	84 guns
Ouryil	
*Rostislav**	84 guns
Varna (or *Kavarna*)	60-gun frigate
Selaftroil	
Silistria	
Sizopol	
*Kulevtcha**	54 guns
*Kagul**	44 guns
Sviatoslav	

Paddle-steamers

Bessarabia paddle-steamer	
Gromonosets	
*Odessa**	4 guns
Elbrose iron paddle-steamer	
*Krym**	4 guns
*Khersones**	4 guns
Taman	
Thunderbearer or *Thunderer*	paddle-steamer
Vladimir	paddle-steamer
Danube	dispatch vessel

Russian Warships in the Baltic, 1854–5

The following Russian warships are known to have been in the Baltic during the campaigns.

Based at Helsingfors/Sveaborg

Russia	120 guns
St George the Conqueror	112 guns
Pultava	84 guns
Prochor	84 guns
Vladimir	84 guns
Brienne	74 guns
Arsis	74 guns
Hezekiel	74 guns
Andrew	74 guns

Based at Cronstadt

Emperor Peter I	120 guns
Enigheten	84 guns
Krasnoe	84 guns
Ganule	84 guns
Volga	84 guns
Empress Alexandra	84 guns
Narva	74 guns
Beresina	74 guns
Borodino	74 guns
Smolensko	74 guns
Finkand	74 guns
Katzbach	74 guns
Ingermanland	74 guns
Kulm	74 guns
Pourgat Azofa	74 guns
Sisoe the Great	74 guns
Villajath	74 guns
Natron-menga	74 guns
Frere Champenoise	74 guns
Michael	74 guns

Appendix 5

British Warships in the Baltic, 1854–5

Those marked * are the original ships that set off under Napier from Spithead in March 1854. Designations and armament figures taken from contemporary *Navy Lists*. Where there is no type designation (for example, screw corvette) the ship was a sailing vessel.

Name of Vessel	Designation	No. of Guns	Dates of Service
Aelous	powder vessel	42	1855
*Ajax**	screw	60	1854, 1855
Alban	steam survey vessel	6	1854
Algiers	screw; used as troop ship	91	1854
*Amphion**	screw frigate	34	1854, 1855
Archer	screw corvette	14	1854, 1855
Ariel	screw	9	1855
*Arrogant**	screw frigate	46	1854, 1855
Badger	steam gunboat	3	1855
Basilisk	steam sloop	6	1854, 1855
Beacon	mortar vessel	1	1855
Belleisle	as hospital ship	6	1854, 1855
Biter	steam gunboat	2	1855
Blazer	mortar vessel	1	1855
*Blenheim**	screw ship	60	1854, 1855
Boscawen		70	1854
Bulldog	steam sloop	6	1854, 1855
Caesar	screw ship	91	1854, 1855
Calcutta		84	1855
Carron	mortar vessel	1	1855
Centaur	steam frigate	11	1855
Colossus	screw	81	1855
Conflict	screw corvette	8	1854, 1855
Cornwallis	screw block ship	60	1855
Cossack	screw corvette	20	1855
Cracker	mortar vessel	1	1855
Cressy	screw	81	1854, 1855
Cruizer	screw corvette	17	1854, 1855

Name of Vessel	Designation	No. of Guns	Dates of Service
Cuckoo	steam gun vessel	3	1854
Cumberland		70	1854
Dapper	steam gunboat	2	1855
Dauntless	screw frigate	33	1854
Desperate	screw corvette	8	1854, 1855
Drake	mortar vessel	1	1855
*Dragon**	steam frigate	6	1854, 1855
Driver	steam sloop	6	1854, 1855
*Duke of Wellington**	screw	131	1854, 1855
*Edinburgh**	screw	58	1854, 1855
Esk	screw corvette	20	1855
Euryalus	screw frigate	51	1854, 1855
Exmouth	screw	91	1855
Falcon	screw corvette	17	1855
Firefly	steam sloop	4	1855
Firm	mortar vessel	1	1855
Geyser	steam sloop	6	1855
Gleaner	steam gunboat	2	1855
Gladiator	steam frigate/troop ship	6	1854, 1855
Gorgon	steam sloop	6	1854, 1855
Grappler	mortar vessel	1	1855
Growler	mortar vessel	1	1855
Hannibal	screw/troop ship	91	1854
Hardy	mortar vessel	1	1855
Harrier	screw corvette	17	1855
Hastings	screw block ship	60	1855
Havoc	mortar vessel	1	1855
Hawke	screw block ship	60	1855
Hecla	steam sloop	6	1854
Hind	steam gunboat	2	1855
*Hogue**	screw ship	60	1854, 1855
Horatio	screw	24	1855
*Impérieuse**	screw frigate	51	1854, 1855
Jack	gunboat	2	1855
Jackdaw	steam gunboat	2	1855
James Watt	screw ship	91	1854, 1855
Janus	steam gun vessel/troop ship	4	1854
Lark	steam gunboat	2	1855
*Leopard**	steam frigate	18	1854
Lightning	steam survey vessel	3	1854, 1855
Locust	steam vessel	3	1854

Name of Vessel	Designation	No. of Guns	Dates of Service
Magicienne	steam frigate	16	1854, 1855
Magpie	steam gunboat	2	1855
Majestic	screw ship	81	1854, 1855
Malacca	screw corvette	17	1855
Manly	mortar vessel	1	1855
Mastiff	mortar vessel	1	1855
Merlin	steam survey vessel	4	1855
Miranda	screw corvette	14	(1854 – White Sea)
Monarch		84	1854, 1855
Neptune		120	1854, 1855
Nile	screw ship	91	1854, 1855
Odin	steam frigate	16	1854, 1855
Orion	screw ship	91	1855
Otter	steam gunboat	3	1854
Pelter	steam gunboat	2	1855
Pembroke	screw ship	60	1855
Penelope	steam frigate	16	1854
Pickle	mortar vessel	1	1855
Pigmy	steam gun vessel	3	1854
Pincher	steam gunboat	3	1855
Porcupine	mortar vessel	1	1854, 1855
Porpoise	mortar vessel	1	1855
Prince Regent		90	1854
Princess Alice	iron paddle-packet	–	1855
*Princess Royal**	screw ship	91	1854
Prompt	mortar vessel	1	1855
Pylades	screw corvette	21	1854, 1855
Redbreast	mortar vessel	1	1855
Redwing	steam gunboat	2	1855
Resistance	store/troop ship	10	1854
Retribution	steam frigate	28	1854, 1855
Rhadamanthus	steam troop ship	4	1854
Rocket	mortar vessel	1	1855
Rosamond	steam sloop	6	1854, 1855
*Royal George**	screw ship	120	1854, 1855
Royal William	troop ship	120	1854
Ruby	steam gunboat	3	1855
Russell	screw ship	60	1854, 1855
St George		120	1854
*St Jean d'Acre**	screw ship	101	1854
St Vincent	as troop ship	102	1854

Name of Vessel	Designation	No. of Guns	Dates of Service
Sans Pareil	screw ship	71	1855
Sheerness	water tanker	–	1854, 1855
Sinbad	mortar vessel	1	1855
Skylark	steam gunboat	2	1855
Snap	steam gunboat	2	1855
Snapper	steam gunboat	3	1855
Sphinx	steam sloop	6	1854
Starling	steam gunboat	2	1855
Stork	steam gunboat	2	1855
Stromboli	steam sloop/troop ship	6	1854
Surly	mortar vessel	1	1855
Swinger	steam gunboat	2	1855
Tartar	screw corvette	21	1854, 1855
Teazer	gunboat	2	1855
Termagant	screw frigate/troop ship	24	1854
Thistle	steam gunboat	2	1855
*Tribune**	screw frigate	31	1854
Twinger	gunboat	2	1855
Tyne	transport	4	1854
*Valorous**	steam frigate	16	1854
Volage	powder vessel	22	1854
Volcano	steam factory ship	4	1854, 1855
Vulture	steam frigate	6	1854, 1855
Weazel (*Weazle*)	steam gunboat	2	1855
Wrangler	screw dispatch vessel	6	1854
Zephyr	steam gunboat	3	1854

Appendix 6

Napier's Defence

The following letter was written by Sir Charles Napier early in 1855 to Lord Palmerston, and contains a summary of his proceedings during the Baltic campaign of 1854. He vigorously defends his actions in the face of hostile criticism in the British press, in government circles and in the Admiralty:

The command of the Baltic fleet was conferred on me last February [1854] by the Cabinet, which measure, I believe, was approved of by the nation at large. Such a magnificent fleet had not been got together for many years, and no fleet was ever composed of ships of the same magnitude, and with the same means of propulsion. I took that fleet to the Baltic, wretchedly manned, and worse disciplined, and brought it back to the shores of this country in as perfect order as the materials of which it was composed would admit.

During the time I was there, I had great difficulties to contend with – beacons and buoys were removed, and others placed to mislead, and all the lights were extinguished. We went there earlier than a fleet had ever gone before, and stayed later, exposed to the gales and fogs usual at those seasons, without pilots and with imperfect charts. Admirals, captains, and officers ignorant of the navigation; the weather cold and the men imperfectly clad; many too old to go aloft and the young ones quite inexperienced; nevertheless, I managed to get them into Wingo Sound, where I opened Lord Clarendon's orders, delivered to me by the Admiralty.

Acting on those orders, I left Wingo Sound and passed the Belt, notwithstanding the gales and fogs, and anchored in Kioge Bay on the 1st of April, where I, on the following day, received the declaration of war, and a letter from the Admiralty, disapproving of my leaving Wingo Sound, and subsequently one approving of my having done so; and highly complimentary letters from Sir James Graham [First Lord of the Admiralty], for having pushed on to Kioge; there I assembled fourteen sail-of-the-line, declared the blockade, despatched Admiral Plumridge to the Gulf of Finland, and cruisers on the coast of Courland.

On the 12th, after coaling and watering, I took the fleet off Faro; there I left seven sail-of-the-line under Admiral Corry, and proceeded to the Gulf of Finland with the rest.

The weather proved unfavourable for entering the gulf and I rejoined Admiral Corry. I then proceeded to Elsgnabben Bay [Sweden] to set up rigging, and I paid a visit to the King of Sweden, with whom I had a long conference. There Admiral Plumridge joined me, bringing much useful information on the state of the Gulf, which was still closed, as far as Revel and Helsingfors. He was next despatched to the Åland Islands, to penetrate, if possible, to Bomarsund.

We had nothing but gales and fogs in this anchorage: where we were detained ten or twelve days; and, on leaving we were surprised by the fog in the narrowest part of the channel, amongst sunken rocks, and the fleet was in imminent danger; some returned, some anchored, and others pushed on, and, by the blessing of Providence, they all escaped.

After remaining a few days off Gottska Sando, I proceeded to the Gulf of Finland, with nine screw line battle ships, and anchored in Hängo Bay for a few days; from thence I proceeded to Baro Sound, which we were obliged to buoy; from the lighthouse we had a good view of the Russian squadron at Sveaborg, and I did hope the [–] would have given me an opportunity of trying the metal of my men. I hoped the Cronstadt squadron would have taken advantage of the separation of my fleet. Had I caught them amongst the rocks of Baro Sound, I think I should have driven one-half of them on shore, and taken the other half.

Seeing no prospect of their moving, I ordered Admiral Corry to Baro Sound and I proceeded off Sveaborg; and on the 12th of June I sent to Sir James Graham, Admiral Chad's report (which I approved of), and which I presume your Lordship has seen. I then returned to Baro Sound and was joined by the French squadron of nine sail-of-the-line, making in all twenty-eight sail-of-the-line, besides frigates. Much was expected from this fleet; but after deliberating and consulting with the French Admiral, we were of opinion that Sveaborg could not be attacked with success. Captain Sullivan [*sic*, Sulivan] joined here from Bomarsund, having surveyed the various passages leading to the fortifications. I at once proposed to the French Admiral to attack that important fortress with the fleet, which he declined; first, because he doubted the policy of the measure; and secondly, because he was anxious to examine Cronstadt, and offer battle to the Russian fleet.

I wrote to Sir James Graham, announcing our intention of going to Cronstadt, and, if unassailable, to attack Bomarsund on our return. I asked for one or two thousand men, if possible; if not, I thought we could do without. We found Cronstadt unassailable, as we expected – first, from want of water for the large ships; and secondly, from the strength of the fortifications. We, therefore, returned to Baro Sound, and found despatches announcing that an army of 10,000 men were on their road to join us. We did not want them, and they would have been much better employed at Sebastopol. They were much too large a force for Bomarsund, and much too small for Sveaborg; and too late in the season for the latter place.

I immediately reinforced Admiral Plumridge with all the small vessels I could spare, and closely blockaded Bomarsund. Nine sail-of-the-line were left at Nargen to watch Helsingfors, and the body of the fleet proceeded to Ledsund.

It is needless to detail the attack on Bomarsund; your Lordship knows the particulars. It was taken, and promptly done; and the greatest cordiality subsisted between the allied forces, by sea and land. Up to that time, I had received the most unqualified praise from the Admiralty, Sir James Graham, and several of the Cabinet Ministers. Sir James complimented me on being a consummate Commander-in-Chief, and approved of all my conduct as being most judicious.

Bomarsund being taken, the French Admiral and General, accompanied by the French and English Engineers, proceeded to reconnoitre Sveaborg, and they brought back their report, which your Lordship has no doubt seen. Suffice it to say, General Jones's was rejected by the Admirals and the General, and General Niel's was approved of by the General and rejected by the Admirals as impracticable and dangerous.

The only thing within our reach was an attack on Abo; this the French General declined, on account of the cholera having broken out amongst the troops, and the tempestuous weather, which had already begun. He decided on taking the army back to France; they sailed on the 5th; and on that night the second heavy gale came on – fortunately it was fair.

When it was known in England that nothing more was to be done, the people got dissatisfied, and the Government became alarmed. Something must be done, and some one must be blamed; and on the 12th of September out came a letter, dated the 4th, to hold a council of war with my French colleagues and the Admirals I had confidence in, to decide whether any further operations could be undertaken, and trusting we should be unanimous. We were unanimous, that nothing more could be done with the means we had, at this boisterous season. The French General and the army had sailed; but he had already rejected General Jones's plan of landing 5,000 men, and the Admirals had rejected General Niel's plan of attacking Sveaborg with the ships alone.

The Admiralty did not wait for the report of the council; for, on the 16th, out came another order, dated the 9th, to lay General Jones's report before the French General-in-Chief and Admirals in a council of war, and decide whether General Jones's report had so far altered their opinion as to induce them to undertake the operation. Fortunately, the French General (now a Marshal of France) had sailed, and I was saved the pain of asking him to alter the decision he had already taken on General Jones's report, which he most decidedly would have taken as an insult.

The Admiralty, seemingly enamoured with councils of war, had not yet received our report when I received, on the 17th September, a letter dated the 12th (they then knew the army was withdrawn) desiring me to confer with the French Admiral on the feasibility of knocking down Sveaborg (the Gibraltar of the north) in two hours, which was the report of General Niel. The French Admiral felt indignant at being asked to alter an opinion he had already given, and (before that opinion had arrived in London) refused to attend the conference, and decided on withdrawing his fleet, according to the order he had received, dated 29th August (and which was known to our Government on the 1st of September), though he had previously decided on remaining with his screw-ships till I left the Gulf of Finland.

The French Admiral having refused to attend the conference, I called a council of my own Admirals, agreeably to my orders, and they unanimously agreed, after reading General Niel's report, that they saw no reason to change their opinions; and Admiral Martin, who was not present at the first council, after being made acquainted with it, coincided in opinion.

I now hoped the Admiralty would have been satisfied, but the sequel will shew they were not.

A few days after this, the French Admiral sailed for France, with all his squadron and I returned to the Gulf of Finland, and joined Admiral Plumridge at Nargen, where I assembled sixteen sail-of-the-line, including four sailing ships, on the 23rd of September. On the 24th I reconnoitered Reval, and made a report to the Admiralty, with which they were perfectly satisfied; and the following day I reconnoitered Sveaborg, and I made as clear a report as it was possible to make – giving two distinct plans of attack: one with ships alone, which I thought very doubtful of success, and dangerous at this season of the year; and the other which I thought sure of success, if undertaken at a proper time.

I felt quite confident their Lordships would have been perfectly satisfied, as they had been with my report on Cronstadt and Reval, but I was mistaken. My report on Sveaborg reached the Admiralty on 4th of October – two days after the [false] news arrived that Sebastopol was taken, and the very day that the full details appeared in *The Times*. The nation lost their head – they were mad with joy, and so were the Admiralty.

The French squadron was stopped at Kiel, and so was Admiral Plumridge's squadron of sailing ships, whom I had sent home by the wishes of Sir James Graham, and they were ordered to hold themselves ready to rejoin me; and out came a thundering letter to me, perverting my report on Sveaborg, and pretending that I had told their Lordships that I could take Sveaborg with the fleet alone, and goading me on to do it.

I was surprised – I could not believe it possible that my letter could have been misunderstood. My feelings were outraged, and I wrote a full explanation to their Lordships. Their Lordships did not wait to know the effects of their goading letter (and my explanation), whether it had had the effect of driving me to risk Her Majesty's fleet; but the news of the taking of Sebastopol being contradicted, they ordered home Admiral Plumridge's squadron by telegraph – the French squadron being ordered home at the same time forthwith. So that, had I been disposed to have risked the fleet, which I was not, they deprived me of the means of so doing; but yet they had not the frankness to acknowledge their mistake, but wrote me a letter, which would have been much fitter for a special pleader than for a Board to write, and finished by expressing their want of satisfaction that Sveaborg was not attacked after the capture of Bomarsund.

It is needless to trouble your Lordship, further or to comment on Sir James Graham's private letters, which were more insulting than the public ones; or on the insulting reception he gave me – suffice it to say, my flag was ordered to be hauled down, and I was informed my command had terminated.[1]

Major Allied Warships in the Baltic, 1855

British

Following the experiences of the fleet in 1854, all were steam powered.

Name of Vessel	No. of Guns	Commanding Officer	
Duke of Wellington	131	Captain Caldwell	Flagship of Rear Admiral Dundas
Exmouth	91	Captain W.K. Hall	Flagship of Rear Admiral M. Seymour
Retribution	28	Captain Fisher	Flagship of Rear Admiral Baynes
Royal George	102	Captain Codrington	
James Watt	91	Captain Elliot	
Orion	91	Captain Erskine	
Caesar	91	Captain Robb	
Nile	91	Captain Mundy	
Majestic	81	Captain Hope	
Cressy	81	Captain Warren	
Colossus	81	Captain Robinson	
Sans Pareil	70	Captain Williams	
Blenheim	60	Captain W.H. Hall	
Hogue	60	Captain Ramsay	
Ajax	60	Captain Warden	
Hastings	60	Captain Caffin	
Pembroke	60	Captain Seymour	
Cornwallis	60	Captain Wellesley	
Hawke	60	Captain Ommanney	
Russell	60	Captain F. Scott	
Edinburgh	58	Captain Hewlett	
Impérieuese	51	Captain Watson	
Euryalus	51	Captain Ramsey	
Arrogant	46	Captain Yelverton	
Amphion	34	Captain A.C. Key	

Name of Vessel	No. of Guns	Commanding Officer
Horatio	24	Captain Hon. A. Cochrane
Cossack	20	Captain Fanshawe
Tartar	20	Captain Dunlop
Pylades	20	Captain d'Eyncourt
Esk	20	Captain Birch
Malacca	17	Captain Farquhar
Magicienne	16	Captain Vansittart
Odin	16	Captain Willcox
Archer	15	Captain Heathcote
Cruiser	15	Commander G. Douglas
Harrier	15	Commander Story
Falcon	15	Commander Pullen
Ariel	9	Commander Luce
Desperate	8	Commander White
Conflict	8	Commander Brown
Vulture	6	Captain Glasse
Centaur	6	Captain Clifford
Dragon	6	Captain H. Stewart
Bulldog	6	Commander A. Gordon
Basilisk	6	Commander Jenner
Rosamund	6	Commander Crofton
Driver	6	Commander A.H. Gardner
Geyser	6	Commander Dew
Gorgon	6	Commander Crawford
Lightning	3	Lieutenant Campbell

French

Name of Vessel	No. of Guns	Designation	
Tourville	90	screw battleship	Flagship of Admiral Pénaud
Austerlitz	90	screw battleship	
Duquesne	80	screw warship	
d'Assas	16	screw corvette	
Pelican	2	screw gunboat	
La Tempête	2	screw gunboat	

British Warships in the Black Sea, 1854–5

Those marked * also served in the Baltic. For Sea of Azoff, see Appendix 9.

Name of Vessel	Designation	No. of Guns	Dates of Service
Agammenon	screw	91	1854, 1855
Albion	sail	91	1854, 1855
*Algiers**	screw	90	1855
Apollo	troop ship	38	1854
Ardent	paddle-sloop	5	1854, 1855
Arethusa	sail	50	1854, 1855
Arrow	steam dispatch vessel	2	1854, 1855
Banshee	paddle-packet	2	1854, 1855
Beagle	steam gun vessel	2	1854, 1855
Bellerophon	sail	80	1854, 1855
Boxer	gunboat	2	1855
Britannia	sail	120	1854, 1855
Caradoc	steam	2	1854, 1855
Clinker	gunboat	2	1855
Cracker	gunboat	2	1855
Curacao	screw	31	1854, 1855
Curlew	steam sloop	9	1854, 1855
Cyclops	paddle	6	1854, 1855
*Dauntless**	steam frigate	24	1855
Desperate	screw corvette	8	1854, 1855
Diamond	sail	28	1854, 1855
Fancy	gunboat	2	1855
Firebrand	paddle-frigate	6	1854, 1855
Furious	paddle-frigate	16	1854, 1855
Fury	paddle-sloop	6	1854
*Gladiator**	paddle-frigate	6	1854, 1855
*Gorgon**	steam sloop/troop ship	6	1855
Grinder	gunboat	2	1855

Name of Vessel	Designation	No. of Guns	Dates of Service
*Hannibal**	screw/troop ship	91	1854, 1855
Harpy	paddle-gunboat	1	1854, 1855
Hibernia	sail	104	1855
Highflyer	screw	21	1854, 1855
Hind	steam gunboat	2	1855
Hogue	screw	74	1854, 1855
Himalaya	screw troopship	–	1855
Inflexible	paddle-steamer	6	1854, 1855
Leander	sail	50	1854, 1855
*Leopard**	paddle-frigate	10	1854, 1855
London	sail	90	1854, 1855
Lynx	screw	4	1854, 1855
Malacca	screw corvette	17	1854
Medina	steam gun vessel/packet	4	1855
Megaera	iron screw troop ship	6	1854, 1855
Modeste	sail	18	1855
Miranda	steam sloop	15	1855
Niger	screw corvette	14	1854, 1855
Oberon	paddle-sloop	3	1855
*Odin**	paddle-frigate	18	1855
*Princess Royal**	screw	91	1855
Prometheus	paddle-sloop	5	1855
Queen	sail	116	1854, 1855
Recruit	paddle-gunboat	8	1855
*Resistance**	store/troop ship	10	1855
*Retribution**	paddle	28	1854, 1855
Rodney	sail	90	1854, 1855
Royal Albert	screw	121	1854, 1855
*St Jean d'Acre**	screw	101	1855
Sampson	paddle	6	1854, 1855
Sans Pareil	screw	70	1854, 1855
Sidon	paddle	21	1854, 1855
Simoom	iron screw troop ship	18	1854
Snake	steam gun vessel/packet	6	1854, 1855
*Sphinx**	paddle-sloop	6	1855
Spiteful	paddle-sloop	6	1854, 1855
Spitfire	paddle	5	1854, 1855
*Stromboli**	paddle-sloop	6	1855

Name of Vessel	Designation	No. of Guns	Dates of Service
Supply	steam screw storeship	–	1855
Swallow	steam sloop	9	1855
Terrible	paddle	21	1854, 1855
Tiger	paddle	16	1854 (wrecked off Odessa)
Trafalgar	sail	120	1854, 1855
Transit	screw troop ship	–	1855
*Tribune**	screw	31	1854, 1855
Triton	paddle	3	1854, 1855
*Valorous**	paddle-frigate	16	1854, 1855 (the last paddle-frigate built)
Vengeance	sail	84	1854, 1855
Vesuvius	paddle	6	1854, 1855
Viper	steam gunboat	2	1854, 1855
Vulcan	iron screw troop ship	6	1854, 1855
*Vulture**	paddle-frigate	6	1854
Wasp	steam sloop	14	1854, 1855
Weser	paddle-gunboat	4	1855
*Wrangler**	steam gun vessel	2	1855
Wye	storeship	–	1854

Examples of French warships serving in the Black Sea, 1854–5

Name of Vessel	No. of Guns	Designation	
Ville de Paris	114	screw	Flagship of Vice Admiral Hamelin
Valmy	114	sail battleship	Rear Admiral Jacquinot
Friedland	114	screw	
Bayard	80	screw	
Breslaw	80	screw	
Charlemagne	80	screw	
Daim	4	paddle-steam vessel	
Darien	14	paddle-frigate	
Descartes	20	paddle-frigate	
Duguesclin	80	screw	
Duperré	70	sail battleship	

Name of Vessel	No. of Guns	Designation	Role/Commanding Officer
Flambart	4	paddle-steam vessel	
Gomer	20	paddle-frigate	
Jean Bart	74	screw	
Jena	82	sail battleship	
Jemappes	90	sail battleship	
Jupiter	80	sail battleship	
Henri IV	114	sail battleship	
Le Napoléon	90	screw	
L'Aigle	4	steam vessel	
L'Andromaque	56	sail frigate	
L'Inflexible	82	sail battleship	
Lucifer	2	screw steam vessel	
Marengo	70	sail battleship	
Milan	4	steam vessel	
Mogador	8	paddle-frigate	
Montebello	70	sail battleship	
Phlégethon	8	steam corvette	
Pluton	8	paddle-corvette	
Poursuivante	52	sail frigate	
Promethée	4	paddle-steamer	
Psyche	42	sail frigate	
Sémillante	60	sail frigate	
Tage	90	screw battleship	
Trident	70	sail battleship	
Vengeance	56	sail frigate	
Virignie	52	sail frigate	
Zenobie	50	screw frigate	

Appendix 9

Ships Engaged at Kertch and in the Sea of Azoff, 1855

Only those ships marked * actually served within the Sea of Azoff; their crews received the clasp *Azoff* – the only purely naval award – on the subsequent Crimea Medal.

It should also be noted that some of the ships' boats (only) of *Agamemnon, Princess Royal, Algiers, Royal Albert, Hannibal* and *St Jean d'Acre* – not the warships themselves – served briefly off Taganrog in the Azoff Sea in June 1855. The boat crews received the *Azoff* clasp.

Sphinx served in the Kertch expedition but only a prize crew of ten of her men actually served in the Sea of Azoff – for six days in May–June 1855.

The store ship *Industry* similarly served only a short time in the Sea of Azoff between 25 August and 1 September, on one voyage to replenish the stores of the squadron.

The others took part in the expedition to take the straits, Kertch and Yenikale, in May but did not proceed into the Sea of Azoff itself as they were too large to be deployed in its shallow waters.

Commanding officers are those at the beginning of the operations.

The British fleet

Name of Vessel	Designation	No. of Guns	Commanding Officer
Algiers	screw two–decker	90	Captain Chas Talbot
Agamemnon	screw two–decker	91	Captain Sir T. Pasley
*Arrow**	screw gun vessel	4	Lieutenant W.K. Joliffe
Ardent	paddle-wheel sloop	5	Lieutenant W. Horton
Banshee	paddle-wheel dispatch vessel	2	Lieutenant L.R. Reynolds
*Beagle**	screw gun vessel	4	Lieutenant W.N.W. Hewett
*Boxer**	screw gun vessel	2	Lieutenant S.P. Townshend
*Clinker**	screw gun vessel	2	Lieutenant J.S. Hudson
*Cracker**	steam gunboat	1	Lieutenant J.H. Marryatt
*Curlew**	screw sloop	9	Commander Rowley Lambert
*Danube**	steam tender	–	Lieutenant R.P. Caton

Name of Vessel	Designation	No. of Guns	Commanding Officer
*Fancy**	screw gunboat	2	Lieutenant C.G. Grylls
Furious	paddle-wheel steam frigate	16	Captain W. Loring
Gladiator	paddle-wheel corvette	6	Captain R. Hall
*Grinder**	steam gunboat	2	Lieutenant F. Hamilton
*Hannibal**	screw two-decker	91	Rear Admiral Houston Stewart; Captain Hay
Highflyer	screw corvette	21	Captain John Moore
*Industry**	screw transport and supply ship	–	Lieutenant G.H.K. Bower
*Jasper** (wrecked)	steam gunboat	2	Lieutenant J.S. Hudson
Leopard	paddle-wheel frigate	18	Captain G. Giffard
*Lynx**	screw dispatch vessel	6	Lieutenant C.M. Aynsley
*Medina**	paddle-wheel sloop	4	Lieutenant H.B. Beresford
*Miranda**	screw corvette	14	Captain E.M. Lyons
*Moslem**	iron steam tender/ transport	–	Lieutenant J. Simpson
Princess Royal	screw two-decker	91	Lord Clarence Paget
*Recruit**	iron gun vessel	6	Lieutenant G.F. Day
Royal Albert	screw three-decker	121	Flag of Admiral Lyons; Captain W.R. Mends
St Jean d'Acre	screw two-decker	101	Captain Harry Keppel
Sidon	paddle-wheel frigate	22	Captain G. Goldsmith
Simoom	screw troop ship	8	Captain T.R. Sulivan
Tribune	paddle-wheel frigate	31	Captain Hon. J.R. Drummond
Terrible	paddle-wheel frigate	21	Captain J.J. McCleverty
Caradoc	paddle-wheel dispatch vessel	2	Commander S.H. Derriman
Snake	screw gun vessel	4	Lieutenant H.F. M'Killop
*Sphinx**	steam sloop	6	Master S. Braddon
Spitfire	paddle-wheel survey vessel	5	Captain T.A.B. Spratt
*Stromboli**	paddle-wheel sloop	6	Lieutenant C.P. Coles
*Sulina**	iron steam tender	–	Mate C.H. Williams
*Swallow**	screw sloop	9	Lieutenant F.A.B. Crauford
Valorous	paddle-wheel frigate	16	Captain C.H.M. Buckle
*Vesuvius**	paddle-wheel sloop	6	Commander Sherard Osborn
*Viper**	screw gun vessel	4	Lieutenant W. Armytage
*Weser**	paddle steamer	6	Lieutenant J.E. Commerell
*Wrangler**	screw gun vessel	4	Lieutenant H. Risk

The French fleet

Under overall command of Admiral Bruat, the Azoff element under Captain de Sedaiges. Those that served in the Sea of Azoff are marked *; the others were engaged during the initial expedition into the straits and around Kertch and Yenikale.

Asmodée, *Berthollet*, *Brandon** (Lieutenant Cloué), *Cacique*, *Caffarelli*, *Caton** (Lieutenant Vida), *Charlemagne*, *Dauphin*, *Descartes*, *Fulton** (Lieutenant La Suchette), *Lucifer**, *Mégère**, *Milan*, *Mogador*, *Montebello*, *Napoléon*, *Phlégethon*, *Pomone*, *Primauguet*, *Roland*, *Ulloa*, *Vautour*, *Véloce*.

Appendix 10

British Ships Engaged in the Bombardment of Sebastopol, 17 October 1854

Those not designated were sailing vessels. Those marked * actually took part in the bombardment. Others towed sailing ships into line. *Circassian* was a tug.

Name of Vessel	Designation	No. of Guns	Commanding Officer
*Agamemnon**	screw	91	Rear Admiral Lyons; Captain W.R. Mends
*Albion**		90	Commander H.D. Rogers
*Arethusa**		50	Captain T.M.C. Symonds
*Bellerophon**		78	Captain Lord Paget
*Britannia**		120	Rear Admiral Montagu Stopford; Captain T.W. Carter
Circassian	paddle	–	2nd Master E.C. Ball
Cyclops	paddle	6	Master R.W. Roberts
Firebrand	paddle	6	Captain W.H. Stewart
Furious	paddle	16	Captain W. Loring
Highflyer	screw	21	Captain J. Moore
*Lynx**	screw	4	Captain J.P. Luce
*London**		90	Captain Chas Eden
Niger	screw	14	Commander L.G. Heath
*Queen**		116	Captain F.T. Michell
Retribution	paddle	23	Captain Hon. J.R. Drummond
*Rodney**		90	Captain Chas Graham
*Sampson**	paddle	6	Captain L.T. Jones
*Sans Pareil**	screw	70	Captain S.C. Dacres
*Sphinx**	paddle	6	Captain A.P.E. Wilmot
Spiteful	paddle	6	Commander A.F. Kynaston
*Spitfire**	paddle	6	Commander T.A.B. Spratt
*Terrible**	paddle	21	Captain J.J. McCleverty

Name of Vessel	Designation	No. of Guns	Commanding Officer
*Tribune**	screw	31	Captain Hon. S.T. Carnegie
Triton	paddle	3	Lieutenant H. Lloyd
Vesuvius	paddle	6	Commander R.A. Powell
*Trafalgar**		120	Captain H.F. Greville
*Vengeance**		84	Captain Lord E. Russell

The French contingent comprised twelve sailing warships and five major screw vessels, as well as smaller ships. Of these, eleven actually took part in the bombardment: *Napoléon*, *Henry IV*, *Valmy*, *Ville de Paris*, *Jupiter*, *Friedland*, *Marengo*, *Montebello*, *Suffren*, *Jean Bart* and *Charlemagne*.

The Turkish fleet was represented by the *Mahmoudie* and one two-decker.

Casualties in the Naval Bombardment, 17 October 1854

From the *London Gazette* casualty lists:

Name of Vessel	No. Killed or Died of Wounds	No. Wounded
Agamemnon	7	22
Albion	11	69
Arethusa	4	14
Bellerophon	4	15
Britannia	0	9
Cyclops	0	1
Firebrand	0	5
London	4	18
Niger	1	4
Queen	1	7
Retribution	0	2
Rodney	0	2
Sampson	1	2
Sans Pareil	11	59
Sphinx	1	0
Spiteful	2	9
Terrible	1	8
Trafalgar	0	2
Triton	1	4
Vengeance	0	2

This gives a total of 49 killed and 254 wounded. These should be taken as a general indication only since not all casualties were published or published accurately. The account offered by Admiral Dundas himself[1] reports 44 killed and 266 wounded and differs in some details from these *London Gazette* listings.

There may have been other naval casualties of the action, reported late in the *London Gazette* or included in 'general' casualty lists and not specifically in those for the bombardment. Because of the vagueness of some entries, it is possible that there were at least another five killed and fifteen wounded.

Appendix 12

Casualties to the Naval Brigade

From the *London Gazette* casualty lists, various major actions and casual day-to-day incidents:

Name of Vessel	No. Killed or Died of Wounds	No. Wounded
Albion	9	28
Arethusa	2	3
Beagle	0	1
Bellerophon	1	8
Britannia	3	13
Dauntless	0	1
Diamond	5	21
Firebrand	0	1
Leander	22	80
Leopard	0	1
London	12	50
Niger	0	1
Queen	28	110
Rodney	19	78
Trafalgar	2	17
Vengeance	2	9
Wasp	4	27

The majority of these were killed in day-to-day shelling, counter-fire, raids and sniping.

Of the larger actions, it is possible to derive tentatively from these lists:

Action	Date	No. Killed	No. Wounded
Inkermann	5.11.1854	3	4
Siege of Sebastopol assaults			
Quarries	7.6.1855	7	31
1st Redan	18.6.1855	12	45
2nd Redan	8.9.1855	0	23

These should be taken as a general indication only; not all casualties were published or published accurately.

Although the batteries were not always in action, manning the naval guns before Sebastopol was no soft option – as is witnessed by the daily casualties suffered by the Naval Brigade, a steady drain on the men of the navy serving ashore.

Allied Warships in the Pacific, 1854–5

British

Name of Vessel	No. of Guns	Designation
Amphitrite	24	*Leda*-class frigate
Barracouta	6	steam sloop
Bittern	12	sail
Brisk	14	screw
Dido	18	sail
Encounter	14	screw corvette
Hornet	17	screw sloop
Pique	40	fifth-rate frigate
President	50	frigate
Sybille	40	sail
Spartan	26	sail
Styx	6	steam sloop
Tartar	21	screw corvette
Trincomalee	24	*Leda*-class sail frigate
Virago	6	paddle-steamer
Winchester	50	sail

French

Name of Vessel	No. of Guns	Designation
L'Artémise	30	sail corvette
L'Alceste	54	steam frigate
L'Eurydice	22	sail frigate
La Forte	56	sail frigate
L'Obligado	12	sail brig
Sibylle	52	sail frigate
Constantine	22	sail corvette

Appendix 14

Victoria Crosses Awarded for the Baltic, Crimea and Sea of Azoff

The VC was instituted by Royal Warrant on 29 January 1856 and announced in the *London Gazette* on 5 February 1856. However, it was made retrospective to include the Baltic and Crimean campaigns of 1854–5; the earliest action for which a VC was awarded was that on 21 June 1854 when Mate Charles Lucas aboard *Hecla* off Bomarsund in the Baltic threw overboard a live shell, saving many lives. The first awards were not announced in the *London Gazette* until 24 February 1857 and the first naval recipient to appear in its pages was Lieutenant C.W. Buckley, rewarded for gallantry in the Sea of Azoff in May and June 1855. However, the first naval VC actually presented was that to Lieutenant Henry Raby who received his medal – awarded for gallantry in the storming of the Redan – from Queen Victoria at the ceremony in Hyde Park on 26 June 1857 when no less than sixty-two VCs were presented for service in the Russian War.

All the following awards were announced in the same *London Gazette* on 24 February 1857.

Buckley, Commander Cecil William.
Action: 29 May and 3 June 1855, Azoff.
For two instances of gallantry. At Genitchi on 29 May 1855, Buckley of HMS *Miranda*, with Lieutenant H.T. Burgoyne of *Swallow* and Gunner John Roberts volunteered to land and destroy important stores under the fire of the enemy. At Taganrog on 3 June 1855, Buckley and Bosun Henry Cooper of *Miranda* led a landing party which fired government stores and buildings under heavy fire. (Burgoyne, Roberts and Cooper also received the VC.)

Burgoyne, Commander John Talbot.
Action: 29 May 1855, Azoff.
See Buckley, above.

Bythesea, Commander John.
Action: 9–12 August 1854, Baltic.
With Stoker William Johnstone, landed on the island of Wardo to capture a Russian emissary with dispatches. After three days in hiding, attacked the Russian escort and captured the dispatches and three prisoners.

Commerell, Commander John Edmund (later Sir, GCB).
Action: 11 October 1855, Azoff.
Commander of *Weser*. For gallantry in crossing the Isthmus of Arabat at night and destroying large quantities of stores on the shores of the Sivash under close fire. Qartermaster W.T. Rickard received the VC for the same action.

Cooper, Boatswain Henry.
Action: 3 June 1855, Azoff.
See Buckley, above.

Curtis, Boatswain's Mate Henry.
Action: 18 June 1855, 1st Redan, Crimea.
See Raby, below.

Daniel, Midshipman Edward St John.
Action: for repeated acts of gallantry, Crimea.
Of HMS *Diamond*. For volunteering to bring gunpowder from a wagon under heavy fire and later for bravery serving alongside Captain Peel at Inkermann. For devotion to the wounded Captain Peel during the assault on the Redan whilst under heavy fire. (VC forfeited February 1867.)

Day, Lieutenant George Fiott.
Action: 17 September 1855, Azoff.
From HMS *Recruit*. For gallantry during a series of reconnaissances behind enemy positions at Genitchi to establish the location of Russian batteries and gun vessels. He carried out a similar reconnaissance on 19 September. (He also received the French *Légion d'honneur* and Turkish Order of the Medjidie.)

Dowell, Lieutenant George Dare, Royal Marine Artillery.
Action: 13 July 1855, Baltic.
Of HMS *Ruby*. See Ingouville, below. For going to the assistance of George Ingouville off Viborg and helping to rescue the crew of a damaged cutter and towing the boat out of range.

Gorman, Able Seaman James.
Action: 5 November 1854, Inkermann, Crimea.
See Reeves, below.

Hewett, Lieutenant William Nathan Wrighte (later Sir).
Action: 26 October 1854 and 5 November 1854, Crimea.
For great gallantry when Mate of *Beagle* when he was instrumental in repelling a Russian attack on his Lancaster battery, 26 October 1854. And for gallantry, then as Lieutenant, in action at Inkermann.

Ingouville, Captain of the Mast George.
Action: 13 July 1855, Baltic.
For gallantry with boat parties from *Arrogant* in action with gunboats and batteries at Viborg. Although wounded, he recovered a damaged cutter under heavy fire.

Johnstone, Stoker William.
Action: 9–12 August 1854, Baltic.
See Bythesea, above.

Kellaway, Boatswain 3rd Class Joseph.
Action: 31 August 1855, Azoff.
Kellaway, Bosun of *Wrangler*, was part of a landing party near Mariaupol which was ambushed and driven back. He rescued the Mate, Charles Odevaine, under heavy fire and despite putting up a brave resistance, both were captured.

Lucas, Mate Charles Davis.
Action: 21 June 1854, Baltic.
When Mate of HMS *Hecla* during an attack on Bomarsund, picked up and threw overboard a live Russian shell which had landed on the deck, thereby saving many lives. (The first action for which the VC was awarded.)

Peel, Captain William.
Action: 18 October 1854, 5 November 1854, 18 June 1855, Crimea.
For repeated acts of gallantry. On 18 October 1854, picking up and throwing away a live shell, with its fuse burning, from amongst powder cases by a magazine. At Inkermann on 5 November 1854 he joined officers of the Grenadier Guards in defending their colours in the Sandbag Battery. During the assault of the Redan on 18 June 1855, he volunteered to lead an assault party and did so until wounded. (Later KCB.)

Raby, Lieutenant Henry James.
Action: 18 June 1855, 1st Redan, Crimea.
During the first attack on the Redan on 18 June 1855, aided by two sailors, Raby went out under very heavy fire to bring in a wounded soldier of the 57th Regt. (Also awarded the French *Légion d'honneur* and later CB.)

Reeves, Seaman Thomas.
Action: 5 November 1854, Inkermann, Crimea.
For gallantry in defending a Lancaster battery during the Battle of Inkermann. Was one of five sailors (two of whom were killed) who mounted the gun emplacement to repel an attack by firing down into advancing Russians under a very heavy fire.

Rickard, Quartermaster William Thomas.
Action: 11 October 1855, Azoff.
See Commerell, above.

Roberts, Gunner John.
Action: 29 May 1855, Azoff.
See Buckley, above.

Scholefield, Able Seaman Mark.
Action: 5 November 1854, Inkermann, Crimea.
See Reeves, above.

Shepherd or Sheppard, Boatswain's Mate John.
Action: 15 July and 16 August 1855, Crimea.
As Bosun's Mate of *St Jean d'Acre*, twice attempted, under exceptionally dangerous circumstances, to row into Sebastopol harbour to place an explosive charge against a Russian warship. (Also awarded the Conspicuous Gallantry Medal (CGM) for the Crimea.)

Sullivan, Boatswain's Mate John.
Action: 10 April 1855, Crimea.
For repeated gallantry, in particular on 10 April 1855 in placing a marker flag to direct artillery fire onto concealed enemy guns, whilst himself under heavy fire. (Also awarded the CGM, the *Légion d'honneur* and Italian *Al Valore Militare* for the Crimea.)

Taylor, Captain of the Forecastle John.
Action: 18 June 1855, 1st Redan, Crimea.
See Raby, above.

Trewavas, Seaman Joseph.
Action: 3 July 1855, Azoff.
Trewavas, of *Beagle*, cut the hawsers of the floating bridge at Genitchi under close and heavy fire by which he was wounded. (He also received the new CGM for the same action.)

Notes

Introduction

1. Later joined by the Italian state of Sardinia.
2. Now part of Romania.
3. According to A.W. Kinglake, the French made most of the running in this. As the newly created Emperor (1852) Napoleon III sought national and personal prestige without really expecting that a war would follow; A.W. Kinglake, *The Invasion of the Crimea*, Cabinet Edn (9 vols, Blackwood, London, 1888), Vol. 2, Ch. 9.
4. The dockyards were completely destroyed by the allies in September 1855.
5. The stance of Austria was of particular importance; in the event, she never joined the allied coalition but the fact that she might be drawn into the war against Russia was something that the Tsar had to keep in mind throughout the diplomatic tussles and the war itself. Austria's intervention against Russia would have caused a major military problem for the Tsar. As it was, by agreement with the Sultan, Austrian forces occupied Moldavia and Wallachia following the eventual Russian withdrawal.
6. The extensive fighting – less successful for the Turks – in the Caucasus, between the Black Sea and the Caspian Sea, included the epic but ultimately unsuccessful defence of Kars in 1855, which was conducted by the English officer Sir William Fenwick Williams in Turkish service. Some thought was given in 1855 to providing significant military aid to the Turkish campaign on the Asiatic coast of the Black Sea but in the end it was left in the hands of Turkish forces. See Captain A.C. Dewar, *The Russian War 1855: Black Sea* (Navy Records Society, London, 1945), pp. 111–12.
7. These fears and the threat of an allied attack on St Petersburg through the Baltic meant that Russia had to divert tens of thousands of troops to the north, far away from any use in the Crimea. Forces amounting to between 200,000 and 300,000 men have been suggested.
8. See A. Seaton, *The Crimean War: A Russian Perspective* (Batsford, London, 1977), pp. 283–4.

Chapter 1

1. Nevertheless, the Sardinian contingent of over 15,000 men with 2,000 horses and 36 guns under General La Marmora was brought largely by British ships from northern Italy to the Crimea early in 1855.
2. A multiplicity of new designs for engines and boilers were being proposed and tried.
3. See below, p. 9.
4. For example, the British *Megaera* and *Simoom* of 1846–9.
5. All the warships employed during the war were wooden constructions, with the exception of the three French 'floating batteries' which came into use late in 1855; their British counterparts saw no action in the war. 'Ironclad' warships came later.
6. Captain S. Eardley-Wilmot, *Life of Vice Admiral Lord Lyons GCB* (Sampson Low, London, 1898), p. 120.
7. Turkish forces engaged in their campaign in the Caucasus, between the Black Sea and the Caspian, were supplied and reinforced largely – but not exclusively – by Turkish vessels.
8. Reigned 1689–1725.
9. Often ascribed to Peter is the statement that 'a ruler that has but an army has one hand, but he who has a navy has both'.

10. Reigned 1822–55.
11. The paddle-steamer gunboat *Pruth*, for example, was built by Lairds of Birkenhead in 1851 and two other Russian warships, the *Witjas* and *Woijn* were being built in England when war began and were seized by the Admiralty to be taken into the British fleet as the *Cossack* and *Tartar*.
12. For example, with the construction of *Le Napoléon*, the first purpose-built steam screw battleship.
13. The remarkable mass-production of warships in 'The Great Armament' in the winter of 1855 gave clear evidence of Britain's industrial and technological superiority.
14. With the failure of their support for the Egyptian ruler Mehemet Ali in the recent Eastern Crisis. The allied naval bombardment of St Jean d'Acre in 1840 had also seen the first significant use of steam-powered warships in action.
15. E.A. Seymour, *My Naval Career and Travels* (Smith Elder, London, 1911), p. 11.
16. The growing obsolescence of the old ship-of-the-line, indeed of all major wooden warships, became apparent during the Russian War – for example, with the use of the three French armoured floating batteries at Kinburn (see p. 136ff.), but was not fully accepted until the 1860s with the use of ironclads during the American Civil War.
17. In 1815, the Royal Navy had 90,000 men (70,000 sailors and 20,000 marines) on its payroll. This figure declined steadily after 1816, to reach a level around the 30,000s in the 1830s; it rose somewhat in view of Anglo-French crises in the 1840s to reach approximately 45,000 by 1853 (33,000 sailors and 12,500 marines). As war with Russia developed, the figures rose significantly – 63,000 in 1854, 70,000 in 1855 and a planned 76,000 for 1856. The end of the war saw another drastic reduction, but the strength of Royal Navy and Royal Marine personnel was retained at around the 60,000 mark for the rest of the century. See D. Lyon and R. Winfield, *The Sail and Steam Navy List* (Chatham Publishing, London, 2004), pp. 13–14.
18. *The Times*, 8 August 1853.
19. See Chapter 2 for the invaluable service rendered by this ship as a survey vessel in the Baltic in 1854.
20. Seymour, *My Naval Career and Travels*, p. 8.
21. Such as *Nemesis*.
22. And were much used in these roles during the Russian War.
23. They still, of course, retained sailing capabilities. Steam power was really reserved for navigation in harbour or places where fine control was needed. Long voyages were still done under sail.
24. Vide the speed trial between the new screw vessel *Archimedes* and the navy's fastest paddle-steamer the *Vulcan* in 1839, which *Archimedes* easily won and the more famous trial of strength between the screw *Rattler* and the paddle-sloop *Alecto* in 1845.
25. The first were *Blenheim*, *Hogue*, *Edinburgh* and *Ajax*. Others examples are *Russell*, *Cornwallis*, *Hawke*, *Pembroke* and *Hastings*.
26. Many conversions were carried out during the war – *Colossus*, *Centurion* and *Mars* were wartime conversions.
27. Other examples of new screw warships were *Prince of Wales*, *Royal Albert*, *Royal George* (all of 120 guns and complement of 1,100 men) and the slightly later *Royal Frederick*, *Victoria* and *Howe*.
28. Some of the Russian Black Sea Fleet carried these weapons and they were used at Sinope in November 1853; see p. 43.
29. The British developed their own form of shell-firing gun as a result, introduced into the Royal Navy in 1838. Another response was the establishment of the School of Gunnery (HMS *Excellent*) in 1830. New oval-bored 'Lancaster guns', named after their inventor, were also developed in time for use in the Crimean War. They were highly regarded for their range, power and accuracy but were not always reliable, with a tendency for the shell to jam in the barrel and cause a backfire.
30. They had already been introduced into the East India Company service and iron paddle-steamers like *Nemesis* (1839) and *Phlegethon* had served in the Bengal Marine in operations off China, 1840–2 and in Burma, 1852.
31. There were problems with compass deviation, weight ratios, balance and corrosion.
32. *Megaera* and *Simoom* were used as troop ships during the Crimean War. Other examples are the supply and store ships *Perseverance* and *Supply* and the gunboats *Caradoc* and *Rocket*.

33. Still, of course, in existence and now moored in the Historic Dockyard at Portsmouth.
34. See contemporary *Navy Lists*.
35. *The Times*, 11 August 1853.

Chapter 2

1. The allies continued to hope that Sweden, with its own powerful fleet, said to include several hundred gunboats, could be induced to join the alliance against Russia. Strong and continuing pressure was put on the Swedish King Oscar, but to no avail, even after the fall of Bomarsund in August 1854. Sweden did not need a permanent enemy in the form of Russia.
2. The paddle-steamer *Sidon* was largely his design.
3. Launched in 1852, the *Duke of Wellington* was a magnificent sight, much commented on at the time. A huge vessel, she towered over most of the other ships in the fleet, especially the newer steam frigates. Despite her size, she was fast and elegant. See *The Times*, 11 August 1853, for an impression of the ship.
4. Lowry Corry served from 1805, seeing extensive service during the French Wars and was promoted to commander in 1815. In 1820, he was appointed Flag Captain to Sir Henry Blackwood on the East Indies station and in 1835 took command of the *Barham*. He later commanded a squadron off the coast of Spain, for which he was highly commended and then retired on half-pay. In September 1844, he was put in command of the new steam frigate *Firebrand* to conduct experiments in the use of steamships and in the same year was given command of the *Leopard*, serving in her on the Home, Lisbon and Mediterranean stations. Appointed rear admiral in 1852, and then placed in command of the Channel squadron, Corry was appointed second in command of the Baltic Fleet in 1854.
5. 1788–1868. Henry Ducie Chads served in the Napoleonic Wars at Martinique (1810) and was captured by the Americans during the 1812–14 war. He went on to serve in the West Indies, Burma and East Indies. Rear admiral in the Baltic; KCB 1855 and admiral 1863.
6. 1787–1863. James Hanway Plumridge served on *Defence* at Trafalgar and saw a great deal of service against the French. MP for Falmouth 1841–47 and rear admiral 1852. Appointed KCB in 1855 for services in the Baltic and promoted to admiral 1857.
7. Alexander Ferdinand Parseval-Deschênes (1790–1860).
8. Of which only one, the battleship *Austerlitz*, was screw driven.
9. Steam preponderance was given to the Baltic fleet.
10. C.R. Low, *Her Majesty's Navy* (Virtue, London, n.d., *c.* 1893), p. 270. Many junior officers had little regard for Napier; Captain Harry Keppel, for example, called him 'The Old Donkey' and had little but contempt for him.
11. See Appendix 6. Napier was not slow to defend himself or to launch attacks on his accusers, especially those in the Admiralty.
12. See, for example, G.B. Earp (ed.), *The History of the Baltic Campaign of 1854* (repr. Naval and Military Press, Uckfield, 2009), pp. 18–20.
13. It was 'a rotten system of manning' according to Rear Admiral Maurice Berkeley, quoted in D. Bonner-Smith and A.C. Dewar (eds), *The Russian War: Baltic and Black Sea 1854* (Navy Records Society, London, 1943), p. 212.
14. Training novice seamen was easier in times of peace than when forced by the needs of war. Hence Napier's constant emphasis on training up his men, especially in basic seamanship and gunnery.
15. For example, in 1852–3, the introduction of Continuous Service with twelve or ten-year terms and service pensions and, slightly later, the introduction of a standard naval uniform for lower ranks. 'Continuous Service' made it possible for a sailor to make a profession of the navy for the first time but its effects were not really apparent by 1854.
16. The Danish government actually forbad its men from serving with the British fleet. See Earp, *The History of the Baltic Campaign*, p. 89.
17. Captains serving in the Baltic in 1854 regularly 'picked up' local fishermen or boatmen to use as pilots or guides as they stopped and searched merchant vessels. In June 1854, for example,

Captain Hall of *Hecla* led an attack on Bomarsund using the services of a local pilot, taken from a fishing boat which the warship had stopped. See p. 25.

18. It was a fleet, said one commentator, 'for the most part manned with the refuse of London and other towns, destitute even of clothing'. Without the ex-Coast Guard men, it was said, the squadron would not have been able to put to sea at all. E. Napier, *The Life and Correspondence of Admiral Sir Charles Napier, KCB* (Hurst and Blackett, London, 1862), p. 225; Earp, *The History of the Baltic Campaign*, p. 19.

19. Earp, *The History of the Baltic Campaign*, p. 16.

20. Hamilton Williams, *Britain's Naval Power* (Macmillan, London, 1898), p. 84. And it was not, of course, deemed to be in any way a 'secondary' theatre of war, although it really has fallen out of view in terms of British naval campaigns.

21. 'Much criticised' according to Sir W.L. Clowes, *The Royal Navy: A History from Earliest Times to the Death of Queen Victoria* (7 vols, Sampson Lowe Marston, London, 1903), Vol. VI, p. 414.

22. Training his largely inexperienced crews in gunnery was a major consideration for Napier.

23. See p. 165ff.

24. Another weakness was the inability to carry out operations on land if required. Apart from the relatively small complements of Royal Marines borne on the ships, the fleet did not carry a force of soldiers capable of serving ashore.

25. The Russians had indeed reinforced their fleet in the Baltic, but the rumours proved to be greatly exaggerated. Napier, *The Life and Correspondence of Admiral Sir Charles Napier*, p. 223.

26. The courts of Sweden and Denmark determined to remain strictly neutral and did not allow the entry of the warship fleets to their main ports, though facilities were granted in all the ports of the neutral powers for the purchase of provisions, except materials of war. British warships frequently report landing at small towns on the east coast of Sweden to buy provisions and take on water. King Oscar of Sweden was courted diplomatically on formal and informal levels – his fleet of 26 major warships and an estimated 300 gunboats would have been very useful, to say nothing of ports and supplies. But he repeatedly made it clear that whilst he might welcome visits from 'friendly' warships, he could not risk allowing Sweden to join the Anglo-French alliance; Sweden, after all, would have to live with the Russians as neighbours after the war.

27. See, for example, the orders given to Napier in Bonner-Smith and Dewar (eds), *The Russian War: Baltic and Black Sea 1854*, pp. 46–7.

28. Napier, *The Life and Correspondence of Admiral Sir Charles Napier*, p. 232. An 'unprotected state' because so many of Britain's warships had been drawn away from the Channel and home defence to the Baltic or elsewhere.

29. Williams, *Britain's Naval Power*, p. 86. See also Sir James Graham's letter to Napier, 10 April 1854, quoted in Napier, *The Life and Correspondence of Admiral Sir Charles Napier*, p. 238.

30. Quoted in Napier, *The Life and Correspondence of Admiral Sir Charles Napier*, p. 235.

31. Quoted in ibid., p. 239.

32. See Captain B.J. Sulivan's scathing attack on those anxious simply to 'have a shot at something or try to get up a fight for the chance of getting their names mentioned', P. Collister, *The Sulivans and the Slave Trade* (Collings, London, 1979), p. 71.

33. What were usually called 'Russian' merchant vessels, many destroyed or seized to be taken back to Britain as prizes and sold with their cargoes, were often Finnish – though still technically 'enemy' ships. The British blockaders did not seize Russian property carried on 'neutral' vessels (for example, American or Danish) as they had done in earlier wars, for fear of antagonising other states. Since Britain was a major exporter and importer of Russian and Finnish goods, it is a moot point as to whether all this actually hurt British trade more than Russian. Russia relied far more on overland trade routes and could replace much of her lost sea trade with that carried overland.

34. Opinions of this vary, but some estimates put the Russian troop presence retained in the Baltic area and for the defence of Cronstadt and St Petersburg at up to 300,000 men who would not therefore be capable of deployment in other important theatres (for example, in the Crimea).

35. Now Hanko.

36. Now part of Latvia.

37. Now Liepaja.
38. Frequently occurs as Revel in contemporary British accounts; now Tallinn, the capital city of Estonia.
39. In their modern Finnish versions these are now Raahe, Oulu and Tornio.
40. See Priest's report on the action in Bonner-Smith and Dewar (eds), *The Russian War: Baltic and Black Sea 1854*, pp. 70–2 and on his similar activity at Uleaborg on pp. 74–7.
41. M. Levien (ed.), *The Cree Journals* (Webb & Bower, Exeter, 1981), p. 231.
42. Ibid., p. 232.
43. See George Giffard's report to Admiral Plumridge in Bonner-Smith and Dewar (eds), *The Russian War: Baltic and Black Sea 1854*, pp. 73–4 and the reports of his subordinates on this round of devastation, pp. 74–80.
44. The journals and letters of naval officers seem understandably divided between the fire-eaters, happy to see 'total war' waged in any way, and many who felt that it was simply unjustifiable to harm local communities and small-scale traders whose activities would hardly affect the war but whose livelihoods depended on their trade.
45. Now Kokkola.
46. There is a good account of this action in Levien (ed.), *The Cree Journals*, p. 236. Surgeon Cree was aboard the *Odin* at the time.
47. So-called because they were carried, inverted, over the paddle wheels on the warships. They were large and handy boats but difficult to launch.
48. Levien (ed.), *The Cree Journals*, p. 236.
49. The boat is still on display in the town – the only surviving paddle-box boat from a British paddle-warship. The graves of nine Royal Marines killed in the attack are still tended in the town.
50. The prisoners seem to have been treated well enough. All who had been wounded were tended in a hospital at Gamla Karleby, whilst the rest were sent on to Helsingfors. After staying at Karleby for five weeks, the wounded were removed to Imola, about 70 miles inland, on the approach of the British steamer *Leopard*. On 21 September, following an agreement on the exchange of prisoners, they were sent by carts to Abo and then to Ledo Sound in a small steamer and thence to rejoin the fleet at Nargen.
51. The effects of the weather need to be borne in mind. During the Baltic campaigns, thick fog and severe winds frequently delayed movements. As an example, see Levien (ed.), *The Cree Journals*, p. 223ff. for frequent references to bad weather and to the persistence of ice.
52. Variously spelled; now Suomenlinna, 'the fortress of the Finns'.
53. Now Viipuri, Turku and Pernu.
54. A novel feature of this campaign was the Russian use of contact and electric mines at Cronstadt. Each contained up to 700lb of powder and up to 300 are believed to have been laid by 1855. See p. 99.
55. Bartholomew James Sulivan (1810–90) played an important role in the Baltic campaigns. He came from a large and distinguished family of naval officers, several of whom served in the Russian War. Appointed CB for service in the Baltic, he was promoted to KCB in 1869, vice admiral in 1870 and retired as an admiral in 1877.
56. Quoted in Collister, *The Sulivans*, p. 47.
57. See Sulivan's report to Napier, 28 June 1854, quoted in Bonner-Smith and Dewar (eds), *The Russian War: Baltic and Black Sea 1854*, pp. 85–7.
58. 'Any attack upon Cronstadt appears to me, with our means, perfectly impossible': Napier to Admiralty, 1 July 1854, quoted in Bonner-Smith and Dewar (eds), *The Russian War: Baltic and Black Sea 1854*, p. 85.
59. Apparently with the full agreement of his senior subordinates.
60. See their letter to Napier in Bonner-Smith and Dewar (eds), *The Russian War: Baltic and Black Sea 1854*, p. 87.
61. The two became known as Nya Skarpans and Gamla Skarpans (New and Old Skarpans). They were more or less destroyed in the fighting in 1854 and little now remains of them.

62. Usually called Nottich in British accounts.
63. Also known as 'Fort Tzee', i.e. Fort 'C'.
64. See B. Greenhill and A. Giffard, *The British Assault on Finland* (Conway Maritime Press, London, 1988), Chapter 2 for a detailed account of the development of the fortified site.
65. The French Admiral is later said to have commented that Sulivan, for all the hard work he carried out as surveying officer, 'must be made of iron' (Collister, *The Sulivans*, p. 48). He certainly played a major part in the Baltic operations.
66. Commanders were well aware of the career advantages offered by a good report on their actions and the 'approbation' of the Admiralty.
67. Presumably Notvik.
68. Levien (ed.), *The Cree Journals*, p. 239.
69. Later to become Rear Admiral Charles Davis Lucas, VC. Born in 1834, he died in 1914.
70. See Hall's account of his Bomarsund attack in Bonner-Smith and Dewar (eds), *The Russian War: Baltic and Black Sea 1854*, pp. 82–4.
71. See the detailed account of Hall in his dispatch to Plumridge, in Bonner-Smith and Dewar (eds), *The Russian War: Baltic and Black Sea 1854*, pp. 82–4.
72. See Napier's comment to the Admiralty reproduced in Bonner-Smith and Dewar (eds), *The Russian War: Baltic and Black Sea 1854*, p. 81: 'If every Captain when detached chose to throw away all his shot and shell against stone walls, the fleet would soon be inefficient'. On his return to Bomarsund for the main attack on the forts in August, Edmund Cree commented that the action had 'only showed them [i.e. the defenders of Bomarsund] their weak points which they have had time to repair' (Levien (ed.), *The Cree Journals*, p. 242).
73. Often occurs simply as Ledsund or Led Sound.
74. 1795–1878. Achille Baraguay d'Hilliers was the son of one of Napoleon's generals. He was made a Marshal of France for the capture of Bomarsund.
75. The novel sight of French soldiers crowded aboard British warships did not fail to arouse comment. The British sailors and steamers carrying the force were *Hannibal, Algiers, St Vincent, Royal William, Termagant, Gladiator, Sphinx* and *Janus*. All of these ships were to be sent back to Britain as soon as they had delivered the expeditionary force.
76. Including one of the highly regarded Lancaster guns.
77. H.N. Sulivan, *Live and Letters of Admiral Sir Bartholomew James Sulivan, KCB* (Murray, London, 1896), p. 169.
78. Accounts vary as to the number of guns mounted in the smaller Bomarsund forts.
79. Colonel Fortescue Graham, RM was another long-serving veteran, whose career spanned the Peninsular War and North America, the Carlist Wars and China. Created CB for the Bomarsund campaign, he was later advanced to KCB and full general before his death in 1880.
80. Which frequently went aground. See Bonner-Smith and Dewar (eds), *The Russian War: Baltic and Black Sea 1854*, p. 92.
81. A total of eleven ships eventually took part in the actual bombardment, forming a shallow crescent to the southeast of the main fort.
82. This fear was repeatedly expressed, but nothing seems to have materialised.
83. Suitably praised by Chads and Napier. See Bonner-Smith and Dewar (eds), *The Russian War: Baltic and Black Sea 1854*, pp. 94–6.
84. They were all later recovered by naval divers and men of the sappers and miners.
85. Captain of the Main Top George Privett and Ordinary Seaman Thomas Barber.
86. See Collister, *The Sulivans*, p. 50.
87. There is some variation regarding the ships that actually took part in the bombardment in the various accounts of the action. This list is from Napier's dispatch to the Admiralty, 16 August 1854, quoted in Bonner-Smith and Dewar (eds), *The Russian War: Baltic and Black Sea 1854*, p. 97.
88. And the personal yacht of the Emperor, *La Reine Hortense*. This had brought General Baraguay d'Hilliers from France to the Baltic and had occasionally been used to carry dispatches and in reconnaissance.

89. A 'beautiful fire' in Napier's dispatch to the Admiralty, 16 August 1854, quoted in Bonner-Smith and Dewar (eds), *The Russian War: Baltic and Black Sea 1854*, p. 97.

90. Napier's dispatch to the Admiralty, 19 August 1854, quoted in Bonner-Smith and Dewar (eds), *The Russian War: Baltic and Black Sea 1854*, p. 98.

91. The allies had fairly light casualties during the whole operation – fifty-four killed and wounded, the great majority being French infantry (seventeen killed); Russian losses are not known, but they suffered very badly in all the bombarded forts.

92. A remarkable feature of this attack was the number of civilian 'sightseers' who came up in small, private vessels simply to watch the proceedings, some from as far way as Britain.

93. The major warships were firing at range of over 2,000 yards and did nothing like the damage wrought by the closer siege guns.

94. The naval bombardment of Bomarsund – and of the sea forts at Sebastopol – had been at comparatively long ranges.

95. Today, only fragments survive – though a popular and much-visited tourist attraction on the islands. The outline of the great semicircular fort is discernible, but with only a few low fragments of its outer (seaward) wall remaining and the barracks blocks forming its rear just about traceable. A main road now runs right through the site. The ruins of Bränklint, Notvik and Prästö forts also survive.

96. Completed by Rear Admiral Martin. Prästö was completely demolished on 30 August, Notvik on the 31st and the great fort on 2 September. Bränklint, of course, had blown up in a huge explosion on 14 August. All the other Russian works on the site and large quantities of unused building material were destroyed by 14 September by the sappers and miners under Captain King.

97. A separate 'Ålands Convention', agreed by the allies in March 1856 and demilitarising the islands, was incorporated into the Treaty of Paris which ended the war.

98. A mine and its workers' village in Northumberland were named 'Bomarsund' in honour of the event.

99. Many of the men taken at Bomarsund were Finnish.

100. Apart from the officers, they were reportedly in poor physical condition when captured and not regarded as fine examples of Russian and Finnish conscripts! Some were accompanied by their wives and all were given a subsistence income and allowed considerable freedom of movement, on parole, during the day. See *Illustrated London News*, 1854, p. 1140. A memorial to the Russian who died in Lewes was later set up by the Tsar and still survives there.

101. There had been all sorts of rumours that Russian ships and/or troops would come to the aid of Bomarsund.

102. See his *Memorandum on the Defence of Abo* in Bonner-Smith and Dewar (eds), *The Russian War: Baltic and Black Sea 1854*, pp. 105–6.

103. This plan became the basis for the actual attack on Sveaborg in 1855. See p. 102ff.

104. Also known as 'fortress of the six islands'. See detailed description on p. 101ff.

105. Now Suomenlinna – 'the fortress of the Finns'.

106. The only ships in Napier's fleet capable of shallow-draught work as gunboats for an attack on Sveaborg were six sloops of the *Arrow* class serving with the fleet – each armed with two of the new 68-pounder Lancaster guns. Six more were ordered and under construction in Britain, these constituting the shallow-draught *Gleaner* class of screw gunboats. At approximately 216 tons each, mounting 1 68-pounder, 1 32-pounder and 2 24-pounders, they would have a crew of 36, 2 of them officers. These small vessels would normally be commanded by a lieutenant or even a master, giving very junior officers opportunities for command and initiative. Space below decks on these new ships was very limited – machinery, coal, boilers, water tanks and engines took up much of their space. Boats like these and the soon-to-be-constructed mortar boat fleet could destroy stone buildings and drop shells through the roofs of forts where the guns of the larger ships firing with a horizontal trajectory and at long range would not do the damage. These gun vessels – eventually built in large numbers – made possible the successful bombardment of Sveaborg in

1855. Some of the new, light gun vessels were employed with great success in the Azoff campaign, especially from the *Dapper* class, of which more than 95 were built before the war ended.

107. A naval 'Council of War' held aboard *Duke of Wellington* at Ledo Sound on 12 September vetoed any thought of an attack on Sveaborg. A detailed plan had been laid out by General Harry Jones, Royal Engineers, to attack Sveaborg – which he thought a perfectly feasible goal – but Napier believed that the adoption of his scheme would be 'mad'. See Bonner-Smith and Dewar (eds), *The Russian War: Baltic and Black Sea, 1854*, pp. 111–23. This view was repeated at a meeting of the allied admirals on 18 September. Napier had put forward his own views on the subject in detail in a letter to the First Lord Sir James Graham on 18 July.

108. See Admiralty letter to Napier, 23 September 1854, outlining the preliminary plans to remove warships from the theatre of war. Bonner-Smith and Dewar (eds), *The Russian War: Baltic and Black Sea, 1854*, pp. 131–2.

109. *The Times*, for example, carried a blistering attack on Napier on 4 October.

110. *The Times* published a detailed article on 15 September denouncing Napier's return to Britain without doing more against the fortresses at Sveaborg and Cronstadt: 'this cessation of hostilities [is] ill-timed ... we have just learned our strength and the enemy his weakness'.

111. The ruins were visited by *Firefly* and *Amphion* in May 1855 and apart from the removal of dressed stone to repair local churches and buildings, nothing had been done to repair the forts or re-occupy the site by that date. It was later stated that the area was being used as a depot for food and stores by the Russians.

112. Low, *Her Majesty's Navy*, p. 271.

113. Just one example is Captain B.J. Sulivan, a man who was not blind to Napier's shortcomings and was frequently critical of him. He nevertheless supported the general line of Napier's policy and had only contempt for those at home who made bald assertions about what should be done without the responsibility of having to act on the spot. 'What the newspapers say in leading articles ... is great nonsense and only misleads people. If our fleet had madly tried to attack Cronstadt and had been beaten and partly destroyed, as it must have been, the papers would have been the first to cry out about our knocking our ships to pieces against stone walls.', quoted in Collister, *The Sulivans*, p. 51.

114. The figures and even the significance of this are disputed. Some claim that up to 300,000 Russian or Finnish troops were thus tied down and that it represents a major achievement of the Baltic operations. For example, H. Seton-Watson, *The Russian Empire 1801–1917* (Clarendon Press, Oxford, 1967), p. 324.

Chapter 3

1. The initial British fleet assembled here comprised seven powerful ships-of-the-line – the 90-gun sailer *Britannia* (flagship of Vice Admiral Dundas), the 120-gun *Trafalgar*, the *Albion*, the *Rodney*, the *Vengeance*, the *Bellerophon* and the 90-gun screw steamship *Sans Pareil*.

2. See Appendix 2 for the ships involved.

3. This naval action had important reverberations. It has been said that the use of the new explosive shells clearly heralded the demise of the unarmoured wooden warship – which some contemporary observers clearly foresaw. Recent writing has tended to play down the importance of the new weaponry in this particular action.

4. See, for example, Eardley-Wilmot, *Life of Vice Admiral Lord Lyons GCB*, p. 135.

5. Now usually Bosporus.

6. Seymour, *My Naval Career and Travels*, p. 12.

7. The former was the Russo-Turkish treaty that allowed Russia predominance in the Black Sea and had closed the sea to foreign warships. The treaty was badly received by Britain and France. The Straits Convention, imposed by Britain, closed the Bosphorus and Dardanelles to all warships, effectively sealing the Russian fleet within the Black Sea.

8. Quoted in Eardley-Wilmot, *Life of Vice Admiral Lord Lyons GCB*, p. 145.

9. Now Trabzon.

10. Eardley-Wilmot, *Life of Vice Admiral Lord Lyons GCB*, pp. 155–6. The town is now known as Kulevi.

11. Ibid., p. 148.

12. Seymour, *My Naval Career and Travels*, p. 12.

13. Sir James Whitley Deans Dundas (1785–1862). Born in December 1785, he entered the navy in 1799 serving in the Mediterranean, off the coast of France and in the North Sea. Lieutenant 1805, commander 1806 and captain October 1807; served in the Baltic and North Sea until 1815. Took the surname Dundas on marriage in 1808. From 1815 to 1819 commanded the frigate *Tagus* in the Mediterranean and later served off Portugal. From 1836–8 commanded *Britannia* at Portsmouth and appointed CB in 1839; rear admiral November 1841. Liberal MP for various boroughs 1832–52 and on the Board of Admiralty 1846–52 when he became Senior Lord. In January 1852, Dundas was appointed to command the Mediterranean Fleet and in December advanced to vice admiral. He accepted what was to be a supporting role for his naval forces in the Black Sea campaign of 1854. He ferried the armies to the Crimea, supported them with transport, men and guns and reluctantly agreed to the naval bombardment of Sebastopol on 17 October 1854. He retired at the end of 1854 when his tenure in command of the Mediterranean Fleet expired and was appointed GCB in July 1855 after his return to England. Promoted to admiral in December 1857, he saw no further service and died at Weymouth in 1862.

14. There was felt to be some saving grace in the known fact that his tenure would cease in December 1854 when he would no doubt be succeeded by his second-in-command, the more highly regarded Sir Edmund Lyons.

15. See instructions to Dundas, Bonner-Smith and Dewar (eds), *The Russian War: Baltic and Black Sea 1854*, pp. 246–7.

16. Ibid.

17. Ibid., p. 249. British merchant vessels were also, of course, forbidden to carry out any trade with Russia or through Russian ports and neutrals were similarly warned on 9 June. Turkish control of the narrow Bosphorus and Dardanelles made this blockade of trade with the Black Sea rather more straightforward than the blockade of the Baltic.

18. Of these, Lieutenant Burke later travelled to Shulma and Routschouk, where he was killed in action. He was the first British officer to be killed in the Russian War. See W. Porter, *History of the Corps of Royal Engineers* (9 vols, Institute of Royal Engineers, Chatham, 1951), Vol. 1, pp. 10–18.

19. See W.H. Russell's disparaging account, *The British Expedition to the Crimea* (Geo. Routledge, London, 1877), pp. 40–1. The *Illustrated London News*, 1854, p. 206, reported that 'although wretchedly built, Varna has one of the best ports on the Black Sea'. It suffered major damage by fire in the autumn of 1854.

20. Lord Paget of *Bellerophon*, Lord Russell of *Vengeance* and Captain Eden of *London* were especially praised by Lord Raglan. See Eardley-Wilmot, *Life of Vice Admiral Lord Lyons GCB*, p. 176.

21. The young William Peel of *Diamond* was amongst very many who chafed at the lack of action or any chance for 'glory' as the huge armada lay just about idle as months went by. See D. Crane, *Men of War* (Harper Press, London, 2009), p. 219.

22. Russell, *The British Expedition to the Crimea*, p. 398.

23. The French fleet received notification of their country's declaration of war on Russia on that day. Their commander, Admiral Hamelin (1796–1864), had initially refused to join the expedition until the fact of the declaration of war was known.

24. Edmund Lyons (1790–1858). Born 1790; joined the frigate *Active* 1803, serving in the Dardanelles and East Indies 1807–13. Commander March 1812. Unemployed until 1828, served in the Mediterranean during the Greek War of Independence. In 1829, in *Blonde*, he cruised the Black Sea, the first British warship to visit Sebastopol, the Caucasus and Odessa. Twenty-five years later Lyons was to be the only senior officer with experience of this sea. In 1835 appointed British Minister at Athens, where he remained for fifteen years. Created baronet in 1840 and in 1844 appointed civil GCB. Rear admiral January 1850. In November 1853 appointed second-in-command of the Mediterranean Fleet under Dundas, with his flag aboard *Agamemnon*. Dundas was well aware that Lyons was a man of ability and delegated to him the command of the 'inshore

squadron' and liaison with the land forces under Raglan, whilst Dundas remained with the main fleet. Lyons advised Raglan to adopt Balaklava as the base of the British army and led a squadron in the attack on Sebastopol on 17 October 1854. Lyons succeeded to the command in January 1855. It was Lyons who secured French agreement to the occupation of Kertch and the Sea of Azoff in May 1855. Although opportunities for purely naval operations declined, Lyons led the expedition against Kinburn in October 1855. In June 1855 he lost his son, Captain Edmund Lyons, who died after being wounded in an attack on Sevastopol. Appointed a military GCB in July 1855 for his services. After the Treaty of Paris Lyons served out his term as commander in the Mediterranean. Created Baron Lyons of Christchurch in June 1856 and a vice admiral in March 1857, he died in November 1858 at Arundel Castle.

25. 1798–1881. In February 1855 succeeded Prince Menshevik in command at Sebastopol until Gortshakoff took over.
26. Soon afterwards lost off Odessa. See p. 51.
27. This ship's name frequently occurs as *Samson* but is *Sampson* in the 1855 *Navy List*.
28. A 50-gun 'fourth rate' under Captain C.R. Mends and one of the last of the sailing frigates.
29. This ship's name frequently occurs as *Sanspareil*.
30. This is believed to be the last occasion when an English man-of-war went into action under sail. See Seymour, *My Naval Career and Travels*, p. 13.
31. *Illustrated London News*, 1854, p. 49.
32. There had been coastal bombardments during the Eastern Crisis of 1839–40, notably of Acre.
33. One or two allied ships remained off Odessa throughout the war as part of the general blockade of the port and of the mouths of the Danube. *Niger* was there again in June 1855; in July 1855, *Spiteful* alone boarded no less than fourteen merchant vessels off Sulina. See Dewar, *The Russian War 1855: Black Sea*, pp. 237–8.
34. See also the loss of the *Jasper* in the Sea of Azoff, p. 125.
35. Not related to the George Giffard who served in the Baltic.
36. For a detailed account, see Greenhill and Giffard, *Steam, Politics and Patronage*, pp. 15–23.
37. See Seymour, *My Naval Career and Travels*, p. 17.
38. Ibid.
39. Kaffa Bay near the Strait of Kertch was one point examined, though there were sizeable Russian forces nearby: Eardley-Wilmot, *Life of Vice Admiral Lord Lyons GCB*, p. 165.
40. Lyons considered that some of the larger coastal towns like Anapa and Soujak Kaleh were not worth attacking at this time since their occupation would serve no purpose and would divert resources. Also, they locked up significant Russian garrisons which might have been more usefully deployed against the allies elsewhere. The meant that operations against the Circassian coast were never very extensive, certainly not until later in the war when the last remaining Russian garrisons were gradually reduced or driven off. See Eardley-Wilmot, *Life of Vice Admiral Lord Lyons GCB*, p. 176.
41. Ibid., pp. 171–2.
42. This seems to be the only occasion on which Russian ships left the safety of their harbour in the face of allied encroachments and the only engagement of its type in the Black Sea. Seymour, *My Naval Career and Travels*, p. 15.
43. *Firebrand*, *Niger*, *Vesuvius*, *Retribution* and *Sidon* were engaged on this work at various times.
44. Eardley-Wilmot, *Life of Vice Admiral Lord Lyons GCB*, pp. 178–9.
45. Ibid., p. 193.
46. Ibid., p. 192; see also *London Gazette* dispatch, 9 February 1855, p. 46970. The sailors and sappers were awarded the Turkish 'Medal of Glory' (1853) in gold for officers and silver for other ranks. It is sometimes called 'the Danube Medal' in British references.

Chapter 4

1. Williams, *Britain's Naval Power*, p. 76.
2. It is usual to credit the highly efficient Mends, later Naval Director of Transport (1862), for most of the planning.

3. Now generally Yevpatoria.

4. Dundas' flagship, *Britannia*, for example, lost 50 men in a night and 3 French 3-deckers lost 352 men; the French army is said to have lost around 4,000 men. See Seymour, *My Naval Career and Travels*, p. 17 and Eardley-Wilmot, *Life of Vice Admiral Lord Lyons GCB*, p. 190.

5. Eardley-Wilmot, *Life of Vice Admiral Lord Lyons GCB*, p. 196.

6. Quoted in Eardley-Wilmot, *Life of Vice Admiral Lord Lyons GCB*, p. 196.

7. Williams, *Britain's Naval Power*, p. 76.

8. See Kinglake, *The Invasion of the Crimea*, Vol. 2, p. 297. He claims that it was not British practice to load the warships with troops.

9. Seymour commented: 'Some people have, I believe, blamed them for not coming and attacking our transports, but when the comparative force of the allied squadrons and of the Russians is considered, I think any such charge is absurd.' Seymour, *My Naval Career and Travels*, p. 20.

10. An estimated 35,000 Russians were attacked by 57,000 allied troops. There were 6,000 Russian casualties.

11. The French ships that bombarded Russian lines were *Mouette*, *Mégère*, *Cacique*, *Canada*; also present nearby were *Roland*, *Lavoisier*, *Descartes*, *Spitfire*, *Vauban*, *Montebello*, *Ville de Paris* (with Admiral Hamelin aboard) and *Caton*. The only British ship near this French squadron was *Britannia*, with Admiral Dundas observing the battle.

12. C.C.P. Fitzgerald, *Life of Vice Admiral Sir George Tryon, KCB* (Blackwood, London, 1897), p. 47.

13. Ibid.

14. Clowes, *The Royal Navy*, Vol. 6, p. 432; Lyons claims that over 2,000 were landed (Eardley-Wilmot, *Life of Vice Admiral Lord Lyons GCB*, p. 212); see also the account of the field after the battle by Captain T.A.B. Spratt of *Spitfire* in Eardley-Wilmot.

15. Sending the Russian wounded to one of their own ports rather than holding them as prisoners of war elsewhere was much applauded as a humane gesture on the part of Dundas.

16. Apparently, the Russian defender Todleben believed that the failure to launch an immediate strike against Sebastopol before its defences were ready was the greatest mistake the allies made. See Seaton, *The Crimean War*, p. 133.

17. Admiral Dundas went to see the sunken ships for himself on the 23rd. See the detailed account of the barriers erected by the Russians in Lyons' letter to the Admiralty on 17 March 1855, quoted in Dewar, *The Russian War 1855: Black Sea*, pp. 105–6.

18. Williams, *Britain's Naval Power*, p. 77.

19. Remarkably, Sebastopol was never fully blockaded – only the main town on the south of the inlet was under blockade by the allies. The Russians were able to send reinforcements and supplies into the city from the north side throughout the siege.

20. The fleet intended to support land operations in the Crimea as opposed to operating more widely around the Black Sea.

21. Token resistance from the old Genoese fort on the heights above the harbour was soon ended by *Agamemnon*. Lyons' skill in taking the large warship into the narrow bay was greatly admired.

22. It eventually had five wharves – one to land ordnance, one for taking off the sick and wounded, one ('Vesuvius Wharf') for landing troops, one ('Diamond Wharf') for landing guns and one for hauling up smaller vessels for repair. It also had its own complement of small tugs and lighters to work within the harbour and a depot ship, *Sir Robert Sale*. See Dewar, *The Russian War 1855: Black Sea*, pp. 3–4 and Lyons' description of the facilities in ibid., pp. 62–6.

23. 1807–55. He had commanded the Russian squadron at Sinope and was to be killed by a sniper during the siege of Sebastopol.

24. Widely regarded as the leading spirit behind the defence, he was killed in the first great bombardment of Sebastopol on 17 October.

25. Franz E.I. Todleben (or Totleben), 1818–84. General 1869 and later planned the siege of Plevna in the Russo-Turkish war of 1877–8. Created count for this service in 1878. Later commander-in-chief of the Russian army.

26. Kinglake, *The Invasion of the Crimea*, Vol. 4, p. 219: 'the commanders of the Anglo-French fleet agreed with the Russians that Sebastopol was safe against an attack from the sea'.

27. See Eardley-Wilmot, *Life of Vice Admiral Lord Lyons GCB*, p. 218.
28. HQ of Sir Colin Campbell's Highland Brigade, which included the 93rd Highlanders, tasked with the defence of Balaklava.
29. Both part of the 'Left Attack' siege positions.
30. See Clowes, *The Royal Navy*, Vol. 6, p. 435: 'Seldom had the navy so much to do on land'.
31. *Diamond's* guns under Peel were formed into a battery known as 'the Koh-i- Noor', named after the famous 'mountain of light' diamond taken from the Sikhs in 1849; it is now in the late Queen Mother's crown.
32. Quoted in Eardley-Wilmot, *Life of Vice Admiral Lord Lyons GCB*, p. 229.
33. Fitzgerald, *Life of Vice Admiral Sir George Tryon*, p. 54.
34. See, for example, Captain Stephen Lushington's letter to Admiral Lyons, 4 March 1855, in which he reports 'the good health of the whole brigade; the sick list does not exceed nineteen, without one serious case. Number victualled, 1,000', quoted in Dewar, *The Russian War 1855: Black Sea*, p. 92.
35. Fitzgerald, *Life of Vice Admiral Sir George Tryon*, p. 53.
36. 'No naval commander would be warranted in crippling his fleet for the sake of attempting mere mischief against sea forts at a range of 800 yards', Kinglake, *The Invasion of the Crimea*, Vol. 4, p. 259.
37. See Raglan's letter to him, quoted in Kinglake, *The Invasion of the Crimea*, Vol. 4, pp. 264–5 and Bonner-Smith and Dewar (eds), *The Russian War: Baltic and Black Sea 1854*, pp. 341–2.
38. See A. Lambert, *Battleships in Transition* (Conway, Oxford, 1984), p. 46; Williams, *Britain's Naval Power*, p. 80 and Seymour, *My Naval Career and Travels*, p. 24.
39. And exploded some of their magazines.
40. Bonner-Smith and Dewar (eds), *The Russian War: Baltic and Black Sea 1854*, p. 210.
41. See Appendix 10.
42. For example, *Britannia* and *Queen* were both towed by *Vesuvius*, *Albion* by *Firebrand*, *Trafalgar* by *Retribution*, *London* by *Niger*, *Vengeance* by *Highflyer*, *Rodney* by *Spiteful*, *Bellerophon* by *Vulcan* and *Arethusa* by *Triton*. Related in Eardley-Wilmot, *Life of Vice Admiral Lord Lyons GCB*, p. 241.
43. Seymour, *My Naval Career and Travels*, p. 23.
44. Expertly piloted by 2nd Master E.C. Ball.
45. *The Times*, 18 October 1854.
46. Seaton, *The Crimean War*, p. 131.
47. Eardley-Wilmot, *Life of Vice Admiral Lord Lyons GCB*, p. 239.
48. Williams, *Britain's Naval Power*, p. 81.
49. And a possible indication of what an attack on Cronstadt might entail.
50. Seymour, *My Naval Career and Travels*, p. 26.
51. Since he really did not approve of the whole plan to pit his wooden ships at anchor against harbour defences, he had instructed his captains to 'haul off without delay' if their ships were seriously damaged during the action. Quoted in Lambert, *Battleships in Transition*, p. 46.
52. Because so many of her crew were ashore with the Naval Brigade, she could not man or operate her upper deck guns, so sustaining fewer casualties than she might have done. Eardley-Wilmot, *Life of Vice Admiral Lord Lyons GCB*, p. 251.
53. There is some variation in the stated casualties, whether officially published in the *London Gazette* or in ships' officers' accounts. See Appendix 11.
54. Seaton, *The Crimean War*, p. 133.
55. Pavel Petrovitch Liprandi, 1796–1864. Served against the French in 1813–14 and against the Turks 1828–9. Had already fought in Wallachia before being transferred to the Crimea.
56. This major sortie was a serious effort but has received little attention. Given the fact that the Russian army that had attacked Balaklava the day before was still in position, the allies' right flank was again under serious threat.
57. He claimed that he had only 600 effective men in the forward positions.
58. Stephen Lushington's dispatch. For his gallantry, Hewett was immediately promoted and eventually received the Victoria Cross.

59. After Inkermann, French forces were deployed to hold the right flank.
60. See Appendix 14.
61. As one French general called it when he visited the site.
62. Eardley-Wilmot, *Life of Vice Admiral Lord Lyons GCB*, p. 264.
63. It was completely moved to Kamiesch shortly afterwards because of the lack of shelter off the Katcha. Surgeon Cree, visiting the area in June 1855 commented on 'the crowds of ships jammed close together in the narrow bay or creek [and] the French wooden town, a queer place, all bustle and noise – French cafes and shops, French girls in some of them', Levien (ed.), *The Cree Journals*, p. 252.
64. Seymour, *My Naval Career and Travels*, p. 30.
65. Wooden planking for the construction of proper huts did not begin to arrive in quantity until January and February 1855.
66. Wood, writing in the *Fortnightly Review* in 1897.
67. See, for example, Bonner-Smith and Dewar (eds), *The Russian War: Baltic and Black Sea 1854*, pp. 372–3.
68. Though he had been proved correct – wooden ships battering themselves against granite forts really could not achieve much.
69. He had already been promised the post on Dundas' retirement; Eardley-Wilmot, *Life of Vice Admiral Lord Lyons GCB*, p. 129.
70. Bruat died at Toulon on his way home from the Crimea in November 1855.
71. The *St Jean d'Acre* ('*Jenny*') is a fine example of one of the new screw warships employed during the Russian War. Ordered in 1851 and launched in 1853, she was a handsome 2-decker mounting 101 guns and with a crew of 900. She was 238 feet long and displaced 5,499 tons.
72. Seymour, *My Naval Career and Travels*, p. 36.
73. Another unusual plan was tried on 18 July – Petty Officer Shepherd of *St Jean d'Acre* devised a plan to create a sort of 'one-man torpedo' using a collapsible canvas canoe and carrying an iron case filled with explosive and a fuse, with loops at each end to allow fixing amidships under water. Shepherd had a truly dangerous time paddling his way through Russian defences and warships to within 400 yards of a Russian three-decker, but he was eventually forced to retreat when Russian boats threatened to locate him. Shepherd tried again a few days later but was forced to give up the enterprise. He was awarded the Victoria Cross for his bravery.
74. Quoted in Eardley-Wilmot, *Life of Vice Admiral Lord Lyons GCB*, p. 285.
75. Bonner-Smith and Dewar (eds), *The Russian War: Baltic and Black Sea 1854*, p. 9.
76. The Russians were very adept at repairing any serious damage overnight. See Bonner-Smith and Dewar (eds), *The Russian War: Baltic and Black Sea 1854*, p. 128.
77. See, for example, Captain Lushington's letter to Lyons, 14 April 1855, quoted in Bonner-Smith and Dewar (eds), *The Russian War: Baltic and Black Sea 1854*, p. 118.
78. His funeral there on the 25th was a major social event drawing in some of the highest dignitaries and commanders from all the allied forces, including the entire complement of *Miranda*. Rear Admiral Lyons received a touching letter of sympathy from the Queen and Prince Albert.
79. Levien (ed.), *The Cree Journals*, p. 254.
80. Succeeded in command of the Naval Brigade by Captain Harry Keppel (1809–1904) on 21 July 1855 when Lushington was promoted. Keppel was a highly experienced officer, well connected, well thought of and known for his personal courage and his dedication to his duty and to his men. After a highly distinguished career and laden with honours, he was appointed full admiral in 1869, Grand Cross of the Bath in 1871 and Admiral of the Fleet in 1877. He was known as 'the Father of the Fleet' by the time of his death at the age of 95 in 1904.
81. William Peel (1824–58), son of Sir Robert Peel, the Conservative Prime Minister. Born in 1824, he entered the navy in April 1838 and served in operations off the coast of Syria in 1840. After service off China, South America and in the Pacific, was promoted lieutenant in 1844 and commander in 1847. Captain in 1849. After expeditions to Palestine, Egypt and along the Nile 1850–2, he commissioned the new frigate *Diamond* in 1853, serving in the Mediterranean and the Black Sea. Served with the Naval Brigade 'before Sebastopol' and repeatedly distinguished

himself, being appointed CB in July 1855 and was one of the first recipients of the Victoria Cross in 1857. His most famous service, however, came in India during the Indian Mutiny. In September 1856 he commissioned the steam-frigate *Shannon* for service in China but on news of the outbreak in India was dispatched to Calcutta with a detachment of marines and soldiers. At Calcutta, Peel formed a Naval Brigade and was present in many significant actions during the fighting upcountry, in particular in the Lucknow operations. In January 1858 he was nominated KCB. During the second Relief of Lucknow in March 1858 Peel was wounded by a musket ball; he reached Cawnpore en route to England but contracted smallpox and died on 27 April. Peel, a brave and effective leader, was very much the archetypical Victorian hero, whose early death deprived the navy of an exceptionally able officer.

82. This was one of the actions for which he was awarded the Victoria Cross.
83. Quoted in Dewar, *The Russian War 1855: Black Sea*, p. 201. See also Lushington's dispatch of 18 June on the action, in ibid., pp. 202–3. He spoke of 'the most murderous fire I have ever witnessed' and listed 7 officers (including Peel and Evelyn Wood) wounded, along with 41 other ranks, and 1 officer and 9 seamen killed.
84. 1792–1868. Another Peninsular War and Waterloo veteran. Chief of Staff in the Crimea, he succeeded Raglan as Commander-in-Chief with some reluctance. Appointed GCB and general on the fall of Sebastopol, he resigned his command in November 1855.
85. Quoted in Levien (ed.), *The Cree Journals*, p. 256. The allies were of course 'sapping' up to the Russian lines, to bring themselves and their guns closer to the enemy.
86. For example, on 15 August, the new mortar boats *Firm*, *Hardy* and *Flamer* were deputed to 'take off the fire of the Quarantine Fort from the battery that our French allies are constructing opposite to it' and to shell Fort Alexander: Admiral Lyons to Admiralty, 17 August 1855, quoted in Dewar, *The Russian War 1855: Black Sea*, p. 272.
87. With another 25,000 at Eupatoria. All British troops were withdrawn from the port by December 1854.
88. See Lyons' letter to the Admiralty, 5 February 1855, in which he relates that the Italian contingent to be transported to the Crimea in British ships will 'probably' comprise 15,500 men 'of all arms', 2,000 horses, 36 guns and 264 wheeled vehicles.
89. Cree noted on the 30 August: 'Through my glass today I noticed that a statue that used to stand in front of what we call the Clubhouse in Sebastopol has been removed and furniture being carried over the bridge of boats to the north side. A promising sign!', Levien (ed.), *The Cree Journals*, p. 258. Admiral Lyons correctly judged that this construction work was to enable the evacuation of the city, not to bring in reinforcements and supplies. See his letter in Dewar, *The Russian War 1855: Black Sea*, p. 271.
90. Fitzgerald, *Life of Vice Admiral Sir George Tryon*, p. 63.
91. Seymour recalled: 'The morning of the 9th showed the city obscured by smoke from the conflagration and lit up with occasional explosions', Seymour, *My Naval Career and Travels*, p. 29.
92. Quoted in Eardley-Wilmot, *Life of Vice Admiral Lord Lyons GCB*, pp. 349–50.
93. Ibid., p. 357.
94. Ibid., p. 353.
95. Ibid., p. 354; Dewar, *The Russian War 1855: Black Sea*, pp. 302–3, 317–18.

Chapter 5

1. The lateness of the notification was criticised in the Commons and in the press. It effectively allowed a large number of traders who had already entered the ports of the White Sea before 1 August to come and go without being molested. Since the allied blockading squadron set off in June, it was in fact powerless to stop this trade until the formal declaration was made. See, for example *The Times*, 30 August 1854, p. 5.
2. *Miranda* was originally destined for the Baltic Fleet in May 1854 but never served in the Baltic, being deployed in the White Sea. At the end of the season's operations there, in September 1854 she headed for Portsmouth and after refitting and re-supplying made for the Black Sea. She reached Balaklava on 11 November 1854 and joined the fleet operating against Sebastopol. Most

of her crew of about 230 served in the White Sea, the Black Sea and the Sea of Azoff and received the Crimea Medal with clasps *Sebastopol* and *Azoff* – and they certainly earned both. What is more interesting, however, is that the 1854 crew of *Miranda* – and it was mainly the same officers and men who went on to serve with her in the Black Sea – were also given the Baltic Medal. This is remarkable because she never actually served within the Baltic. Indeed, Captain K.J. Douglas-Morris, in his *Naval Medals 1796–1857* (pivately published), p. 343, makes the point that she was 'never attached at any point to the Baltic Fleet' in 1854 or 1855 and was 'the only ship to earn the Baltic Medal without having sailed or steamed anywhere near those particular territorial waters'. Her consorts in the White Sea, HMS *Brisk* and *Eurydice* did not get the Baltic Medal. In fact, the crews of those ships, like those that operated only in the Pacific, received no medal for that part of the war against Russia.

3. Bad weather frequently hampered the activities of the allied squadron: there were continual reports of 'brisk gales, thick fogs and very strong currents'; the crews had 'quite enough to do to keep the vessels out of danger', *Illustrated London News*, 1854, p. 225.
4. Now more commonly Archangelsk.
5. As many as sixteen gunboats and five slightly larger ships.
6. *Illustrated London News*, 1854, p. 336.
7. It had successfully defended itself against Swedish attacks in the past.
8. *Illustrated London News*, 1854, p. 336. Some were released if, as neutrals, their papers and cargoes were in order; 'enemy' vessels were generally seized and burned along with their cargoes. Very few were sent to England as prizes.
9. Of *Miranda*'s 375 seizures, only 3 were sent back to Britain.
10. Williams was to render equally good service in *Miranda* buoying the Straits of Kertch during the Azoff campaign a year later. See p. 118.
11. The whole campaign was, not surprisingly, equally criticised in the Russian press as a pointless war largely waged against innocent civilians. See, for example, the Russian comments quoted in *The Times*, 9 September 1854, p. 8.
12. Lyons maintained that he was receiving fire from defenders within the town and was thus compelled to fire on them. He was actually in a perilous situation himself; the ship frequently grounded during the attack and only made its way back up the narrow Kola River with the greatest difficulty. If the river banks had been defended, *Miranda* would have been in serious trouble.
13. *Illustrated London News*, 1854, p. 336.
14. Two months earlier than that of 1854.
15. One of the many Franklin search expeditions.
16. Double its 1854 garrison.
17. See letters to *The Times*, 9 September 1854, quoting Russian sources on the effects of the blockade and on 7 November 1855, p. 6.
18. For example, *The Times* on 6 November 1855 relating reports in the French *Moniteur* of 4 November.
19. Many villages adopted the sensible policy of simply carting goods further inland, beyond observation.

Chapter 6

1. A Russian presence in the Pacific region was only established after the mid-seventeenth century.
2. 'One of those advanced posts which for the past half century it has been the policy of Russia to establish on the frontier of her dominions', *Illustrated London News*, 1854, p. 534.
3. Alaska, discovered by Vitus Behring in 1712, was of course a Russian possession, its trade dominated by the Russian-American Company. It remained Russian until purchased by the USA in 1867.
4. The great modern port of Vladivostok did not develop until after the war of 1854–6.
5. 1803–88.
6. The Russian Pacific fleet usually wintered in San Francisco.

7. Still in existence and now preserved in Hartlepool.
8. Quoted in G. Dodd, *Pictorial History of the Russian War* (Chambers, Edinburgh and London, 1856), p. 189.
9. *The Times*, 24 October 1854, p. 7.
10. It was estimated that the allied flotilla fired 3,000 rounds of shot and shell during the day. See *Illustrated London News*, 1854, p. 534.
11. The latter apparently carrying six Russian officers and $200,000, as reported in the *Illustrated London News*, 25 November 1854, p. 534.
12. Japan at this time was still very much an unknown and 'closed' state, only on the verge of its 'opening' to the West and was not involved in the campaigns.
13. One of the few Japanese ports that was 'open' to foreigners as a result of an Anglo-Japanese treaty of 1854.
14. It was not even realised at this date that Sakhalin was an island, not a peninsula.
15. With *Winchester*, *Spartan* and *Tartar*, later joined by *Styx*.
16. *The Times*, 8 October 1855.

Chapter 7

1. He spent the few remaining years of his life trying to defend his actions in Parliament (he was MP for Southwark) and in print. He refused to accept the Grand Cross of the Order of the Bath (GCB) which was offered to him.
2. Quoted in D. Bonner-Smith, *The Russian War: Baltic 1855* (Navy Records Society, London, 1943), p. 4.
3. Ibid.
4. See Bonner-Smith, *The Russian War: Baltic 1855*, p. 5.
5. See Appendix 7.
6. The Queen, in the steam yacht *Fairy*, did go to see the advanced squadron set sail.
7. *The Times*, 3 April 1855, quoted in Bonner-Smith, *The Russian War: Baltic 1855*, p. 6. The writer speculated that 'for anything we know, the departure of the Baltic fleet may be an annual ceremony for many a year to come'.
8. Sir Richard Saunders Dundas (1802–61). Born 1802, he became a volunteer on the frigate *Ganymede* in 1817. Lieutenant 1821; commander 1823; captain 1824. Served in the Mediterranean, off North America, the East Indies and Australia. In *Melville* he served in the First Opium War and for his services was nominated a CB. Promoted rear admiral in July 1853 and in February 1855 appointed commander-in-chief of the fleet in the Baltic. Dundas attended the allied council of war in Paris in January 1856 and was made a KCB on 4 February. After a period as second-in-command of the Mediterranean Fleet he joined the Admiralty as Second and later First Sea Lord. Promoted to vice admiral in February 1858, he died in London on 3 June 1861. He was not related to Admiral J.W.D. Dundas who commanded the Black Sea Fleet.
9. Terms reproduced in Bonner-Smith, *The Russian War: Baltic 1855*, p. 29.
10. Admiral Baynes sailed from the Nore with the heavy blockships, the gunboats and the mortar vessels on 5 June and only reached Nargen on 14 July.
11. Captain Yelverton in *Arrogant*, with *Cossack*, *Esk* and *Tartar*, operated off Courland at this time.
12. For example, *Cossack* under Captain E.G. Fanshawe captured six vessels on 26–7 May, three of which were run aground by their own crews and then burned by the British. Captain Nicholas Vansittart in *Magicienne* entered Biorko Bay, shelled Russian infantry on the shore and sank two vessels laden with granite destined for the defences of Cronstadt. A more serious incident was the attack on sizeable batteries at Narva by Rear Admiral Seymour in *Exmouth*, assisted by *Blenheim* and – given an opportunity to try their guns – by the gunboats *Pincher* and *Snap*.
13. One oft-repeated justification for the Baltic operations in 1854 and 1855 was that they tied down so many Russian and Finnish troops and resources.
14. Quoted in Bonner-Smith, *The Russian War: Baltic 1855*, p. 8. See also his report in ibid., pp. 59–61. It seems to have been concluded very quickly that Cronstadt would not be a target in

this year's campaign and attention switched to Sveaborg. See also Dundas' report to the Admiralty on the reconnaissance in ibid., pp. 43–6.

15. *Merlin* became the first ever victim of the new form of weapon when she was damaged by a mine whilst closely reconnoitring Cronstadt on 9 June 1855. The first 'minesweeping' operations also occurred during this campaign. As unknown and largely invisible weapons, the threat of underwater mines was taken very seriously by the allies. See Dundas to Admiralty on 'sweeping' operations off Sveaborg in August in Bonner-Smith, *The Russian War: Baltic 1855*, p. 185.

16. This was a mass-production of warships of all kinds on a scale never before seen – a good example of an industrialised nation turning its resources to war. Over 200 new gunboats, 11 armoured floating batteries (copied from French patterns used in the Black Sea in 1855) and 100 mortar vessels and rafts were laid down and completed, ready for use in the new campaign season of 1856. New steam battleships were also prepared, for example, HMS *Conqueror*.

17. See correspondence on the whole incident reproduced in Bonner-Smith, *The Russian War: Baltic 1855*, pp. 109–12.

18. When part of the town itself was accidentally burned.

19. *Prompt, Pickle, Rocket* and *Blazer*.

20. Found to be 'in good condition and a work of great strength' but already stripped of its armament and abandoned by its defenders. Yelverton blew it up. Bonner-Smith, *The Russian War: Baltic 1855*, p. 113.

21. Ibid., passim.

22. See Napier's letter below, p. 105.

23. Sveaborg was rebuilt and refortified and remained an important part of the defence network of the Gulf of Finland and the approaches to St Petersburg. The fortifications are intact for the most part, except for those on the island of Länsi Mustasaari, which were never repaired after the Crimean War bombardment. The fortress of Sveaborg/Suomenlinna was transferred to civil administration in 1973 and has undergone repairs since then. The site was added to the UNESCO World Heritage list in 1991 and is now one of Helsinki's most important tourist attractions.

24. A further consignment of heavy mortars was sent out on *Sans Pareil* on 24 August but they and the existing mortar vessels with Dundas' fleet were sent home after the attack on Sveaborg: 'a visible sign that "offensive operations" were over'. Bonner-Smith, *The Russian War: Baltic 1855*, p. 10–11.

25. There was a constant need to be aware of the slight possibility that with British and French naval forces engaged elsewhere, the Russian fleet at Cronstadt would sally out to strike at the allies.

26. The British element was listed and named by Dundas in his letter to the Admiralty, 13 August 1855, see Bonner-Smith, *The Russian War: Baltic 1855*, p. 184.

27. Collister, *The Sulivans*, pp. 66–7; Sulivan, *Life and Letters of Admiral Sir Bartholomew James Sulivan*, p. 318ff.

28. *Stork* and *Snapper*, operating to the far right of the allied line on the 9th and moved to the far left on the 10th, carried Lancaster guns and concentrated their fire on the Russian warships blocking two of the island channels.

29. About forty were claimed to have been burned or damaged.

30. Quoted in Bonner-Smith, *The Russian War: Baltic 1855*, p. 187. His report on the attack is given in ibid., pp. 185–90.

31. In terms of potential Anglo–French naval conflict in the future, Preston and Major comment that 'the gunboat and mortar bombardment of Sveaborg was so similar to the planned [British] attack on Cherbourg as to make the presence of the French forces alongside the British bizarre', B. Perrett, *Gunboat! Small Ships at War* (Cassell, London, 2000), p. 9.

32. Intended as a diversionary attack, it really served no purpose other than to damage the ships, which took numerous hits.

33. In 1854 the only ships in Napier's fleet capable of shallow-draught work as gunboats for Sveaborg were the six ships (sloops) of the *Arrow* class with the fleet – each armed with two of the new 68-pounder Lancaster guns. A further 6 were ordered (the *Gleaner* class screw gunboats) and able to take part in the bombardment of Sveaborg in 1855, followed by 20 (later raised to over 90) of

the highly successful *Dapper* and related *Albacore* classes. This was at that time the largest construction programme for one type of warship. The *Dapper* gunboats were extensively and effectively used in the Azoff campaign. The real need was for high-angled mortar fire to pierce defences from long range. Usually ships' guns, firing on a more or less flat trajectory, needed to be brought in close to be effective – their massive broadsides would hopefully outweigh the steady and accurate fire from static defences well served, but the ships would suffer commensurate damage at close range.

34. Napier, *The Life and Correspondence of Admiral Sir Charles Napier*, p. 162.
35. Informants later reported that 'the batteries were very little injured'. See Captain Hewlett to Dundas, 7 September, in Bonner-Smith, *The Russian War: Baltic 1855*, p. 271. See a Russian account of the bombardment in ibid., pp. 273–7.
36. In *Pickle*, *Mastiff* and *Growler*.
37. On 21 August their Lordships at the Admiralty transmitted their 'great satisfaction' on the success of the operation.
38. An industrialised power turning its technology to the mass-production of armaments, mainly ships in this case. Not only gunboats and mortar vessels were built, but also vital ancillary craft like store vessels, depot vessels, factory and repair ships etc. Britain demonstrated in this instance its overwhelming superiority in industrial and construction processes.
39. These could, nevertheless, be employed in an attack on French bases like Cherbourg. The grand Naval Review at Spithead on 23 April 1856, part of the victory celebrations, included a mock attack on a shore fortress largely conducted by gunboats and mortar vessels.
40. Many had suffered severely from their use in two solid days of bombardment and urgently needed repair. They were towed home after 21 August.
41. See Captain Henry Otter's report on the attack, which was spread over five days, in Bonner-Smith, *The Russian War: Baltic 1855*, pp. 245–7.
42. 'Although the result of this expedition is in itself insignificant, still it is humiliating to the enemy to see a town 15 miles inland, defended by a considerable body of troops, and a fort, obliged to succumb to a force not exceeding 130 men', Captain High Dunlop's report to Dundas, 13 August 1855, in ibid., pp. 225–7.
43. See his report in ibid., pp. 199–200.
44. See ibid., pp. 231–3 for Captain Ommanney's account.
45. Report to Dundas on 12 August 1855 in ibid., pp. 234–6.
46. 'With the exception of the church', Ommanney's report to Dundas, 15 August 1855, in ibid., p. 251. Ommanney's biggest success was 'the unconditional surrender' of the town of Pernau, intimidated by his ships, *Hawke*, *Archer*, *Conflict* and *Cruiser*, on 12 September.
47. See reports in ibid., pp. 259–61.
48. All enumerated in ibid., pp. 267–8.
49. Earl Hardwicke, quoted in ibid., p. 11.
50. Variously estimated at 60–80,000 men, mainly French.
51. Bonner-Smith, *The Russian War: Baltic 1855*, p. 12. The Duke of Cambridge considered that the plan for a naval attack on Cronstadt and a land campaign against St Petersburg in 1856 was 'so impracticable that it will not be entertained by anybody', ibid., p. 14.
52. C. Ponting, *The Crimean War: The Truth Behind the Myth* (Chatto & Windus, London, 2004), p. 254.

Chapter 8

1. Frequently occurs in contemporary sources as Azov.
2. Sometimes called 'the Lazy Sea'.
3. 'This has really more the attributes of an extensive marsh than an inland sea for in many places the water is only a few inches deep', Eardley-Wilmot, *Life of Vice Admiral Lord Lyons GCB*, p. 301.
4. The former British Consul at Kertch, Charles Cattley, was able to provide valuable information on the area and its trade. See Ponting, *The Crimean War*, p. 264. He was retained on Lord Raglan's staff.

5. Prince Gorchakov, the Russian commander in the Crimea, believed that the allied seizure of Perekop by a force in the Sea of Azoff striking either across the Spit of Arabat or from Genitchi would isolate the Crimea and lead to the defeat of the Russian army. But no move against Perekop was ever attempted. See Seaton, *The Crimean War*, p. 189. Similar views were expressed regarding possible allied operations inland from Eupatoria. There seems to have been some surprise amongst the Russian high command that the allies restricted themselves to what was nothing more than coastal raiding in the Sea of Azoff.

6. Reinforcements for the army in the Crimea were certainly drawn from the Kertch-Taman command during the war. Seaton, *The Crimean War*, p. 188.

7. Dewar, *The Russian War 1855: Black Sea*, pp. 435–9.

8. Armand Joseph Bruat (1796–1855). Called by Lyons 'an enterprising, dashing fellow with moral courage enough withal to resist being persuaded or provoked into doing what he does not consider right and proper'; Lyons quoted in Eardley-Wilmot, *Life of Vice Admiral Lord Lyons GCB*, p. 359. Died at Toulon on his way home from the Crimea in 1855.

9. Its final stage from Varna was laid by the cable steamer *Argus* with the assistance of HMS *Spitfire* and *Terrible* and was brought ashore near Balaklava. It was not a success – constantly breaking – and Varna actually remained the effective end of the cable system.

10. 1809–95. Had extensive military service in Algeria and was an important supporter of Louis Napoleon. Commanded a Division in the Crimea under Marshal St Arnaud and succeeded to the command on St Arnaud's death. Served in the Italian campaign of 1859 and later became a Marshal of France.

11. For British correspondence on the recall, see Dewar, *The Russian War 1855: Black Sea*, pp. 132–3 and 143–4.

12. At this stage, Napoleon III was contemplating the bold idea of a completely new campaign in the Crimea, leaving the siege of Sebastopol as a side-show and launching allied forces deeper into the Crimea to confront Russian forces. This was discussed in an allied council in London in April and found considerable support but was never put into practice. See ibid., pp. 10–11.

13. There seems to have been universal dissatisfaction with 'the fact' of this telegraph, especially amongst the French who seemed to suffer more from its use, and a feeling that there was too much long-distance interference with those on the spot who were more clearly in command of the facts. The situation continued – Pélissier was later forbidden 'by wire' from an attack on Anapa later in 1855, but seems simply to have ignored it. See Kinglake, *The Invasion of the Crimea*, Vol. 9, pp. 81–2 and Dewar, *The Russian War 1855: Black Sea*, p. 11.

14. 1794–1864. Made a Marshal of France and Duc de Malakoff for his command in the Crimea. French Ambassador to London 1858–9 and later Governor of Algeria.

15. 42nd Highlanders, 71st Highland Light Infantry, 79th and 93rd Regiments and contingents of cavalry (10th Hussars), marines, engineers, artillery and transport.

16. Sulivan, *Life and Letters of Admiral Sir Bartholomew James Sulivan*, p. 7. Nothing came of it.

17. Son of Admiral Lyons and already well known for his exploits in the White Sea in HMS *Miranda*.

18. 1790–1865. Another Peninsular War veteran. Lieutenant general in 1851 and KCB in 1852. Commanded the Light Division in the Crimea and the British contingent that was sent to Kertch in 1855. Later commander-in-chief in Ireland.

19. Extensive remains of these fortifications still exist.

20. See W.H. Russell's damning account of the allied excesses in Russell, *The British Expedition to the Crimea*, pp. 269–80.

21. Ibid., p. 275.

22. This is as the name appears in the *Navy List*; also occurs as McKillop, especially in Dewar, *The Russian War 1855: Black Sea*.

23. Which brought immediate promotion to M'Killop.

24. George Williams, the very able Master of the *Miranda*, had navigated the same ship down to Kola in her White Sea expedition. He received the *Légion d'Honneur* for his services during the war.

25. Lyons' dispatch printed in Dewar, *The Russian War 1855: Black Sea*, p. 164.

26. There were nevertheless a few sizeable coastal forts around the Sea of Azoff, Arabat being the largest.
27. See opinion in Kinglake, *The Invasion of the Crimea*, Vol. 9, p. 84.
28. Williams, *Britain's Naval Power*, p. 99. In fact Sebastopol seems to have been well supplied and stocked and the damage to foodstuffs did not immediately tell on the garrison; it may have had more effect on Russian armies operating to the east of the Black Sea.
29. This unfortunate town was to be attacked no less than six times during the summer of 1855; many others were repeatedly 'visited' and damaged.
30. Lyons finished them off with 'submarine explosions' and further damage was done to the remains of the hulls and machinery in July 1855 by *Ardent* and *Boxer*.
31. It later transpired that even these had been scuttled or burned.
32. Sometimes occurs as Ghenitchesk.
33. The only sea route into and out of the Putrid Sea was via the Tchongar Strait at the north of the Spit, opposite Genitchi. This was 'closed' by a floating bridge later destroyed by the British. See p. 124.
34. See his report, Dewar, *The Russian War 1855: Black Sea*, p. 172.
35. See Russell's caustic comments in his *The British Expedition to the Crimea*, p. 280.
36. This process is absolutely typical of many that took place in the Sea of Azoff in the summer of 1855.
37. Captain Lyons to Rear Admiral Lyons, 29 May 1855: *London Gazette*, 1855, p. 2299. See Appendix 14.
38. It was this flotilla that had been enlarged by Peter the Great to form the Black Sea Fleet, with a new base at Sebastopol.
39. Coles continued his experimentation with new ways of mounting guns on ships. As Captain Cowper Coles, he lost his life in 1870 when his specially designed turret ship *Captain* capsized with all aboard in the Bay of Biscay.
40. Krasnow later described the attack as 'a new act of powerless animosity directed against a peaceful commercial city', quoted in Dodd, *Pictorial History of the Russian War*, p. 455. A British citizen at Taganrog, John Martin, supported the town's governor Count Tolstoi in suggesting that the British were responsible for inhuman acts against women and children and indiscriminate attacks on civil settlements. This accusation, especially coming from a British citizen, caused something of a stir in Britain. See Sherard Osborn's forceful riposte in Dewar, *The Russian War 1855: Black Sea*, pp. 320–3 and 343–4.
41. Admiral Lyons relaying Captain Lyons' report of the attack, 7 June 1855, quoted in Dewar, *The Russian War 1855: Black Sea*, p. 185.
42. See Captain Lyons' letter to Admiral Lyons, 3 June 1855, for a detailed account of the attack in ibid., pp. 179–81. The only allied casualty was one Royal Marine, severely wounded.
43. But the Russians were apparently surprised that the allies did no more than coastal raiding in the Sea of Azoff: 'the allied operation degenerated into the raiding of coastal towns and of fishing settlements on the Sea of Azov coast, the capture or burning of Russian merchant vessels and the sending of a small expedition to Anapa on the Black Sea coast. The allied troops remained virtually idle in the area until 19 October 1855 when they were withdrawn', Seaton, *The Crimean War*, p. 189. There was some surprise that the allies did not use the western shores – for example, around Genitchi – as a base for land operations deeper into Russian territory, especially towards Perekop.
44. Various spellings occur, now usually Mariupol.
45. Also occurs as Yesk, and nowadays as Yeysk.
46. See *London Gazette*, 1855, pp. 2492–3 for Captain Lyons' dispatches on these actions.
47. Quoted in Eardley-Wilmot, *Life of Vice Admiral Lord Lyons GCB*, p. 306.
48. Now Novorossisk.
49. A force of 2,000 French and 1,000 British soldiers with British artillery was assembled under command of Sir George Brown.

50. There were 10,000 men between the two ports with British and French officers attached, supported by a small Anglo-French infantry and cavalry force – squadrons of the British 10th Hussars and most of the 71st HLI remaining at Kertch.

51. Rear Admiral Sherard Osborn (1822–75) served from 1837 and saw extensive service in the Far East and in Arctic waters in 1850–1 and 1852–4. Early in 1855 he commanded *Vesuvius* in the Black Sea and at the capture of Kertch and after the death of Captain Lyons became senior officer in the Sea of Azoff. On 18 August he was advanced to captain, appointed to the *Vesuvius*, in which he remained as senior officer in the Sea of Azoff until the end of the war. Received the CB, the *Légion d'Honneur* and the Turkish Mejidieh. In 1857 Osborn commanded the paddle-frigate *Furious* in operations at Canton. After peace had been concluded, he carried Lord Elgin to Tokyo to conclude a treaty that opened Japan to relations with the West. In 1861, appointed to *Donegal* in the Gulf of Mexico during the Mexican war and in June 1862 agreed to command a Chinese squadron for the suppression of piracy on the Chinese coast but the command never materialised. In 1864 Osborn commanded *Royal Sovereign*, with a new turret system for mounting its heavy guns. In 1871 he commanded *Hercules* in the Channel. In May 1873 reached the rank of rear admiral. He continued to take great interest in Arctic exploration, suggesting a new Arctic expedition in 1873 and serving on its advisory committee. On 3 May 1875, as the ships were about to sail, Osborn went to Portsmouth to see them off. He died suddenly three days later at his home in Berkeley Square, London and was buried in Highgate Cemetery.

52. Seaman Joseph Trewavas of Mousehole in Cornwall actually cut the hawsers, under a heavy rifle fire, and was one of those who received the Victoria Cross for this action. See Appendix 14.

53. Now commonly Berdyansk.

54. Now usually Genichi.

55. He was promoted to captain for these services.

56. *Jasper*, *Wrangler*, *Cracker*, *Beagle*, *Curlew*, *Grinder*, *Swallow*, *Fancy*, *Boxer*, *Vesuvius* and the French *Milan* (under Captain de Cintré) and *Mouette* under Captain de l'Allemand. See the dispatches on the action quoted in Dewar, *The Russian War 1855: Black Sea*, pp. 224–33; these were also published in the *London Gazette*, 1855, p. 3080.

57. The only other significant loss was that of *Tiger* off Odessa early in the war. See p. 51.

58. Too hastily, according to some. See Clowes, *The Royal Navy*, Vol. 6, p. 461 and Eardley-Wilmot, *Life of Vice Admiral Lord Lyons GCB*, p. 333. Some thought that Hudson should have awaited the arrival of the rest of the squadron to help free his ship. He was later 'admonished' by the Admiralty for the loss but his career seems to have suffered no harm in the long run.

59. See Osborn's report, printed in Dewar, *The Russian War 1855: Black Sea*, pp. 263–5.

60. Williams, *Britain's Naval Power*, p. 100.

61. 150 tons in one attack on 31 August in the Bay of Arabat.

62. Quoted in Dewar, *The Russian War 1855: Black Sea*, pp. 301–2.

63. Kellaway received the VC for this incident. He had attempted to rescue Odevaine under heavy fire, but both (along with Thirston) had been surrounded and captured.

64. See Burgoyne's detailed account of the action and the circumstances of the men's capture in his report to Commander Osborn, 1 September 1855, quoted in Dewar, *The Russian War 1855: Black Sea*, pp. 287–90. The prisoners were sent to Taganrog and were well treated. See also Odevaine's letter to Burgoyne, forwarded by the military commander at Taganrog, ibid., pp. 311.

65. Lyons to Admiralty, 12 September, quoted in ibid., p. 308.

66. Or Phanagoria.

67. See the account of these operations in Captain Hall's report to Admiral Lyons, 3 October 1855, quoted in Dewar, *The Russian War 1855: Black Sea*, pp. 332–4 and Osborn's account in ibid., pp. 334–6.

68. Dispatch of 25 October 1855; quoted in P. Duckers and C.N. Mitchell, *The Azoff Campaign* (Squirrel, Harrow, 1996). But contrast this view with that of Russell, who was highly critical of the waste of food and supplies, which could have been used by the allies in the Crimea – at a time when grain was being bought from the USA to ship to the Black Sea. Russell, *The British Expedition to the Crimea*, p. 280.

69. See Appendix 14.
70. Quoted in Eardley-Wilmot, *Life of Vice Admiral Lord Lyons GCB*, p. 332.
71. Even Osborn had to admit at the end of October that 'there do not appear to be any stores of corn, hay or provisions left within reach of our vessels', Dewar, *The Russian War 1855: Black Sea*, p. 377. This did not stop his squadron destroying 'enormous quantities of grain and forage ... extending over 2 miles along the coast near Gheisk liman' on 5 and 6 November – amongst the last actions of the Azoff squadron, ibid., p. 402.
72. And again proving the value of the light steamers.
73. Quoted in Eardley-Wilmot, *Life of Vice Admiral Lord Lyons GCB*, pp. 235–6.

Chapter 9

1. Its terms and limits are reproduced in Dewar, *The Russian War 1855: Black Sea*, p. 81.
2. Also described as 'a Martello tower'.
3. Hopes that the allies might be able to raise local communities against their Russian masters were frequently expressed but did not come to anything. A Circassian force did attack a fort near Soujak Kaleh when it was under bombardment by Captain Giffard in March 1855 but played no further role in the attack on the town. See also Dewar, *The Russian War 1855: Black Sea*, pp. 155–6 on possible Circassian involvement.
4. The local Circassians had entered the town when the Russian garrison left and destroyed what remained. Captain John Moore to Admiral Lyons, 2 June 1855, quoted in ibid., pp. 155–6.
5. Eupatoria remained under occupation throughout the war and was repeatedly attacked. Some Russian leaders believed that the town would be used as a base for allied operations inland and that working from Eupatoria an allied force could isolate and destroy the Russian Crimean army. See Seaton, *The Crimean War*, pp. 183–4. It was in fact never used as a base of for further operations by the allies. To comply with a wish of General Pélissier, Admiral Lyons ordered 'a considerable portion of our fleets' to the port on 22 September 1855, after the fall of Sebastopol, 'for the purpose of leading the enemy to believe that the allies are assembling a large force in the neighbourhood' (see his letter to the Admiralty, in Dewar, *The Russian War 1855: Black Sea*, p. 315). Though some consideration was being given to the possibility of using Eupatoria as a new advanced base in the spring of 1856 as the allies considered their strategy for the coming year, their plans were negated by the ending of the war in March 1856.
6. Amongst others, *Megaera*, *Leander* and *Firebrand* did duty off Eupatoria in 1855.
7. After redeployment, there were something like 55,000 Turks 'before Sebastopol' and the rest at Eupatoria.
8. Carried to the Crimea in British ships: 'as the French contribute so largely to the efficiency of this expedition by the strength of their army, they may reasonably expect us to do all we can with our fleet', Admiral Lyons, 2 January 1855, quoted in Dewar, *The Russian War 1855: Black Sea*, p. 53. Over 40,000 Turkish troops, 3,000 horses and 97 guns were landed in February–March 1855.
9. *Henri IV* served as a sort of coastal fort before her guns were removed and landed for use ashore.
10. For an account of the losses etc., see Dewar, *The Russian War 1855: Black Sea*, pp. 85–6.
11. It was said that the depressing news of the defeat at Eupatoria contributed to the death of Tsar Nicholas I; Kinglake, *The Invasion of the Crimea*, Vol. 8, p. 59; Seaton, *The Crimean War*, p. 185. His last act was to dismiss Prince Menshikov as commander in the Crimea following this failure at Eupatoria. Menshikov was succeeded temporarily by Osten-Sachen (Governor of Odessa during the British naval attack in 1854), who had been in command at Sebastopol since 22 December 1854; the new Russian commander in the Crimea was to be Prince M.D. Gorchakov.
12. Blown up by the allies in a series of huge explosions.
13. Claims successfully deflected by Admiral Lyons. See for example his letter to the Admiralty on 12 January 1855, quoted in Dewar, *The Russian War 1855: Black Sea*, p. 59.
14. See p. 78.
15. Frequently occurs as Kimburn or Kimbourn in British accounts. Now more usually Kim-Bournu or Kil-Bouroun.
16. Now more commonly Nicolayev.

17. There was some criticism of the fact that the important city of Odessa was not attacked later in the war. But this was largely because it had by then been cleared of Russian trade and shipping and the allied admirals saw no point in attacking it if it were not to be occupied or used as a base for further operations. Odessa clearly expected an attack when the Kinburn fleet arrived nearby in October 1855.

18. Comprising HMs 17th, 20th, 21st, 57th and 63rd Regiments with 950 Royal Marines under Colonel Hurdle.

19. Two others were also being prepared, the *Congreve* and the *Foudroyante*. Using the French plans, the British constructed five similar vessels, armour plated and carrying fourteen guns – *Aetna* (which accidentally burned on the stocks), *Meteor*, *Thunder*, *Glatton* and *Trusty* – but none saw action. Two – *Glatton* and *Meteor* – were towed out to the Black Sea but arrived off Kinburn a week after the action.

20. The appearance and use of these new warships suitably impressed naval observers around the world and great claims were made for them as the forerunners of a new type of armoured ship. As a result of their successful use at Kinburn, the French began to armour wooden warships – though they were not in service by end of the war – and it is notable that no more purely wooden major warships were built by France from then on. Naturally, their revolutionary design provoked a considerable stir in the Admiralty and there was much talk of the death of the wooden warship: 'their very existence was an ominous warning that the day of the wooden line-of-battle ship was drawing to a close', Williams, *Britain's Naval Power*, p. 102. However, there has since been some dispute as to the *actual* value of the French floating batteries, some suggesting that their impact was exaggerated to flatter the Emperor. Nevertheless, Admiral Lyons, although he recognised that the mortar boats had done all the damage and that the line-of-battle ships had finished the job, regarded the French batteries as impressive vessels which would no doubt have completely demolished the fort for very little damage to themselves; see Eardley-Wilmot, *Life of Vice Admiral Lord Lyons GCB*, pp. 368–9. George Tryon equally considered that 'the palm and honour of this late attack decidedly belongs to the French floating batteries'; Fitzgerald, *Life of Vice Admiral Sir George Tryon*, p. 65.

21. Principally the *Spitfire* under Captain Thomas A.B. Spratt.

22. Armand Joseph Bruat, 1796–1855. He died of cholera aboard *Montebello* at Toulon whilst returning home from the Crimea.

23. 1791–1875. Previously senior officer at Malta. Served at Walcheren in 1809, off Jamaica 1817–18 and in the Eastern Mediterranean in 1839–40. Later commander-in-chief North America and at Devonport. GCB 1865 and admiral of the fleet, 1872.

24. Levien (ed.), *The Cree Journals*, p. 263.

25. Under Captain Willcox, with fire being directed by Captain Digby, RMA.

26. Levien (ed.), *The Cree Journals*, p. 263.

27. And those only from the bursting of a British gun.

28. These were closest to forts at 700–800 yards and noticeably took many hits – over 130 – but were not seriously damaged because of their thick iron armour and suffered comparatively few casualties. Cree noted how 'it was strange to see the shot striking their iron sides and then flying off again, generally split into pieces', Levien (ed.), *The Cree Journals*, p. 263. The gunboats, including *Arrow* and *Lynx*, both of which were armed with the new and powerful Lancaster guns, fired from about 800–900 yards.

29. The mortar and gun vessels fired at ranges of between 600–2,800 yards depending on their type and armament.

30. Levien (ed.), *The Cree Journals*, p. 263.

31. For Lyons' account of the attack, see Dewar, *The Russian War 1855: Black Sea*, pp. 346–8; see also Rear Admiral Houston Stewart's account in ibid., pp. 349–51.

32. But they were allowed to bring away their personal possessions and the officers kept their swords: it was a very civilised surrender arrangement.

33. See, for example, Clowes, *The Royal Navy*, Vol. 6, p. 472. Other sources give much higher figures for the Russian losses.

34. Fitzgerald, *Life of Vice Admiral Sir George Tryon*, p. 65.
35. Levien (ed.), *The Cree Journals*, p. 264.
36. Fitzgerald, *Life of Vice Admiral Sir George Tryon*, p. 65.
37. See, for example, Houston Stewart's account in Dewar, *The Russian War 1855: Black Sea*, pp. 355–6 and the Surveying Officer Captain T.A.B. Spratt's detailed report on the Dnieper and Bug in ibid., pp. 373–5.
38. Ponting, however, considers that the attack was 'designed primarily to provide the illusion of military activity before the winter set in', Ponting, *The Crimean War*, p. 304.
39. Some remained on station after the peace treaty to observe the carrying out of some of its military and naval clauses.
40. No detailed plans for a campaign of this nature in the Baltic seem to exist.

Conclusion

1. See Dewar, *The Russian War 1855: Black Sea*, p. 22.
2. Putting into use the hugely enlarged fleet of new gun and mortar vessels produced by 'The Great Armament'.
3. Taking advantage of Turkey's involvement elsewhere, there was a brief Greek revolt in the spring of 1854, which British and Turkish warships helped to suppress. But it has been said that neither the allies nor the Russians properly exploited the potential to raise disaffected nationalities – the Bulgarians and Rumanian in the Danubian Provinces against the Turks or the Finns, Circassians or Poles against the Russians. Their impact could have been influential. Seton-Watson, *The Russian Empire 1801–1917*, p. 330.
4. A separate Åland Convention was incorporated into the treaty, demilitarising the islands. The Russian naval base at Bomarsund was never rebuilt.
5. As vital to the defences of St Petersburg.
6. Opinions on their actual strength, power and value varied widely.

Appendix 1

1. *The Times*, 12 August 1853. For a detailed descriptions of the fleet, its programme of exercise and manoeuvres, see *The Times* for the first two weeks of August 1853.

Appendix 6

1. Reproduced in Napier, *The Life and Correspondence of Admiral Sir Charles Napier*, pp. 403–9.

Appendix 11

1. See Eardley-Wilmot, *Life of Vice Admiral Lord Lyons GCB*, pp. 253–4.

Bibliography

Allen's Navy List, London, 1855.

Bonner-Smith, D., *The Russian War: Baltic 1855*, Navy Records Society, London, 1943.

Bonner-Smith, D. and Dewar, A.C. (eds), *The Russian War: Baltic and Black Sea 1854*, Navy Records Society, London, 1943.

Brackenbury, G., *The Campaign in the Crimea* (Series I and II), Colnaghi, London, 1855–6.

Brooks, R., *The Long Arm of Empire*, Constable, London, 1999.

Clowes, Sir W.L., *The Royal Navy: A History from Earliest Times to the Death of Queen Victoria*, 7 vols, Sampson Lowe Marston, London, 1903.

Collister, P., *The Sulivans and the Slave Trade*, Collings, London, 1979.

Crane, D., *Men of War*, Harper Press, London, 2009.

Dewar, Captain A.C., *The Russian War 1855: Black Sea*, Navy Records Society, London, 1945.

Dodd, G., *Pictorial History of the Russian War*, Chambers, Edinburgh and London, 1856.

Douglas-Morris, K.J., *Naval Medals 1796–1857*, privately published, Milton Keynes, 1987.

Duckers, P. and Mitchell, C.N., *The Azoff Campaign 1855*, Squirrel, Harrow, 1996.

Eardley-Wilmot, Captain S., *Life of Vice Admiral Lord Lyons GCB*, Sampson Low, London, 1898.

Earp, G.B. (ed.), *The History of the Baltic Campaign of 1854*, repr., Naval and Military Press, Uckfield, 2009.

Fitzgerald, C.C.P., *Life of Vice Admiral Sir George Tryon, KCB*, Blackwood, London, 1897.

Gardiner, R. (ed.), *Steam, Steel, Shellfire: The Steam Warship 1815–1905*, Conway, Maritime Press, 1992.

Greenhill, B. and Giffard, A., *The British Assault on Finland*, Conway Maritime Press, London, 1988.

——, *Steam, Politics and Patronage: The Transformation of the Royal Navy, 1815–54*, Conway Maritime Press, London, 1994.

Hill, R., *War in the Ironclad Age*, Cassell, London, 2000.

Kinglake, A.W., *The Invasion of the Crimea*, Cabinet Edn, 9 vols, Blackwood, London 1888.

Lambert, A., *Battleships in Transition*, Conway, Oxford, 1984.

——, *The Last Sailing Battle Fleet*, Conway, London, 1991.

Lambert, A. and Badsey, S., *The War Correspondents: the Crimean War*, Sutton, Stroud, 1994.

Levien, M. (ed.), *The Cree Journals*, Webb & Bower, Exeter, 1981.

Lloyd, C., *The British Seaman*, Collins, London, 1968.

Low, C.R., *Her Majesty's Navy*, Virtue, London, n.d., *c.* 1893.

Lyon, D. and Winfield, R., *The Sail and Steam Navy List*, Chatham Publishing, London, 2004.

Napier, Major General E., *The Life and Correspondence of Admiral Sir Charles Napier, KCB*, Hurst and Blackett, London, 1862.

Nolan, E.H., *The Illustrated History of the War against Russia*, 2 vols, Virtue, London, 1857.

Perrett, B., *Gunboat!: Small Ships at War*, Cassell, London, 2000.

Ponting, C., *The Crimean War: The Truth Behind the Myth*, Chatto & Windus, London, 2004.

Porter, W., *History of the Corps of Royal Engineers*, 9 vols, Institute of Royal Engineers, Chatham, 1951.

Preston, A. and Major, J., *Send a Gunboat: the Victorian Navy and Supremacy at Sea 1854–1904*, Conway, London, 2007.

Reilly, W.E.M., *An Account of the Artillery Operations of the Royal Artillery and Royal Naval Brigade before Sebastopol, 1854–55*, HMSO, London, 1859.

Russell, W.H., *The British Expedition to the Crimea*, Geo. Routledge, London, 1877.

Seaton, A., *The Crimean War: A Russian Perspective*, Batsford, London, 1977.

Seton-Watson, H., *The Russian Empire 1801–1917*, Clarendon Press, Oxford, 1967.

Seymour, E.A., *My Naval Career and Travels*, Smith Elder, London 1911.

Stuart, V., *Beloved Little Admiral: Admiral of the Fleet Sir Henry Keppel*, Hall, London, 1967.

Sulivan, H.N., *Life and Letters of Admiral Sir Bartholomew James Sulivan, KCB*, Murray, London, 1896.

Tyrell, H., *The History of the Present War with Russia*, 3 vols, London Printing Co., London, 1856.

Williams, Hamilton, *Britain's Naval Power*, Macmillan, London, 1898.

Williams, H. Noel, *The Life and Letters of Admiral Sir Charles Napier, KCB*, Hutchinson, London, 1917.

Wood, Sir E., *The Crimea in 1854 and 1894*, Chapman and Hall, London, 1895.

——, *From Midshipman to Field Marshal*, Methuen, London, 1912.

The Dictionary of National Biography

Illustrated London News, 1854–6

London Gazette, 1854–6

The Navy List (various types and dates)

The Times, 1854–6

Index